HENRY IV

PARTS ONE AND TWO

EDITED BY
NIGEL WOOD

OPEN UNIVERSITY PRESS
BUCKINGHAM·PHILADELPHIA

Open University Press
Celtic Court
22 Ballmoor
Buckingham
MK18 1XW

and
1900 Frost Road, Suite 101
Bristol, PA 19007, USA

First Published 1995

A catalogue record of this book is available from the British Library

ISBN 0 335 15690 8 (pb)

Library of Congress Cataloging-in-Publication Data
Henry IV, part one and two / edited by Nigel Wood.
        p.   cm. — (Theory in practice)
    Includes bibliographical references and index.
    ISBN 0–335–15690–8
    1. Shakespeare, William, 1564–1616. King Henry IV. 2. Henry IV,
King of England, 1367–1413 — In literature. 3. Historical drama,
English — History and criticism. 4. Kings and rulers in literature.
I. Wood, Nigel, 1953– . II. Title: Henry IV. III. Title: Henry 4,
part one and two. IV. Title: Henry four, part one and two.
V. Series: Theory in practice series.
PR2809.H45 1995
822.3′3—dc20   94–23678

Typeset by Colset Pte. Ltd., Singapore
Printed in Great Britain by St Edmundsbury Press,
Bury St Edmunds, Suffolk

THEORY IN PRACTICE SERIES

General Editor: Nigel Wood, School of English, University of Birmingham

Associate Editors: Tony Davies and Barbara Rasmussen, University of Birmingham

Current titles:

Don Juan
Henry IV
Mansfield Park
A Passage to India
The Prelude
The Tempest
The Waste Land

Forthcoming titles include:

Antony and Cleopatra
Hamlet
Measure for Measure
The Merchant of Venice
To the Lighthouse

Contents

The Editor and Contributors

JONATHAN GOLDBERG is Sir William Osler Professor of English Literature at The Johns Hopkins University. His recent books include *Writing Matter: From the Hands of the English Renaissance* (1990) and *Sodometries: Renaissance Texts, Modern Sexualities* (1992). He is co-editor with Stephen Orgel of the Oxford Authors *Milton* (1991), and editor of and contributor to *Queering the Renaissance* (1993).

RONALD R. MACDONALD teaches Renaissance English literature at Smith College in Northampton, Massachusetts. He is the author of *The Burial–Places of Memory: Epic Underworlds in Vergil, Dante, and Milton* (1987) and *William Shakespeare: The Comedies* (1992), a contribution to the Twayne's English Authors Series.

KIERNAN RYAN taught at the universities of Geneva and Oxford before taking up his present post as Fellow and Director of Studies in English at New Hall, University of Cambridge. He is the author of *Shakespeare* (1989; 2nd edn 1995) and the editor of *King Lear: Contemporary Critical Essays* (1993). His most recent book is *Ian McEwan* (1994), and he is currently working on a study of Shakespearian comedy and romance.

PETER WOMACK lectures in English Literature at the University of East Anglia. He is the author of *Ben Jonson* (1986) and *Improvement and Romance: Constructing the Myth of the Highlands* (1989). He is now working (with Simon Shepherd) on a cultural history of English drama.

NIGEL WOOD is lecturer in English at the University of Birmingham. He is the author of a study on Jonathan Swift (1986), and of several essays on literary theory, has co-edited essays on John Gay (1989), edited a selection from Frances Burney's diaries and journals (1990), and is editor of the *Theory in Practice* volumes on *Don Juan*, *The Prelude*, *Mansfield Park* (all 1993), *The Waste Land* and *A Passage to India* (both with Tony Davies, 1994) and *The Tempest* (1994).

Editors' Preface

The object of this series is to help bridge the divide between the understanding of theory and the interpretation of individual texts. Students are therefore introduced to theory in practice. Although contemporary critical theory is now taught in many colleges and universities, it is often separated from the day-to-day consideration of literary texts that is the staple ingredient of most tuition in English. A thorough dialogue between theoretical and literary texts is thus avoided.

Each of these specially commissioned volumes of essays seeks by contrast to involve students of literature in the questions and debates that emerge when a variety of theoretical perspectives are brought to bear on a selection of 'canonical' literary texts. Contributors were not asked to provide a comprehensive survey of the arguments involved in a particular theoretical position, but rather to discuss in detail the implications for interpretation found in particular essays or studies, and then, taking these into account, to offer a reading of the literary text.

This rubric was designed to avoid two major difficulties which commonly arise in the interaction between literary and theoretical texts: the temptation to treat a theory as a bloc of formulaic rules that could be brought to bear on any text with roughly predictable results; and the circular argument that texts are constructed as such merely by the theoretical perspective from which we choose to regard them. The former usually leads to studies that are really just footnotes to the adopted theorists, whereas the latter is effortlessly self-fulfilling.

It would be disingenuous to claim that our interests in the teaching of theory were somehow neutral and not open to debate. The idea for this series arose from the teaching of theory in relation to specific texts. It is inevitable, however, that the practice of theory poses significant questions as to just what 'texts' might be and where the dividing lines between text and context may be drawn. Our hope is that this series will provide a forum for debate on just such issues as these which are continually posed when students of literature try to engage with theory in practice.

Tony Davies
Barbara Rasmussen
Nigel Wood

Preface

Thanks are due to the students of the Theory seminar at the Shakespeare Institute (University of Birmingham) at Stratford-upon-Avon who have helped me straighten certain matters out and complicate others. Professor Tom McAlindon kindly showed me his work on the Histories, which proved invaluable. As has become usual, I am indebted to all the contributors, who have helped make this a genuinely collaborative enterprise, and Alison, Naomi and Amber who, I am sure, will not want to hear of Henry IV for a long time.

Nigel Wood

How to Use
this Book

Each of these essays is composed of a theoretical and a practical element. Contributors were asked to identify the main features of their perspective on the text (exemplified by a single theoretical essay or book) and then to illustrate their own attempts to put this into practice.

We realize that many readers new to recent theory will find its specific vocabulary and leading concepts strange and difficult to relate to current critical traditions in most English courses.

The format of this book has been designed to help if this is your situation, and we would advise the following:

(i) Before reading the essays, glance at the editor's introduction where the literary text's critical history is discussed, and

(ii) also at the prefatory information immediately before the essays, where the editor attempts to supply a context for the adopted theoretical position.

(iii) If you would like to develop your reading in any of these areas, turn to the annotated further reading section at the end of the volume, where you will find brief descriptions of those texts that each contributor has considered of more advanced interest. There are also full citations of the texts to which the contributors have referred in the references. It is also possible that more local information will be contained in notes to the essays.

(iv) The contributors have often regarded the chosen theoretical texts as points of departure and it is also in the nature of theoretical discussion to apply and test ideas on a variety of texts. Turn, therefore, to question and answer sections that follow each essay which are designed to allow contributors to comment and expand on their views in more general terms.

A Note on
the Texts Used

Quotations from *1 Henry IV* are from the Oxford University Press edition, edited by David Bevington (1987), and from *2 Henry IV* from the Cambridge University Press edition, edited by Giorgio Melchiori (1989).
  In addition, the following Shakespeare editions have been consulted:

As You Like It	ed. Alan Brissenden (Oxford, 1993)
Cymbeline	ed. J.M. Nosworthy (London, 1955)
Henry V	ed. Gary Taylor (Oxford, 1982)
1 Henry VI	ed. Michael Hattaway (Cambridge, 1990)
2 Henry VI	ed. Michael Hattaway (Cambridge, 1991)
3 Henry VI	ed. Michael Hattaway (Cambridge, 1993)
King John	ed. R.L. Smallwood (Harmondsworth, 1974)
The Tragedy of King Lear	ed. Jay L. Halio (Cambridge, 1992)
The Tragedy of Macbeth	ed. Nicholas Brooke (Oxford, 1990)
The Merchant of Venice	ed. Jay L. Halio (Oxford, 1993)
A Midsummer Night's Dream	ed. R.A. Foakes (Cambridge, 1984)
Much Ado About Nothing	ed. Sheldon P. Zitner (Oxford, 1994)
Richard II	ed. Andrew Gurr (Cambridge, 1984)
Richard III	ed. E.A.J. Honigmann (Harmondsworth, 1968)
The Sonnets and Love's Complaint	ed. John Kerrigan (Harmondsworth, 1986)

Introduction

NIGEL WOOD

'We are Time's subjects, and Time bids be gone' claims Hastings in *2 Henry IV* (1.iii.110), and yet, by Act IV, according to Westmoreland, he is brought 'to the correction of [the King's] law' (IV.ii.85). Hastings's pithy dictum offers an exhortation to seize the day, while simultaneously exhibiting an anxiety that human motivation, however fervent, might be beside the point: subject to no king, he is still ruled by circumstance and the fathomless power of Time. Is it Henry IV or some always hidden ironic temporal process that brings Hastings to the block? If the latter, then is Time always on the side of Authority against Rebellion? Does it have a purpose? For Henry IV, there are clear reasons why a reliance on a metaphysical right to power is impossible, of course, as, in usurping the throne from Richard II, he feels he has forfeited God's direct aid. Similarly, his perspective on History suggests its crucial indecipherability:

> O God, that one might read the book of fate
> And see the revolution of the times
> Make mountains level, and the continent,
> Weary of solid firmness, melt itself
> Into the sea; . . .
>   . . . how chance's mocks
> And changes fill the cup of alteration
> With divers liquors!
>
>   (*2 Henry IV*, III.i.44–8; 50–2)

So much is this the case that even the 'happiest youth' on his setting out would learn to be circumspect, and even 'shut the book and sit him down and die' (III.i.55).[1] However careful one may be to describe and so frame Time linguistically, by metaphor or proverbial emblem, this is only apparently successful. The 'book of fate' does not in fact exist; cups can hold the 'liquors' of mutability, but the contents are still unknowable. A verbal performance can only demonstrate an eventual failure to catch Time on the wing – especially when the case is language in the service of theatrical gesture.

The promise of History is that Time may be rendered significant when one allows events to speak for themselves, and intelligible when one traces human motivation and its results in patterns of cause and effect. When Hotspur upbraids Worcester and Northumberland for their part in Richard II's fall, he imagines the shameful verdict of History, when proven testimonies that they helped in the usurpation might 'fill up chronicles in time to come'. This need not be the verdict of posterity, however, as he is clear that 'time [yet] serves wherein' they might 'redeem/. . . banished honours' (*1 Henry IV*, I.iii.171; 180–1). For Hotspur Time is not yet History until his own death, when 'life' becomes 'time's fool' and Time itself, 'that takes survey of all the world,/Must have a stop' (V.iv.80–2). This moment of tragic irony all but confirms Hotspur as hero and reminds the audience of his determination to 'dive into the bottom of the deep' and ignore Worcester's 'secret book' of sound advice, his apprehension of a 'world of figures' instead of 'the form of what he should attend' (I.iii.203; 188; 209–10).

This attempt at self-fashioning, one could claim, is not actually seriously entertained by Shakespeare. After all, the very first audiences knew that Hotspur was the stuff of History, and so could appreciate that all 'deeps' bottom out. Moreover, one could claim that attendance at a play entails a surrender to a highly structured experience, where all freedoms are provisional ones. History plays inevitably take Time as their subject matter, and so they may be historiography by other means. If followed to its conclusion, however, this portrays Shakespeare's hands as closely bound by (and in) the book of History. Holinshed or Hall may be widely read and authoritative chroniclers of the events here covered by Shakespeare, but to regard drama as a chronicle or Tudor pageant is to miss a crucial point. Theatrical representation does not merely conjure up the axiomatic and traditional – if it does, then it is likely that it does so in order to confute or challenge it. Even if one were to come across a dramatic portrayal of historical events that tallied exactly with one's own knowledge of the period derived from

other sources and media, one would still have to concede that the
re-presentation not only holds such 'events' up to an audience's judgement, drawn to the venue by the promise that History was now to be
staged not repeated, but also that 'History' second time around is con-
cocted by those who selected the arena, those who constructed the set
and designed the costumes, and the one who cast the roles. One could
go further. Whenever a record of the past passes beyond the barest annal
it becomes a form of narrative. Indeed, one could make the claim that
even the choice of *this* as opposed to *that* fact with which to start the
account involves a prior choice of frame within which to present one's
History and the results that may be forthcoming from it.

We either regret the lack of verisimilitude involved in this translation, and pull the History play back in line with what is an acceptable
historical account, or welcome the boldness of statement that is at the
very least implicit in the staging, and so celebrate the constant tension
between preserving the past and exploiting it. Thus it is no surprise to
find certain chronicled events prominent in the History plays as
Shakespeare could not here invent a battle of Illyria or of Belmont or
parody to an extreme degree an audience's understanding of recent
history. One is not being an illegitimate artist if one treats the past
as a powerful fund of symbols and archetypes rather than as a series
of 'finished', autonomous events. Indeed, this appropriation of the
past could be a poetic duty, hardly surprising when one considers the
fact that *historia* then signified 'story' and that a *History* indicated both
the attempt to describe the past faithfully *and* to use the colours of
rhetoric to narrate it. When outlining his project in composing the
Faerie Queene (1590), Edmund Spenser clearly regarded his romantic
allegory as a 'History', and himself a 'Poet historical', to be numbered
alongside other 'antique Poets historicall', such as Homer and Virgil.
A 'Historiographer' 'discourseth of affayres orderly as they were donne,
accounting as well the times as the actions', whereas a Poet need
only have recourse to 'thinges forepaste' while 'diuining of thinges
to come' so as to arrive at a 'pleasing Analysis' ('A Letter of the
Authors . . . To the Right noble, and Valorous Sir Walter Raleigh . . .',
Spenser 1977: 737–8). For Sidney in his *Apology for Poetry* (1595),
it was the especial excellence of poetry that it exceeded the 'truth
of a foolish world' to which historians were 'captived', for, laden
with 'old mouse-eaten records', they had to authorize their versions
'upon other histories, whose greatest authorities are built upon the
notable foundation of hearsay' (Sidney 1965: 111, 105). Although not
included in the Folio division of Histories, the Quartos of *Merchant*

of Venice (1600) and *King Lear* (1608) were advertised as 'Histories'.[2]

One of the matters that this contextual information illustrates concerns the relative validity (and expected success) of History in its task of framing Time and so making its passage comprehensible. Spenser's 'Poet historical' treats historical records as signifiers of wider metaphysical import, and also as destined to provide fallible evidence for our present predictions – like the equivocations of Macbeth's Witches. Henry IV only makes it as far as the Jerusalem chamber. This vanity that accompanies the desire to order Time is a literary commonplace, usually an adjunct to religious homilies against human presumption.[3] All might eventually be vanity, according to this topos, but there were several degrees of assent to this idea, and the occasional denial. When Warwick responds to Henry IV's figure of the 'book of fate', he is far less pessimistic about historical prophecy:

> There is a history in all men's lives
> Figuring the natures of the times deceased,
> The which observed, a man may prophesy,
> With a near aim, of the main chance of things
> As yet not come to life, who in their seeds
> And weak beginning lie intreasurèd.
> Such things become the hatch and brood of time, . . .[4]
>
> (*2 Henry IV*, III.i.79–85)

Henry seems reassured, and returns to an assessment of affairs of state with renewed attention: 'Are these things then necessities?/Then let us meet them like necessities' (III.i.91–2), yet, on reckoning the enemy power, Warwick contradicts his sovereign, and lays the blame on the inevitable encroachment of Rumour, which 'doth double, like the voice and echo,/The numbers of the feared' (III.i.96–7), and, personified in the Induction to the play, sets a keynote of sophistry and polyphonic misinformation.[5] In practice, necessity is obscured by false reports, even if 'the main chance of things' seems within grasp – indeed, *must* appear so, if we are to act at all.

This level of doubt may seem a little hyperbolic, for both parts of *Henry IV* are destined, one might think, to conclude with Henry V's coronation, yet this is hardly the meat of the enterprise as the Art that lies in the writing of History is realized only when these connected events signify something other than themselves, and exhibit *difference* – between the expected account and what is finally delivered, between individual motivation and an overall pattern traced by the Poet/ Historian. In Pierre Macherey's terms, this gradually unfolding form of 'knowledge' is 'not the discovery or reconstruction of a latent meaning, forgotten or concealed', but rather 'something newly raised up, an addition to the reality from which it begins' (Macherey 1978: 6). Thus we may retain the critical edge of Shakespeare's poetic histories by finding its historiography a pretext in every sense.

Critical Judgement and the History Play

From the writing of *Richard II* (1595) to that of *Henry V* (1598–9) the target audience for dramatic accounts of recent history must have been a large one. For example, there were at least three plays registered on Henry V from 1587 to 1596 (see Taylor 1982: 1–5), and *1 Henry IV* went through seven Quarto editions before the 1623 Folio (two in 1598, and then one in 1599, 1604, 1608, 1613 and 1622). Shakespeare's theatrical associations were also well established by 1595. The Chamberlain's Men were performing regularly at the Globe, and were protected by a well-placed peer at Court, the Lord Chamberlain, whose tasks included the organization of courtly entertainment and taking the reports of the Master of the Revels. While not quite 'rude Mechanicals', the company must have anticipated an invitation to Court. This did not mean that they were conformist – or, indeed, that the Histories were safe chronicle material. The events of 1599–1600 provide an instructive example. When occupying the Curtain Theatre as a temporary base, they revived *Henry V*, and marked the occasion with the inclusion of inflammatory lines for the Act V Chorus in clear praise of the Earl of Essex (V.0.26–34). Despatched to Ireland to tame the Earl of Tyrone in March of that year, Essex actually had a disappointing campaign, and was put under house arrest for a year on his return in September. It is entirely possible that the company were sympathetic to the Earl's aristocratic Puritan faction (in opposition to the Admiral's Men at the Rose), a view reinforced by the topicality of *Richard II*. On the eve of the Earl's abortive rebellion (8 February 1601), a specially commissioned performance of the play, drawing on a series of clear parallels between the decadence of Richard's advisers and Elizabeth's, took place and involved them thereafter in protracted legal wrangling. The invitation to perform at court came – the day before Essex's execution (24 February). As Peter Thomson points out, 'It was through such theatrical timing that Elizabeth I sometimes bit her biters' (Thomson 1992: 71). Also, in February 1599, one John Hayward dedicated his *The First part of the life and reign of King Henry the IIII* to Essex, and went to the Tower of London in the summer of 1600. Nearer to home, it is clear that Shakespeare's choice of the name of Falstaff was not his first, and that extrinsic historical pressures determined a late switch from Oldcastle. There are still vestiges in the Folio text of the first scheme. In Falstaff's first scene, Hal puns on 'my old lad of the castle' (*1 Henry IV*, I.ii.40–1), the 1600 Quarto bears the assignment of a speech at *2 Henry IV*, I.ii.96, to *Old.*, and the Epilogue to Part 2, protesting perhaps too much, refers to an 'Oldcastle' who 'died martyr', and that Falstaff 'is not the man' (Epil., 24–5).[6] The historical Sir John Oldcastle was a Lollard leader martyred during Henry V's reign, and the descendants of his widow had climbed into influential positions in Elizabethan politics. Sir William Brooke, the seventh Lord Cobham, had been Lord Chamberlain from August 1596 to his death in March 1597, a post principally responsible for the licensing of plays. Falstaff must have seemed a much safer option, but the initial decision to name a historical personage as the Falstaff figure shows a daring and desire to engage with contemporary politics – and also a satirical motive to deal dismissively with Protestant fundamentalists.

As a key to some Ur-Falstaff, however, noting this late change is crucial. It may account for the occasional narrative detail where Falstaff seems to have unexpectedly bridged the gap between Court and Tavern, especially the high-powered council at *1 Henry IV*, Act V, scene i. Oldcastle had been a 'meetely good man of war', according to John Stow, in his *Annales of England* (Stow 1592: 550–1), and John Bale's account of Oldcastle's death regarded him as a '*blessed Martyr of Christ*', according to the title page, which also portrays him with sword and shield – see Taylor (1983: 93–7); but see also Goldberg (1992a) for an alternative view on Taylor's editorial decision to reinstate Oldcastle instead of Falstaff. The very least one could say is that Shakespeare did not frame his accounts of recent history in a hermetically sealed form: they were sensitive to an audience's deep-seated prejudices and could therefore manipulate them. To a degree, this is borne out by certain contemporary non-chronicle sources (or influences). *The Famous Victories of Henry the Fifth* (printed in 1598) was an anonymous play that showcased the slapstick comic talents of Richard Tarlton, who had died in 1588, and presented Hal in a more unflattering light than in Shakespeare's texts, taking trouble to show the future monarch boxing the ears of the Chief Justice, and being sent to prison as a result. *The Famous Victories* showed a relish for the lawlessness that Shakespeare tempers and loads on to Falstaff and company. So well-known must Shakespeare's use of Oldcastle have been that when Michael Drayton and Anthony Munday (among others) compiled *1 Sir John Oldcastle* for the Admiral's Men in 1599, its Prologue went out of its way to exonerate the damaged memory of their hero (see Bevington 1987: 3–10). The vogue for dramatized history did not imply purely antiquarian interests.

There is ample evidence to suppose that the history play was not a suddenly popular form, even if it grew to maturity in the 1590s. Ribner (1957: 33–67) gives a full account of the form's first specimens, a gradual development from the morality play, replacing the moral and spiritual crisis of an 'Everyman' figure with that of the nation – see also R.L. Smallwood's 'Shakespeare's Use of History', in Wells (1986: 143–62) and Dean (1990) for some revealing information on Elizabethan two-part histories. For the second tetralogy, there is little doubt that allegorical imaginations were at play, most certainly in the audiences and why not for Shakespeare? Margot Heinemann crystallizes the full democratic potential for the form (and Richard's deposition in particular) when she claims that the audience were thereby encouraged to think and debate fundamental issues of state: 'It is not the answer [as to whether kings may be deposed] but the question that subverts. The drama gives people images to think with, and thus reinforces confidence in their own ability to understand and discuss conflicts of state' ('Political Drama', in Braunmuller and Hattaway 1990: 177). The conflicts, however, are not ones designed to be diluted by some final homage to present distributions of power.

This is perhaps to be inferred from another History play that can be dated from this period of composition, *King John* (probably 1593–4). As R.L. Smallwood makes clear in his Introduction to the Penguin edition (1974, 11–16), it is a play that, at the same time as it is less obviously political in theme than its sources, is also clearly intended to suggest a contemporary Elizabethan context. The shock of the Bastard's ironic commentary at the court in Act I, scene i and his parodies of the claims to legitimacy might remind us of a first draft of Edmond from *King Lear*:

> QUEEN ELEANOR: The very spirit of Plantagenet!
> I am thy grandam, Richard. Call me so.
> BASTARD: Madam, by chance, but not by truth; what though? . . .
> Who dares not stir by day must walk by night,
> And have is have, however men do catch;
> Near or far off, well won is still well shot,
> And I am I, howe'er I was begot.
>
> (*King John*, I.i.167–9, 172–5)

In Act V, scene vii, John dies (unhistorically) of poison in the Abbey garden at Swinstead.

The insistence on a bastardized first person can cut both ways, either as an undercutting of political seriousness or as the new radical Promethean voice, punishable but heroic. This insistence on the first person marks the second tetralogy, as do the possibilities for parody. One thinks of the daring potential in *1 Henry IV*, Act II, scene iv, where it is the prince's understanding of the mock court at Eastcheap (more an Elizabethan reality than a Plantagenet one) that the state could be taken 'for a joint-stool', the 'golden sceptre for a leaden dagger' and the crown for a 'pitiful bald' cushion (II.iv.367–9). This is reminiscent of the paper crown that mocks York in *3 Henry VI*, Act I, scene iv, or the emptying of the crown's significance that Richard II senses at *Richard II*, IV.i.181–221. Phyllis Rackin has documented how self-reflexive these Histories could be, one eye on an original source, the other on a contemporary application (Rackin 1990: 1–39). In this, they have been fruitfully read as 'carnivalesque' explorations of social turbulence (see Holderness 1992: 130–77) and attempts at redefining ideas of kingship (Howard 1994: 129–53).

Ceremony ceased to have quite so magical a hold on the mythical imagination. The 'idol ceremony' identified by Henry V (*Henry V*, IV.i.228) was not an isolated sentiment. If this is scepticism, then it is certainly a benign form, but as Richard C. McCoy conjectures, this was even the atmosphere of the Elizabethan court (' "Thou Idol Ceremony": Elizabeth I, *The Henriad*, and the Rites of the English Monarchy', in Zimmerman and Weissman 1989: 240–66). If this present phase of radical reassessment seems to take the political intent as evident, we shall see how comparatively recent this emphasis has been, and how this hinged on the separation of its ceremonial function (the idea that one gathered to see a play confirm one's cultural identity) from its dramatic potency (the idea that drama can only truly take place once questions of identity and inheritance are being seriously debated outside the theatre).

To be purist: the decision to edit a volume of studies on the *Henry IV* plays would seem to offer a premature hypothesis, namely, that there might be an organic link between both, and possibly also a close association with the other works that comprise the second tetralogy, *Richard II* and *Henry V*. There also hovers around this delimitation of interest a questionable assumption that, because the Folio demarcated Histories from both Comedies and Tragedies, it follows that these plays possess distinct generic properties. The critical history of these plays inevitably

involves broader questions of integrity and continuity, authorial intention and/or historical circumstance.

There is ample internal evidence to lead us now to regard both plays
as distinct dramatic units, but of an extended scheme. The promised
rejection of Falstaff Shakespeare kept back until Part 2, and there are
clear indications that, as early as Act IV of Part 1, there are preparations
for a prolonged treatment of Henry IV's post-Shrewsbury problems.
The otherwise unnecessary introduction of the Archbishop of York in
Act IV, scene iv, points forward to Prince John's venture in Part 2 and
the rebellion is only in recess at the conclusion of Part 1. John's prediction of Henry V's French campaign that closes the action proper of Part
2 (V.v.98–101) plus the detailed preview of *Henry V* in the Epilogue
(20–6) seem to clinch the matter: as Andrew Gurr has it, *Richard II* was
regarded as 'the initial play in a sequence planned as three or four plays
about the Lancastrian phase of English history' (Gurr 1984: 1). The
heart of the matter is contained in that 'three or four': whether Part 2
was an integral unit from the start, or grew out of a pragmatic judgement (an afterthought), given the ground already covered in Part 1.

Compared to the immense popularity of Part 1, Part 2's single Quarto
printing of 1600 indicates that it was probably less acted, and so less
regarded as possessing its own organic unity. The darker shades of Part
2 – Falstaff's less robust good humour, the political manoeuvring at
Gaultree Forest which might seem a poor substitute for the chivalric
good form surrounding Hotspur's death and Hal's bravery, the
diminished focus on individual actions and values – can be explained as
Shakespeare compiling an acceptable logic out of what was actually left
on the cutting-room floor and so softening us up for the necessity of
putting Falstaff by at the play's conclusion. The most comprehensive
account of the factors that might bring us to that or a similar conclusion
can be found in Giorgio Melchiori's Introduction to his Cambridge edition of Part 2 (especially pp. 1–15), where he unequivocally finds the
play a 'remake' or sequel.

The less flattering, or at least more objective, perspective on regal
authority contained in Part 2 can be explained away, not as Shakespeare's
game plan, but as an unfortunate side-effect of his role as a jobbing
playwright. I will return to this debate on the so-called structural
'problem' in the review below on the critical history of the plays, but
it would be pertinent to isolate some critical consequences of this
preference, all of which question the universality and value given to the
providentialist thesis supposed to lie behind the project of writing the
Histories in the first place. The grand march of History, a favourite

proposition of older Historicists, would involve multi-part dramas, or series of gradually unfolding chronicles, thus representing on a formal level the integration they see present in Historical direction. Identify Part 2 as some inspired *ad hoc* calculation, and this faith is questioned, and becomes a black sheep in the tetralogy, to be excused indulgently, but not taken as seriously as more legitimate family members. Recently there has been a serious re-examination of the supposed links between the plays in terms of the extensive openings in dramatic representation for revisions and revaluations of previous dramatic episodes. Rather than a smoothly unfolding numinous design we actually perceive a series of radical discontinuities, which foster a constantly recursive response, forcing us to reappraise what we thought we had understood. As Harry Berger Jr recognizes, this can still promote the idea of a Henriad, but one where there is a 'process of continuous revision in which earlier textual moments persist like ghosts that haunt and complicate later moments, and thus take on new meaning' ('On the Continuity of the Henriad', in Kamps 1991: 227). Far from privileging an exclusively text-centred attention to echoes and internal allusions, Berger's insight – more fully expressed in Berger (1989) – is alive to the more spontaneous registering of shock and reversal that constitutes dramatic effect. Act I of Part 1 could thus become a different entity and so be seen more accurately, not as we encounter it in the linear sequence, but as we eventually understand it after the close of the particular dramatic unit for which we form an audience. While reminding us that the two plays were probably never performed together in Shakespeare's time (see Crane 1985), Paul Yachnin objects to the implicit values in play whenever critics write of 'structure' instead of 'sequence' in this quarter. This is part of a 'mistaken attempt to force the idea of aesthetic unity upon the genre of Shakespeare's Histories', and shows a failure to recognize the fact that Part 2, in dramatic effect, 'undoes [Part 1], revises its meaning in order to appropriate it to its own darker view of political life' (Yachnin 1991: 163, 171).

This perception is unsettling on two counts: first, it questions the consolation that humans can impose form and will on the surface heterogeneity of events; and second, it ushers in a newly politicized Shakespeare, involved in the struggles of his own time rather than transcending them. In Wolfgang Iser's terms, this centrality of political 'personality' is less a gesture of humanist confidence (although there is much of that impulse elsewhere in Shakespeare's plays) than an effect of the gradually dawning realization that 'events always provide their own momentum, and consequently politics becomes an indispensable necessity'. Though never a universal panacea, such a new-found emphasis on the political provided its own problems, for there was quite abruptly 'nothing politics could fall back on, invoke, or claim as orientation for the pursuit of success' (Iser 1993: 194). Dramatic events occur, but the value awarded them and their eventual results are often in scare-quotes.

Providence and Poetic Drama

As Richmond, Henry VII rings down the curtain on Shakespeare's first tetralogy of Histories with a stirring anthem of thanksgiving for the peace now smiling on England:

> O, now let Richmond and Elizabeth,
> The true succeeders of each royal house,
> By God's fair ordinance conjoin together!
> And let their heirs, God, if Thy will be so,
> Enrich the time to come with smooth-faced peace, . . .
> (*Richard III*, V.v.29–33)

That God should so have answered England's needs in time of civil strife is hardly in question. The present fortunate time where spectators can view war only as a dramatic spectacle derives from the union of York and Lancaster, met in the Tudor regime. As David Bevington acknowledges, Shakespeare's espousal of the Tudor myth is not without reservation, but

> *Richard III* offers a seeming contradiction to the lessons of the *Henry VI* plays that de facto rulers of whatever shortcomings are to be endured in passive obedience. . . . Richard is the scourge of God punishing a nation for its rebelliousness, and his destruction is a sign of God's appeasement. The people themselves do not rise against Richard, and even Henry Tudor's role is tactfully discreet.
> (Bevington 1968: 242)

God's providential intervention and its second cause, Richard's insatiable (and improbably evil) ambition, prevent our identifying the Tudors as historical agents in their own right. Throughout *Richard III*, the power of prophecy works against the local freedoms of powerfully depicted individuals, through either the interventions of Queen Margaret (see especially Act I, scene iii) or moments where fated souls are given premonitory visions (the dreams of Clarence in Act I, scene iv, I.iv and of Lord Stanley, narrated to Hastings by the Messenger, in Act III, scene ii). For Raphael Holinshed, in Shakespeare's most consistently consulted historical source, *The Chronicles of England, Scotland, and Ireland* (2nd edn, 1587; 1st, 1578), the union with Elizabeth of York is actually founded on an astute political decision of Henry's, in Council. Holinshed's allegiances become clear when he describes Henry VII as 'more an angelicall creature, than a terrestiall personage' (Holinshed 1907: 424). Hall, in the parallel passage in his *Union of the Two Noble and Illustre Families of Lancaster and York* (1548), commits himself only as far as to say that peace 'was thought to discende oute of heaven into England' (Bullough 1957–75, III: 301). This is not supremely dramatic material, so it comes as no surprise that it is excised, but what we are left with is an apparently devout homage to God's plans for mankind.

If the first tetralogy (written, *c*. 1590–93) was based on a chronicle history's mingling of event and numinous guidance, then that is not to claim that Shakespeare took up History much as Holinshed had left it. Holinshed's protestant jingoism was infected by, and in turn nourished, topical war fever (see Bevington 1968: 187–95). God often ordains just wars, and was often moving in a mysterious way throughout this most turbulent era. Providence could only produce its effects through second causes, its human agents. For Wilbur Sanders, providential drama eventually robbed Time of its sudden intensities, depending instead on

> a sense of fitness in events, an unseen ripening which is manifested only in symptomatic changes in the political landscape – and since this sense reaches us at an almost pre-conscious level, being apprehended 'musically' as a kind of proportion and symmetry in the temporal ordinance of the action

it eludes the implicit questioning that dramatic representations provide (Sanders 1968: 102; see also 1968: 110–20) – hence the often complete split between vivid and sometimes violent action and interpolated scenes that supply choric commentary on it. One might point to the conflict between Jack Cade and Alexander Iden in *2 Henry VI*, Act IV, scene x, framed by Iden's expression of rural content and Cade's acknowledgement of God's justice, as well as Henry VI's prolonged description of the sway of battle at Towton, punctuated by the entry of both fathers and sons as victims of civil strife at of *3 Henry VI*, Act II, scene v.

What Providence enables, in terms of drama and most other narratives, is the depiction of an ironic distance between the partial knowledge aired by the protagonists and the greater degree of knowledge allowed the audience. Human volition cannot provide for long the means of seizing the day. In their varied ways, Hall, Holinshed and Samuel Daniel – in *The First Fowre Bookes of the Civile Wars Between the Two Houses of Lancaster and Yorke* (1595) – all supplied historical source material that emphasised divine interest in human affairs. This, until relatively recently, led commentators on Shakespeare's second tetralogy to perceive in the plays a mythic power similar to the first: usurpation leads to internal division, which can only be healed ('redeemed') after purgatorial distress by a ruler who rediscovers God's purpose and so modifies his personal goals thereby.[7] Shakespeare is drawn to depict disorder because of its inherent theatricality, but eventually this 'unofficial' delight palls, and the audience is content to rest on the rock of truth – which can be found most easily in a political order that resembles the Elizabethan, by either the Tudor connection or sanctified peace. While this could be a plausible (though generalized) account of the first phase, it raises more problems than it solves where the second is concerned.

To begin with what might seem the most obvious point: Shakespeare moves further away from the Tudor present with the account of the reigns from Richard II to Henry V. At the height of Henry V's prosperity (and England's), the Chorus is on hand to engage our imaginations one last time in looking beyond this act of amity. Queen Isabel invokes God's blessing on Katherine and Henry, to which 'All' say 'Amen' (*Henry V*, V.ii.344-54), but the accents of the Chorus fail to instil confidence in this as the final word. The 'mighty men' of this historical record might here be confined in a 'little room', their exploits too glorious for the 'rough' pen of the dramatist, but Henry is actually destined to have but a 'small time' as the 'star of England' – just a nine years' reign (1413-22) – before the troubles of Henry VI, when this painfully acquired French empire was quickly lost, and the state was once again caught up in civil war. Even if we were to have the Quarto version performed, which omits this epilogue, this doom is still felt to be waiting in the wings. The Folio Chorus, however, offers this closing happy tableau as some recompense for the anarchy portrayed in the first tetralogy, 'which oft our stage hath shown', and hopes that it will gain 'acceptance'. We are reminded of the events that will soon take place just as we are asked to forget them – and this will not be by divine sanction but by an audience's willing suspension of disbelief.

Secondly, it is not clear that the split between divine favour and the Crown is healed by Shakespeare's cycle. A more accurate perspective is that direct Providential power behind historical events comes to be regarded as a consolation that can never be as effective again. History has moved on, the modern state has to forage for itself, and kings should now find the initial right to govern by dint of personal qualities. Heaven will help those who will help themselves. When Richard II finds no angels ready to come to his aid at his deposition, the title of king becomes token:

> What must the king do now? Must he submit?
> The king shall do it. Must he be deposed?
> The king shall be contented. Must he lose
> The name of king? A God's name let it go.
> (*Richard II*, III.iii.143–6)

God may have willed it so, but this strikes at the root of several tropes of identification that characterize the emblematic explanation of natural existence: God's signature may not be as deeply on the world as Richard had imagined.[8] By Act IV image is disjoined from reality, individual perception from common sense:

> ... my grief lies all within
> And these external manners of laments
> Are merely shadows to the unseen grief
> That swells with silence in the tortured soul.
> There lies the substance; ...
> (IV.i.294–8)

Hal may banish Falstaff, but, as we have seen, the real test is whether he has banished the Falstaff within himself, and, perhaps more crucially, whether an audience can actually condone that action. Canterbury provides such a hagiography of Henry at the opening of *Henry V* that we might be in no doubt that 'Consideration' had indeed 'whipped th'offending Adam out of him' (*Henry V*, I.i.29–30). This is the character who announces in this same scene his strategy to deflect Henry's interest from turning church lands to secular philanthropic uses: to engage his attention on claims to French soil. In this he succeeds, especially by reviving the hereditary glories of Edward III – but this foray is presented as policy, and Henry is left ignorant of what he might have done at home. Far from underpinning his providential right to govern, the action centres on Henry's deepest fears that God might *not* intervene (IV.i.276–93) or that the only system of belief that keeps him in authority might be merely a powerful ideology (IV.i.221–40): 'Art thou aught else but place, degree, and form,/Creating awe and fear in other men?' (234–5). In this he both resembles his father in his regard for policy (compare *1 Henry IV*, III.ii.39–91 or *2 Henry IV*, IV.ii.329–47), and allows substantial doubt that he is in power *de jure* as opposed to *de facto*. One might note the Chorus's view of the miracle at Agincourt: 'Fortune made his sword' (Epil., 6).

Lastly, and possibly most revealingly, the peremptory removal of Eastcheap companionship is not total. Falstaff dies off-stage, Nym and Bardolph are hanged, the Boy is (presumably) slaughtered by the French in a manoeuvre not sanctioned in Fluellen's martial rules and Hostess Quickly succumbs to a sexually transmitted disease, but Pistol, rather like Autolycus in *The Winter's Tale*, is a reminder that the New Order will still contain discordant elements. Dishonourably, he will turn to the picking of pockets and the impersonation of a war veteran. Discerning the truth about Agincourt will not be a simple matter.

These formal considerations, selected from internal evidence, take us so far, but an understanding of how Shakespeare made dramatic capital out of orthodox belief demands some careful reference to his source material, and some of the cultural debate of the time. One of the problems stems from the readiness of our own readings to establish Machiavellian individualism as the only alternative to Providential trust. This is not the whole picture. Ever since recognition of the Thirty-nine Articles in 1571, the Church of England had tried to avoid, or at least mitigate, the severity of Calvin's views on predestination, the *locus classicus* being his *De Predestinatione* (1552). The concept of a God creating beings that were inevitably condemned to everlasting torment, no matter what they did, was often unacceptable, even if voiced by authoritative figures.[9] The troublesome Article of 1571 was the seventeenth, 'Of Predestination and Election':

> Predestination to life is the everlasting purpose of God, whereby (before the foundations of the world were laid) he hath constantly decreed, by his counsel secret to us, to deliver from curse and damnation those whom he hath chosen in Christ out of mankind, . . .
>
> (Rivers 1979: 124).[10]

In the political sphere, such a purpose was often ignored rather than refuted. Rather than the more deterministic texts in Romans (8: 28–31; 9: 13–16, 19–21), one could take the second commandment of the Decalogue (Deuteronomy 5: 9–10) to suggest that God takes an active part in human affairs for the promotion of Good and the punishment of Evil. There was, however, a potential gap between spiritual matters and how this private devotion was traceable in a wider temporal scheme. Henry V gestures to this when finding that 'Every subject's duty is the King's, but every subject's soul is his own' (*Henry V*, IV.i.168–70). To render up to Caesar true duty (however that might be interpreted) became a pragmatic matter involving second causes; it did not follow that one's spiritual status was intimately and necessarily involved. Hotspur, though a rebel, could still be honourable.

As Phyllis Rackin has shown, Shakespeare develops something of the agnostic's sense of God in the second tetralogy (see Rackin 1990: 59–85), advancing the safe thesis that 'all things have their first causes in the will of God' but at the same time enjoying double indemnity in exploring 'their second causes in the deeds of men' (1990: 69). Usually this is capable of a perfectly straightforward rationale: drama in this particular form of development dealt with new humanist sympathies that addressed discrete moral questions, dilemmas that would have been all but negligible if viewed through the wide lens of Providence. Differing priorities do not mean contradictions. Similarly, the Tudor myth was peculiarly amenable to a prehistory that stressed individual virtue and vice. For Ornstein (1972: 10–31), theatrical spectacle became all the more powerful as a political critique if we saw its manipulative power – as with the splendidly comic scene where Richard III stage-manages his own rapturous welcome by the citizens of London (*Richard III*, Act III, scene vii). We cannot quite so readily reassemble our faith in what could thereafter be intended as the genuine article.

It is less remarkable in commentaries on the Henriad that where Shakespeare resists Divine Right or Providential theories he is often drawing on equally accepted secular notions. In Richard Hooker's *Of the Laws of Ecclesiastical Polity* (1594; 1597) Natural Law was divine: 'See we not plainly that obedience of creatures unto the law of nature is the stay of the whole world?' (Book I.iii.ii, Hooker 1989: 60). Hooker then goes further than that; the natural can engross the rational, indeed is its test:

> The works of nature are all behoveful, beautiful, without super-fluity or defect; even so theirs, if they be framed according to that which the law of reason teacheth. Secondly those laws are investi-gable by reason without the help of revelation supernatural and divine.
>
> (Book I.viii.ix, Hooker 1989: 81).

Henry IV and V have to do without a sense of Providence. Instead of regarding this quite as they tell us to, as their inherited weakness, we should perhaps be kinder to their resort to policy as a natural *and rational* reaction to an unenviable political predicament.[11] As a representation of man's civil nature, the Henriad, in depicting the lifting of a hereditary curse, implicitly indicates as a result of Bullingbrook's usurpation an unexpected side-effect: the emergence of a more self-sufficient monarchy. Civil law may be 'diverse and variable' and derives from the 'opinion of man; it resteth wholly in his consent', according to Thomas Starkey in his *Dialogue Between Reginald Pole and Thomas Lupset* (*c*. 1533–6), and is not directly inferred from Natural Law, but rather is a test of an individual society's 'diligence and labour' (Starkey 1948: 31–2). Justice and the rule of law are sometimes the only constants in times of rapid change. For example, as a compliment to Elizabeth, Sir Edward Coke's *Reports* (1600) praised her management of an excellent legal system, one that ensured some modicum of continuity.

At this juncture, it should be stressed that I am not advocating that the *Henry IV* plays can be decoded as political allegories *tout court*. On the other hand, Shakespeare's deft changes to his sources do not only signify the work of a dramatist alert to attractive scenes and streamlined plots; the concentration also on the more figurative possibilities in these accounts has a certain resonance that we would do well to recognize. A few examples will suffice. Henry IV commences Part 1 by describing himself as 'shaken' and 'wan with care' (I.i.1), but finds this as one with the macrocosmic disorder that attends civil war. Holinshed similarly notes his 'unquiet reign', but is clear in relating these personal fears to the aftermath of a failed attempt on his life in 1401, so that he could not thereafter 'compose or settle himself to sleep for fear of strangling' (Bullough 1957–75, IV: 181). Falstaff's first scene (Act I, scene ii) is notoriously difficult to locate. The BBC Shakespeare placed it in Eastcheap and had Falstaff snoring behind a curtain at the back of the stage (as first suggested by Wilson 1943: 37), so as to supply a likely enough reason for the opening question – and consequently robbing it of any greater reference to wider temporal matters – whereas those who had taken their Holinshed to heart might have understood it as taking place in the prince's own apartments, deduced from a comment relating to 1411, when he came under review because of the 'great resort of people' who 'came to his house' (Bullough 1957–75, IV: 193). Cocoon it in a recognizable milieu and you both depart from what we know of Elizabethan stage practices and also retreat from the greater symbolic freedoms implicit in the scene. Similarly, by bringing Hotspur's age nearer Hal's (in actuality, he was twenty-three years older), he not only constructs a neater contrast but also loads their later hand-to-hand combat with a thematic conflict: Hotspur as the acceptably honourable and chivalric 'military title capital', who, according to Henry IV, had 'more worthy interest to the state', against the actual blood-line in the prince, 'the shadow of succession' (*1 Henry IV*, III.ii.110, 98–9).

Once these appropriations (among several others) are weighed in the balance, then the plays have a wider remit – not just to direct political matters, but also to less easily traceable cultural debate. As we have seen, Falstaff both is and is not a historical figure. As Fastolf, he is perhaps the 'cowardly knight' in *1 Henry VI* (see I.i.131–4; I.iv.34–6; III.ii.104–9; IV.i.9–47), but also has to receive some of the qualities of Sir John Oldcastle, a Lollard martyr, which would have been a clear case of influence from Holinshed, where he is similarly cast off from Henry V's circle on the latter's accession – 'a valiant capteine and a hardie gentleman' (Bullough 1957–75, IV: 376).[12] On the other hand, Falstaff is hardly just an allegorical personification, 'that reverend Vice' of *1 Henry IV*, II.iv.437. We will see below how this precarious alternation between the unsparing visceral commentator and symbolic figure has been the object of long and sometimes acrimonious debate. There is, however, a more general reflection which is not critical ecumenism for its own sake. Poetic drama is not constituted by its capacity for bearing information or packaged messages about the human condition. A multivalent figure such as Falstaff appears to suggest a myriad of possible readings at the same time as being impressive as a great original, a 'Falstaffian' persona.

Recent work on the dramatic presentation of 'character' has stressed the consequences of portraying a self within the process of a play's duration (see the Endpiece). If it is accepted that our knowledge of a list of *dramatis personae* is only ever secure in the most programmatic Humours comedies, then we receive 'knowledge' of what Hal is by a technique of registering the evidence, say, of his madcap antics and Eastcheap theatricals so as to develop a capacity to forecast what 'type' of actions he is likely to perform or what the basis for change might be. Hal may inform us of his intentions, yet he cannot help but give out lateral signals about himself as he does this. 'He' is gesture at the same time as he is a self-representation. Take the climactic moment in *1 Henry IV*, Act II, scene iv, when Falstaff's impersonation of Henry IV in the Eastcheap mock coronation leads him to offer fatherly advice against the banishing of 'plump Jack'. Hal answers 'I do, I will' (II.iv.462–3). When? At the end of Part 2, one could reply, but, as noted above, even this is not definitive.

Hal's penchant for gazing into the middle distance and constructing an acceptable regal self is characteristic of him. Like Hamlet, he can delay. In Act III, scene ii, when confronted by his anxious father, he is advised to *lose* 'presence', lest our view of it become 'glutted, gorged, and full' (84). He has become 'blunted with community' (76) and a 'common sight' (88), and yet at the same time the 'shadow of succession' (99). One of Hal's answers promises that he 'shall hereafter, . . ./Be more [himself]' (92–3). When? On inheriting the Crown, perhaps, but, then, can character be willed like that? As we have also seen, he then *loses* his being as Falstaff's Hal and starts again as Henry V. He becomes the office in Part 2 and less the individual – despite the earlier promises:

> This new and gorgeous garment, majesty,
> Sits not so easy on me as you think. . . .
> Not Amurath an Amurath succeeds,
> But Harry Harry. Yet be sad, good brothers,
> For, by my faith, it very well becomes you.
> Sorrow so royally in you appears
> That I will deeply put the fashion on
> And wear it in my heart. . . .
>
> (*2 Henry IV*, V.ii.44–5, 48–53)

Is there a distinction between the Harrys? Even the most cursory glance at the latter sentences quoted above reveals a curious identity between father and son. No matter how 'deeply' the fashion of sorrow is worn, the will intervenes, implying choice, not instinct (banished with Falstaff). Henry V rules with his father's vital 'spirits', to 'mock the expectation of the world', and 'Frustrate prophecies', yet any bets that a new king might aim to be regal at his coronation are safe ones. He now feels 'the tide of blood' flowing in him away from 'vanity' and towards extinction of the individual: 'Where it shall mingle with the state of floods,/And flow henceforth in formal majesty' (V.ii.123–32). Majesty has to be form, and yet Henry V believes that it produces personality.

This split between the public and private, the office and the individual, was supposed to have been healed at this point, and yet we see the one subsumed by the other. Is the above any longer Shakespeare's perspective just on Henry V? Or is it a reflection on authority? Is Falstaff mimetic? Seen from this vantage point, the plays pulse with hidden dramatic metaphors. For example, the 'formal' Lord Chief Justice is both a distinct character (in that one actor will represent him) and the very opposite of a character in the Romantic sense of a piece of autonomous life. It is no coincidence that he is increasingly referred to as 'Justice', and, at V.ii.102, kitted out with emblematic signs of office, the 'balance and the sword'. When financial 'reckoning' seems near for Falstaff (for example, in *1 Henry IV*, Act II, scene iv), there is always the distinct possibility that a moral account is being drawn up as well (see Falstaff's own definition of a 'trim reckoning' (*1 Henry IV*, V.i.135), and the Prince's at III.ii.147–52).

If we trace these symbolic moments as part of the relay towards an eventual moment of closure and resolution, then it is granted a significance that is only fully understood within, and judged against, the unity of conception of some immanent idea. For example, Edmond, in *King Lear*, may call his father's belief in the 'wisdom of nature' 'excellent foppery' as if one were 'villains on necessity' (I.ii.92, 104, 107), yet he is the prime example of a character whose plans fail to grasp hold of events. At his death, he acknowledges that 'The wheel is come full circle' (V.iii.164), and even his last atypical gesture, to do some good, 'Despite of mine own nature' (V.iii.218), in trying to save Cordelia from his own orders for execution, comes to nothing. Albany asks for the 'gods' to 'defend her' (V.iii.230), yet we are more impressed by their cruelty than their poetic justice (for a more comprehensive account, see Wilders 1978: 29–52). The play of *King Lear* has a structure, yet the tragedy lies in the portrayal of a potentially motiveless world. There is as much Fortune as Destiny in this.

Falstaff and Historical Order

The critical history of the *Henry IV* plays follows one consistent course: the resolution to make sense of Falstaff's attractiveness and Hal's obduracy in rejecting him. In Barbara Hodgdon's *The End Crowns All* it becomes clear that the most pressing problem posed for directors is that of whether Falstaff is damned the first time we meet him (see Hodgdon 1991: 152–61). The early stage history of the plays is so unequal, with Part 1 a stock favourite and Part 2 grudgingly billed as a sequel, as in Thomas Betterton's adaptation for Drury Lane in 1720. Even then, it was the comic Falstaff that sold the play, as Betterton omitted most of the historical scenes in the first three acts (the only exception being I.iii), and added to the prominence given to Pistol. It was not until David Garrick's influence (1758–70) that Part 2 achieved the kind of sonority accorded Part 1, and that was largely on the back of a sumptuous coronation scene. These are, however, isolated novelties. Due to Thomas Killigrew's astute management of the King's Company mainly at the Red Bull Theatre in Clerkenwell, Part 1 was a staple ingredient of the seasons from 1660 to 1669. Betterton made the part of Hotspur famous in his 1682 revival, but it was his Falstaff in the 1699–1700 season at Lincoln's Inn Fields that set the stamp on the play as a comic masterpiece.

The full Folio text was rarely played, but the nineteenth-century theatre's capacity for scenic magnificence greatly affected the relative emphases placed on History and Comedy. W.C. Macready played King Henry and Charles Kemble the Prince in the 1821 revival of Part 2, which included a glittering (and long-winded) coronation scene, a formal compliment to George IV's own crowning (see Odell 1963, 2: 166–9; Hodgdon 1993: 10). Kemble's own production of Part 1 in 1824 at Covent Garden and the tercentenary tribute in 1864 at Drury Lane both found Falstaff a welcome, but also at times supernumerary, guest at a particularly ceremonial feast. In Frank Benson's 1894 Part 2 at Stratford-upon-Avon, the particular virtues of that play came to the fore, and Falstaff's theatrical fortunes were revived. Benson's own Falstaff was daringly epicurean, and his eventual fate full of poetic justice. Benson went on to present a 'cycle' of Histories at Stratford between 1901 and 1906, yet surprisingly omitted Part 1 to smooth the transition towards *Henry V*.

The vogue for performing and viewing both parts on a single day (or even in a single run) is a twentieth-century taste. Sir Barry Jackson commemorated Shakespeare's birthday (23 April) in 1921 at Birmingham Repertory Theatre with a full text of both plays, and this was followed by a double-header in 1932 to mark the opening of the New Memorial Theatre at Stratford. This ability and willingness to stage 'cycles' of the Histories led to a renewed understanding of how Part 2 could be thematically a part of a wider sense of British destiny. In 1951, Anthony Quayle provided both parts at Stratford as part of the Festival of Britain celebrations and Trevor Nunn similarly opened the Barbican base for the Royal Shakespeare Company in 1982.

The greater acquaintance with Part 2 also tilted Falstaff's role from that of knockabout clown to that of the sadder and wiser humorist. This was the point to Orson Welles's *Chimes at Midnight* – or, in the United States, *Falstaff* (1966). The film was a digest of both parts, but heavily weighted towards the impending rejection. Welles's Falstaff was rarely out of shot, the main exception being the extravagant battle of Shrewsbury which lasted all of ten minutes (see McMillin 1991: 97–9). War was brutal and brutalizing, and Falstaff's often bewildered reaction was carried over into his private dealings with Hal; in the public world of the Plantagenet court it is inconceivable that he could survive – more an object for *pathos* than *praxis*.

As a 'cycle' of History plays (with almost their full texts) has only been a recent proposition, the opportunity for assessing whether the structural unity of the two parts made theatrical sense has been brought up against the stubborn armchair belief that they *should*. The texts' early critical history, however, did not often follow theatrical practice. While the two parts were considered separate items theatrically, most readers were persuaded of their essential unity. Falstaff was a constant point of reference, and often the plays stood or fell according to how his role was regarded. It is heartening to find one of his earliest commentators, John Dryden, fully alive to the contradictory aspects of his persona, for he stood for the progressive resources of non-Humours characteriza-tions. In his *Of Dramatick Poesie, An Essay* (1668), Neander cites Shakespeare as the irregular genius: 'All the Images of Nature were still present to him, and he drew them not laboriously, but luckily . . . he needed not the spectacles of Books to read Nature' (Vickers 1974–81, 1: 138). Falstaff cannot be understood by the textbook enumeration of character types, as he is 'a Miscellany of Humours or Images', and his attractiveness stems from his very being rather than his script: 'for the very sight of such an unwieldy old debauch'd fellow is a Comedy alone' (Vickers 1974–81, 1: 140). By 1679 Dryden (*in propria persona*) had taken Falstaff even more seriously to heart in his 'Grounds of Criticism in Tragedy'. French neoclassical theory had prescribed simplified types in tragedy to allow their representative functions freer rein and the tragic action greater freedom, but Falstaff 'is a lyar, and a coward, and a Glutton, and a Buffoon, because all these qualities may agree in the same man' (Vickers 1974–81, 1: 258). It is tempting to locate Dryden as the period's spokesperson, but he is hardly that. Falstaff is strong medicine to swallow, if his jests actually carry an audience with him. The Rev. Jeremy Collier paused in his wholesale attack on the debauchery of Etherege, Wycherley and Congreve, in his *Short View of the Immorality, and Profaneness of the English Stage* (1698) to tackle the problem of Falstaff's eventual fate. He is consoled by the reflection that Falstaff is a comic part, but admires the eventual unfurling of a '*Unity of Design*', where he 'is thrown out of Favour as being a *Rake*, and dies like a *Rat* behind the Hangings' (Vickers 1974–81, 2: 88).

If Falstaff and Hal are to be distinct not only in social class but also in spiritual composition, then the two plays must exhibit a purpose to throw 'old Jack' off at last. Repeatedly, though, critics of the eighteenth century found Falstaff recalcitrant material. In Nicholas Rowe's *Account of the Life of Shakespeare* (1709), for example, it was a 'Fault' to make Falstaff 'Vicious' while at the same time giving him 'so much Wit as to make him almost too agreeable' (Vickers 1974–81, 2: 195). We may consequently be sorry to see him so cast down by the end of Part 2. Corbyn Morris in 1744 had to forget certain awkward details to conclude that he could be an 'amiable character' and was treated so roughly at the close 'in Compliance with the *Austerity* of the Times, and in order to avoid the Imputation of encouraging *Idleness* and mirthful *Riot* by too amiable and happy an Example' (*An Essay Towards Fixing the True Standards of Wit, Humour, Raillery, Satire, and Ridicule*; see Vickers 1974–81, 3: 122). Here there are none of the intimations of mortality and sickness of Part 2, nor the opportunistic gesture towards Hotspur at the close of Part 1. Increasingly, the century found that Falstaff and Hal were more than types and the result was to explore a divided response in the audience, which, according to Henry MacKenzie in *The Lounger* (1786), entailed an identification with the prince to

> admire while they despised. To feel the power of his humour, the attraction of his wit, the justice of his reflections, while their contempt and their hatred attended the lowness of his manners, the grossness of his pleasures, and the unworthiness of his vice.
>
> (Vickers 1974–81, 6: 441)

In a sense, this is to jump ahead over Johnson's edition (1765) and Maurice Morgann's (at the time) perverse celebration of Falstaff in the *Essay on the Dramatic Character of Sir John Falstaff* (1777). Morgann will be considered more fully in my Endpiece, but it is necessary to note at this point how the *Essay* defends Falstaff from the imputation of cowardice. While not dwelling too much on Part 2, he finds throughout a dramatic tactic of the comic undercutting the moral interest. This is because he appeals to the 'Impressions' of an audience and not their understanding:

> With a stage character, in the article of exhibition, we have nothing more to do; for in fact what is it but an Impression; an appearance, which we are to consider as a reality; and which we may venture to applaud or condemn as such, without further inquiry or investigation? But if we would account for our Impressions, or for certain sentiments or actions in a character, not derived from its apparent principles, yet appearing, we know not why, natural, we are then compelled to look farther, and examine if there be not something more in the character than is *shewn*; . . .
>
> (Morgann 1972: 203)

This isolation of the specifically dramatic function of Falstaff's characterization shelves difficult ethical decisions by hiving them off on to the effects on the rational powers. We behave differently in an auditorium. This perspective is not fully shared by Johnson, but there are passages where he realizes that matters of performance alter the nature of verbal communication. For example, his note to *1 Henry IV*, I.ii.201 (Hal's speech announcing the future renunciation of his 'loose behaviour') finds it 'very artfully introduced to keep the Prince from appearing vile in the opinion of the audience'. Here we see the display of a 'great mind' in the process of 'offering excuses to itself' (Johnson 1986: 170). This distance from Hal is part of Johnson's attempt to comprehend the plays as a scheme, where, as the Headnote to Part 2 has it, they are so 'connected that the second is merely a sequel to the first; [they are] two only because they are too long to be one' (Johnson 1986: 178). This manoeuvre sets up a running dichotomy between Falstaff's powers of 'perpetual gaiety' and his vices which should excite 'contempt' (Johnson 1986: 188).

As the new century dawned, the political aspects of this view of authority grew to prominence. Jonathan Bate's work on the early Romantic period's use of Shakespeare's character studies uncovers a series of parallels waiting to be teased out, the authority of the national poet underpinning certain otherwise controversial doctrines. Hal could figure the Prince Regent in his socializing with the Opposition lobbyists such as Charles Fox (Falstaff?), whose weight seemed a gift to caricaturists (see Bate 1989: 74–86). This partisan use aside, there was a definite swing back towards the need to regard Hal (and Hotspur) as 'the essence of chivalry', in Hazlitt's words in his *Characters of Shakespeare's Plays* (1817). However, his Republican sympathies surface most strongly when he considers Henry V alone in his own play: 'He was fond of war and low company: – we know little else of him. He was careless, dissolute, and ambitious; – idle, or doing mischief' (Bate 1992: 360, 364). With this in mind, Hazlitt is still not alone in lionizing Falstaff's 'masterly presence of mind, an absolute self-possession, which nothing can disturb' (Bate 1992: 358). This preference for Falstaff would eventually engender a complete distrust of Hal. John Masefield, in his *William Shakespeare* (1911), even denied him the status of a hero: 'he is not a thinker, he is not even a friend; he is a common man whose incapacity for feeling enables him to change his habits whenever interest bids him' (Masefield 1911: 112; see also Yeats's verdict on Hal as a man of 'gross vices' and 'coarse nerves', compared to Richard II, who becomes a poet and martyr (Yeats 1961: 108)).

This energetic discovery of satire in the historical action as well as the comic plot emerges exactly when theatrical preference was for the high-flown and rhetorical. One major watershed in critical thinking on the plays occurs when an understanding of History changes, and it is no surprise that, when Hegel's panoramic understanding of global History affects criticism, there should be a move away from character study. Hermann Ulrici's *Shakespeare's Dramatic Art* refuses to recognize individual characters as items of critical attention; at best, they are 'living hieroglyphics' (Ulrici 1876: 236), part of the representation of an age's whole historical process. Before one finds here a blanket homogeneity of approach, Ulrici shows a careful understanding of Falstaff's role, which has 'an ironical character' and works 'to parody the hollow pathos of political history' (1876: 244). Falstaff is merely 'personified parody' (1876: 245).

It is worthwhile pausing to take in the strands of this legacy for more recent ideas on what constitutes a History play. Ulrici identifies the plays as propositions about History – not as History itself. There may seem to be little that is truly controversial about that, but the irony does not cease with Falstaff's banishment. It is still present – erosive and undermining – even at Henry V's coronation. This is a critical problem as well as an opportunity: how can we approach the plays as a play of opposites or as moral debate, if Shakespeare does not appear to be taking sides – if, indeed, the most powerful dramatic force would seem to be a figure hardly recognizable as historical at all? In Falstaff, there could be more to consider than his culpability or wit, as if these were 'personal' qualities. It is the function assigned to the wit and infectious good (or bad) humour that might be the central point.

Falstaff, Hal and the Time of Day

Falstaff's first words are compelling evidence that he lives in a different time zone from Hotspur, and, as we shall see, from Hal:

FALSTAFF: Now, Hal, what time of day is it, lad?

PRINCE HENRY: Thou art so fat-witted with drinking of old sack, and unbuttoning thee after supper, and sleeping upon benches after noon, that thou hast forgotten to demand that truly which thou wouldst truly know. What a devil hast thou to do with the time of the day?

'Hours' are converted to 'cups of sack', 'minutes' to 'capons', 'clocks' to 'tongues of bawds' and 'dials' to 'signs of leaping-houses' (brothels) (*1 Henry IV*, I.ii.1–9). If we were to progress beyond the evident moral distaste here expressed, then we might grant Falstaff's (and, temporarily, Hal's?) experience of time a certain value, for it does not seem that he is to be fooled by time as Hotspur is. Hal does not avoid likening the 'fortune' of his Eastcheap society to that of 'moon's men [that] doth ebb and flow like the sea, being governed as the sea is by the moon' (I.ii.30–1). This tidal and *natural* flow is so cyclical it would seem to cheat that inevitable linear progress towards death that is hidden by Falstaff's initial metaphorical inspiration, here picked up by Hal. Yet it is typical of him to enjoy Falstaff's irresponsible self-display while stemming it and finally closing down its serious options: the amoral freedom from destiny actually obeys a final reckoning, where there is eventually an ebb as low as 'the foot of the ladder' that will lead to 'as high a flow as the ridge of the gallows' (I.ii.35–7). It is not just Hal who is pulled two ways in this scene, for it is often forgotten that Falstaff, too, is not the unregenerate hedonist of (romantic) caricature. The very next line has him assent to the truth of Hal's careful manipulation of his rhetoric, and also proceed with his own prophetic hopes of life when Hal shall be king – 'shall there be gallows standing in England when thou art king? And Resolution thus fobbed, as it is with the rusty curb of old Father Antic the law?' (I.ii.56–8). Will the new King Henry hang thieves and break the circle? This is not an isolated theatrical *geste* either, as he returns in Part 1 to his own version of the fragility of his sustaining illusions[13] at the Eastcheap coronation ('banish not [Falstaff] thy Harry's company – banish plump Jack, and banish all the world' (II.iv.461–2)), when he meditates on 'hell-fire and Dives' whenever he catches sight of Bardolph's beacon of a nose (III.iii.28–31), at the realization that he owes death a life, in the midst of his more familar catechism on honour (V.i.127–8), and also when resolving to 'purge and leave sack' under the new post-Shrewsbury dispensation (V.iv.159–60). A case could be made for Falstaff as the character most hounded by Time's wingèd chariot.

In the more obviously grave Part 2, where Falstaff is frequently separated from fellowship and left to his own more chastened self, his need to believe in Hal's continued protection is desperate. At the point when the Folio has the prince and Poins enter, but now in disguise, Falstaff is chided by Doll Tearsheet for his lack of spiritual preparation. Increasingly, Time's reckoning intimates mortality: 'Peace, good Doll, do not speak like a death's-head, do not bid me remember mine end . . . I am old, I am old' (*2 Henry IV*, II.iv.190–1, 222), the 'chimes at midnight' sound at III.ii.177, and, by Act IV, scene i, his 'natural' behaviour includes the duping of Justice Shallow, rather as a 'young dace' is bait 'for the old pike' – 'Let time shape, and there an end' (IV.i.266–8). The final dismissal by Hal (as Henry V) is not the putting by of the Falstaff of Act I, scene ii, in Part 1.

If Falstaff comes to regard time as Time, a symbol, not just a condition, of earthly existence, then one could maintain that, *if* we were to assess the two plays as a unit, then Shakespeare is gradually writing the 'radical' Falstaff, the libertine rake, out of his script. This would be to construct a streamlined model of dramatic experience that excludes as much as it apparently solves. The more an audience is made to attend to these portents, the more sympathy is likely to mingle with an original admiration and amoral joy at Falstaff's wit. Take the concluding sentiments of Act V, scene i. Falstaff muses on the 'participation of society', witnessed by the increased identity between those in command and those they command – here, between Shallow and his retinue: 'It is certain that either wise bearing or ignorant carriage is caught, as men take diseases, one of another. Therefore, let men take heed of their company' (V.i.59–62). Does he speak hereby of more than he can know? Or, in terms less regulated by the *dramatis personae*, how reminiscent is this of Henry IV's homily to the prince on 'vile participation' that had lost him 'princely privilege', back in Part 1 (III.ii.86–7)? Does he here anticipate the reasons for his own banishment from Hal's favour? This irony is embedded in the experience of the whole play, not the compartmentalized registering of how individual characters 'grow'. A play might shape time (five-act structures, comedies or tragedies) and, in Elizabethan staging, contain more or less consistent actors-as-characters throughout its duration, but this formal description leaves unexplored the multiple and contradictory effects of the theatrical process. Characters are fully known only by dint of the other voices that, in their absence, have just spoken or that will speak (sometimes, not directly or logically connected – 'as men take diseases'), as well as those that provide accompaniment and dialogue for them. When Falstaff aims to store up instances of Shallow's folly for Hal's 'continual laughter', this eternity of shared and continual merriment ('without intervallums'), dissolves the more it is thought on, a span eventually measured by the finite units of the judicial year: until 'the wearing out of six fashions – which is four terms – or two actions' (*2 Henry IV*, V.i.63–5). Falstaff may reach nostalgically for a future of Eastcheap escapades at the same time as provide an audience with evidence of how this, for Hal as well as him, is by now quite out of reach, a passing fashion among

many. When Act V, scene v, portrays Hal's progress as king, his entry
(s.d. 35) is announced in the Folio as '*Enter King Henrie the Fift*'; we
should also bear in mind the fact that Falstaff's 'Hal' is throughout Part
1 'Henry' in the Folio and 'Prince Henry' in the 1598 Quartos. For Part
2, the part is designated 'Prince Henry' in the Folio, and just 'Prince'
in the 1600 Quartos – until its sudden replacement by 'King' to match
the elevated status. Does 'Hal' exist, except in Falstaff's familiarity?

The shock that attends the king's disowning of not only Falstaff and
the Eastcheap crew but also, note, by association, the ineffectual
Shallow at Act V, scene v, is a necessary narrative item, one could argue,
to conclude the account with satisfying finality, to show the regal and
courtly caste system as inevitable and essential to maintain the impersonal good order that could only be in peril if it admitted such members
as Falstaff. As Peter Womack (in this volume) makes plain, though, it
would be a mistake to expect consistent realism in Shakespeare's plots.
If realism calls for a redundancy of detail to signal a possible profusion
of non-figural references, and an attempt to 'ground' the action and
characters in recognizable contexts, then one would be hard put to it
to identify passages that provided totally autonomous agents and
actions – that is, those free of any cross-reference to other areas of the
plays (or those that comprise the second tetralogy) or that could not be
regarded as significant colouring for Shakespeare's larger purpose. This
is before we consider the (conscious or fortuitous) role provided for an
audience that often does not feel unequivocally either for or against the
main protagonists at this point, that may appreciate how necessary the
king's gesture was without relishing its effects, or be glad that true
Authority takes centre stage, or suddenly feel how calculating 'Hal' has
been all along, or perceive the personal loss that Henry must endure to
fulfil his destiny – or, more likely, a mingling of all or some of these
reactions.

There is ample opportunity for symbolic action in a History play, as
the overall pattern of events portrayed is already likely to be in the
public domain. What is far more notable is how the action is to be
judged and how our sympathies are generated throughout. When
Falstaff encounters Henry in Act V, scene v, with his 'God save thy
grace, King Hal, my royal Hal' (V.v.36) he dares to yoke the formal
and untouchable with the idiomatic and personal. Pistol may have
envisaged that '*semper idem*' (a favourite motto of Elizabeth's) will be
appropriate as well as ''tis all in every part' (V.v.24), but the next forty
or so lines demonstrate a new order of radical change and dislocation,
and not just for Falstaff. He may now be old and vain, but Henry's

speech (43–68) illustrates a painful split in 'Hal's' self, a turning away from the immediate and bodily to the abstract concerns of duty and an intense need to exercise the Will to rewrite his own personal history:

> I have long dreamt of such a kind of man,
> So surfeit-swelled, so old and so profane,
> But being awaked, I do despise my dream.
> Make less thy body hence, and more thy grace, . . .
>
> (V.v.45–8)

He is not to be viewed as 'the thing [he] was' because he has 'turned away [his] former self' (52, 54). He has fashioned himself a king.

In Henry's words, here as elsewhere in both parts, there is much of the future tense. It is crucial to trace the *lack* of finality in this dismissal. First, 'telling' an audience might not be as powerful as the impact of the full (non-textual, visual) spectacle of the speech act, which cannot always be successfully conveyed just by a series of cut-and-paste excerpts. Second, Falstaff is promised 'competence of life' (62) and, if he will also remake himself, 'according to [new] strengths and qualities' (65), the hope of a second chance. Falstaff, indeed, is deep in plans for the evening's dining arrangements, and is about to pass these words off as 'colours' (pretences – 82), when the Lord Chief Justice, Prince John and 'Officers' – not Henry – return to convey them all (Shallow included) to the Fleet prison. John may 'like this fair proceeding of the king's' (90) and stress that they '*Shall* all be very well provided for' (92, emphasis added), but not, it would seem, just yet. Holinshed and Stow both mention this magnanimity,[14] yet Shakespeare conveys their testimony in a token manner; the dramatic action has spoken louder.

Lastly, and possibly more revealingly, Henry is not here involved in a performative act. His word *will* be law, but we do not see him enact it yet. It is not literal-minded to find Henry's dream of Falstaff's 'kind' (quoted above) a curiously evasive affair. Falstaff is not mentioned by name. 'I know thee not, old man' (43) sounds clear enough, yet Henry is actually practising a form of verbal *noli me tangere*. Falstaff can be held in perspective as long as he is a type or far-off in a dream. His 'body' needs to be dissolved, much as does Henry's 'former self'. He is not to 'presume' him the '*thing*' he was. What is more, the depiction of the 'surfeit' associated with Falstaff occurs in Henry's dream. Now that he is awake, he might 'despise' Falstaff's importunate reality, one might have thought, not his own capacity for dreaming. Henry banishes this 'former self' quite as much as he does Falstaff, and just as he imagines a time when his erstwhile friend might once again involve him in

'participation' then that will be the time when the Gadshill Hal is
resurrected:

> When thou dost hear I am as I have been,
> Approach me, and thou shalt be as thou wast,
> The tutor and feeder of my riots;
> Till then I banish thee, . . .

(V.v.56–9)

This is to protest too much, perhaps, and certainly not to offer a
definitive exile. The main struggle is within the king's own person. He
has just buried his natural father and now needs to escape his other
father-figure, that unofficial 'tutor and feeder'.[15]

What final shape is here given to the historical action? John's last
speech opens the action yet further with a prophecy that 'civil swords
and native fire' (99) will be borne as far as France, the project of
Henry V, as does the Epilogue, which promises a continuation with 'fair
Katherine of France' and Falstaff, who may well 'die of a sweat' (22–3).
In *1 Henry IV*, our first chance to size up Hal is also an introduction
to the 'private' history of his own development – a path that he regards
as one of his own choosing, where, sun-like, he might break 'through
the foul and ugly mists' of participation, 'when he please again to be
himself'. Just twenty lines later, his father will also vow to be himself,
rather than consistent with his 'condition', 'smooth as oil, soft as young
down' (I.iii.5–7). Hal, similarly, will aim to disappoint the prophecies
of others, yet fulfil none of his own, when he pays 'the debt [he] never
promised' (I.ii.190, 188, 197). Unlike Hotspur, his redemption of Time
is a falsification of 'men's hopes' (199), and an exceeding of his 'word'
with his own person (198). The Time to be saved is, on one level only,
that tainted by the illegitimacy of his father's usurpation, as it picks up
Hotspur's own usage at I.iii.180 (quoted above), and I.iii.206, where
he imagines his resuscitation of 'drowned honour' (205). The main topic
of the scene has been the claim for redemption from Glendower of
Hotspur's brother-in-law, Mortimer – a financial metaphor, but, in
Hotspur's hands, it is heroic and even chivalric.

In what sense does Henry V redeem, or rediscover, himself? Hal
seems to believe that outward shows cannot display his hidden self, so
it would be tempting to ask the question: how can an audience decipher
this real self, if indivisible from the office of king? To speak of the self
does not prove its existence; on the contrary, it could signify its loss.
When in conference with his father, Hal goes through a familiar litany
of self-defence, responding to the accusation that his membership of the

House of Lancaster has become honorary, and that 'the hope and expectation of [his] time/Is ruined' (III.ii.36–7). In Henry IV's discourse, the king's 'presence' is a manipulable asset, 'like a robe pontifical,/Ne'er seen but wondered at' (56–7), which leads to his observation that Hotspur has more of this necessary 'presence' than contained in the direct blood-line. The prince vows to be henceforward 'more [himself]', and declares that this will be the case by an assumption of a chosen persona, 'When I will wear a garment all of blood/And stain my favours in a bloody mask' (135–6). This, when 'washed away' will be a potent form of astringent, to 'scour' his shame (137), the aim being to 'redeem' his good name 'on Percy's head' (132). This eventuality is witnessed and underlined by the king himself at V.iv.47, in gratitude for the saving of his life – an action, not an oath. In combat with Hotspur, Hal can now dub him a rebel and himself the 'Prince of Wales' (61–2).

It is no accident, here, that these accents of redemption should have a Pauline ring. Colossians 4: 5 advises us to 'Walk in wisdom toward them that are without, redeeming the time', and Ephesians 5: 15–16 could have been a text close to Henry IV's heart: 'Walk circumspectly, not as unwise, but as wise,/Redeeming the time, because the days are evil'.[16] Conversion here implies a radical reassessment of the passage of time and how one is figured in it. As we will see below, there is a thematic as well as a commercial point to Hal's backsliding in Part 2 (more opportunities for a reprise of madcap japes), but even as he toys with his good reputation once more, he is frequently clear about the figure he is cutting. Faced with Poins's naïve invitation, for example, to wed his sister, Hal immediately observes his behaviour from without: 'Well, thus we play the fools with the time, and the spirits of the wise sit in the clouds and mock us' (*2 Henry IV*, II.ii.108–9). When informed of the new alarms by Peto, he feels himself 'much to blame/So idly to profane the precious time' (II.iv.294–5).

The above account of Hal's development has largely stayed within the expectations of realism. Hal's 'character' has been assessed by what is directly scripted for him, and, for the sake of closer analysis (so the formula has it), his existence within the play has seemed autonomous, to be approached via our collection of 'real-life' touchstones, equivalent behaviour which we might regard as obeying a parallel course with that depicted in a fictional, dramatic frame. To choose an extreme example, this faith in the validity of direct mimesis has long been the virtue of A.C. Bradley's work on Shakespeare (and, for those antagonistic, its vice, too). Here is his provisional conclusion in his 'The Rejection of Falstaff' (1902; reprinted in Bradley 1909) as to why the Hal that had once laughed with Falstaff could ultimately disown him so suddenly and publicly: 'He had shown himself [in Eastcheap and Gadshill mood] . . . a very strong independent young man, deliberately amusing himself among men over whom he had just as much ascendency as he chose to exert. Nay, he amused himself not only among them, but at their expense' (Bradley 1909: 254). The motivation discovered by Bradley is true of a psychologically consistent case study, and implies that Shakespeare worked within a theatrical tradition that placed superior value on such a private, non-political, non-allegorical process. Bradley regrets the need of the History play to reflect a non-poetic truth, to finish with Falstaff appearing 'no longer as the invincible humorist, but as an object of ridicule and even of aversion'. This relies on an audience that responds in an obedient fashion; what they are told (overtly, textually), they inevitably feel. The fact that we still feel the force of dramatic shock in the rejection scene Bradley cannot but feel as a miscalculation: 'in the creation of Falstaff he overreached himself. He was caught up on the wind of his own genius, and carried so far that he could not descend to earth at the selected spot' (Bradley 1909: 273) – a piece of God's plenty.

On the other hand, what to some can seem like miscalculation, to others can appear realistic and parodying. We have already seen how it is at least viable to conclude that Shakespeare used the History play in a particularly self-conscious way. For Bradley the excess associated with Falstaff upsets the scheme of History. Ronald Knowles identifies a central weakness in Bradley's approach: 'At no time does Bradley recognise how the imperatives of comic role-playing might modify naturalistic explanation in terms of dramatic convention and audience engagement' (Knowles 1992: 41). As an alternative to this search for some level of naturalistic theatre, there was also a call for situating the plays, and Falstaff particularly, within theatre history. E.E. Stoll and John Dover Wilson, especially, accentuated the mythic power of Falstaff. Stoll rejected the call for sympathy on an audience's behalf, but, in finding Falstaff a stage clown *tout court*, he refuses the persona a wider function (see especially Stoll 1927: 472). For Wilson, in his *The Fortunes of Falstaff* (1943), not only was he a *miles gloriosus* or braggart soldier, but an embodiment of Riot or Vanity. Certainly, in the closing passages of the work, Wilson is alive to the immediate and non-allegorical in the dramatic texture, but Hal and Falstaff both develop in a transcendental world of art. For C.L. Barber, Falstaff similarly becomes a lord of misrule, a type rather than an objection (Barber 1959). Wilson found the 'English spirit' alive and well in the plays, which 'ever' requires two ingredients, 'Order as well as Liberty' – and found the action treading carefully between 'the bliss of freedom and the claims of the common weal' (Wilson 1943: 128). Barber (without the Englishness) was equally convinced that the risks taken with Falstaff could be contained within a scheme that kept the office of king eventually uncontaminated. His *Shakespeare's Festive Comedy* (1959) countered a generation of dismissive readings of comic power, and the deft understanding of the embedded traits of saturnalian comedy is a genuinely new departure. As Graham Holderness notices, though (Holderness 1992: 143–4), Barber's determination to have misrule a manageable threat which at the last has an audience gravitate towards Rule shows some strain. Barber may claim that the comedy operates non-satirically, but he also is acutely aware of the 'dangerously self-sufficient everyday scepticism' of Falstaff (Barber 1959: 214).

The movement towards celebrating hard-won order out of the threat of chaos is a sustaining myth about History – and less applicable to the local effects of drama. It is in the work of E.M.W. Tillyard, however, that the more optimistic perspective on the plays and their culture can be found. *Shakespeare's History Plays* (1944) was well timed. A full span of Shakespeare's historical concerns now included the Henry VI plays which could with some safety be identified as his, and this provided Tillyard with an opportunity to analyse them for the first time as a genre and a long-considered project. Following closely his *The Elizabethan World Picture* (1943), this study shared many of its preoccupations: a striving towards a totalizing grasp of complexity until it could be summed up in a 'World Picture' and yet a faith in the humanist model of a suddenly central location for human concerns. Tillyard's understanding of Elizabethan culture was based on a set of correspondences between the macrocosm and the microcosm, Man:

> Of all the correspondences between two planes that between the cosmic and the human was the commonest. Not only did man constitute in himself one of the planes of creation, but he was the microcosm, the sum in little of the great world itself.
>
> (Tillyard 1944: 16)

This world is a purposive one, and is imbued with a providential direction; all is a part of a consuming whole, and Man, while he has a more active power of choice than was usually stated in the Elizabethan homilies, is still constrained by natural order.[17]

So out of favour has Tillyard's thesis become that his work now forms a wide and now inert enough target for the clumsiest cultural materialist to hit. The objections to totality can be easily enumerated – the depiction of a belief to which only the most literate of the population had access, the model of interdependency with a final ruling term of order (God?), the limiting of figurative profusion until it fitted preconceived categories on which varied sentiments 'must have' been based – but the positive global alternatives have not been as forthcoming. According to Hugh Grady, this is the legacy of the modernist Shakespeare (Grady 1991: 177–89), a critical image of the work that stresses polyphony and fracture, which favours periods of radical change rather than those of cultural consolidation. It is also the result of searching analysis based on the Marxist concept of dialectic, an unresolvable struggle between contending forces out of which usually unsought syntheses appear. This is development, but it is not foreknown in detail nor guided by some ideal authority.[18] Tillyard's work requires some notion of basic order, a reflex that Elizabethans simply accepted. As we have seen, this reliance on Providence was by no means universally accepted, and does not account for the emergent features of the History play.

One can take this historical reflection a little further. In answer to John Dover Wilson, William Empson recorded in the *Kenyon Review* for 1953 a series of objections to the tendency to face dramatic effects as if they were likely to be pointing all in one direction. Instead, Empson suggested we try to comprehend what happens when these events are narrated in a dramatic medium, using 'Dramatic Ambiguity' (Empson 1986: 37). The trick is not to overread to discover thinking that the dramatic images never quite serve, nor to rest content when we have located what an audience might have found obvious. Doubt and uncertainty are exactly what an audience immediately receive from the portrayal of Hal, pleasure and vicarious freedom from Falstaff. Here the balance is one of uncertainty, not underlying conviction. If we are asked if Hal actually robbed anybody, if indeed he is the Prince out of *The Famous Victories*, then the safest conclusion is that Shakespeare could have made matters a lot clearer if he had seen fit to (see Empson 1986: 40–2). That is the point where the politics of performance, then as now, individual productions as well as constraining and informing ideologies, takes over – and repays the most thoroughgoing materialist scrutiny of the lot.

CHAPTER 1

Hal's Desire, Shakespeare's Idaho

JONATHAN GOLDBERG

[There is a perennial temptation to so manage the expression of sexual desire that the marginal and heterodox is comprehended only as deviant or perverse. This tyranny of the normal permeates most writing, either as a form of self-censorship or, even deeper, as the observance of what appear to be 'natural' limits to literary expression, outside of which (in more than one sense) lies the incomprehensible. Thus the paucity of direct references to homo-erotic or lesbian desire in early modern culture is no evidence that it did not exist. On the contrary, it testifies only to the fact that twentieth-century terms of difference did not directly apply. As Eve Kosovsky Sedgwick makes clear in her study of *Between Men* (Sedgwick 1985), legal and social repression of homosexual activity effaced, and often still disguises, a myriad of relations between men many of which stop short of full sexual contact. Her preferred term is the 'homosocial', which can embrace tendencies as well as actions.

Jonathan Goldberg here addresses these concerns and so offers a model of how to decipher homosociality within works that do not appear to take sexual identity as a topic. In Michel Foucault's *La Volonté de savoir* (1976, trans. as *The History of Sexuality* (1978)), the inaugural volume in his three-part study of sexual discourses, sodomy in the early modern period (before the eighteenth century) was known as an 'utterly confused category' (Foucault 1978: 101), denoting an intention of those defining rather than those defined. Rather like the term 'atheism', 'sodomy' gestured towards a number of deliberately ill-defined practices, the one constant factor being their illegitimacy. As a quasi-legal term, it reinforced the heterosexual norm, and banished those areas that hindered or questioned 'the strict economy of reproduction'. The result was a powerful prejudice against 'unproductive activities' and 'casual pleasures' that was as much discursive as legal in its repression, the aim being 'to reproduce labor capacity, to perpetuate the form of social relations' (Foucault 1978: 36–7). More was involved than simply a misguided drive towards physical health (the apparent and often stated motive); it was the deployment of a form of overall social correction. Indeed, Foucault goes further: sexuality became a means of exploring the secret and individual drives of desire. As a result, the 'deployment of sexuality' became increasingly more distinct from the 'deployment of alliance', which typified 'a system of marriage, of fixation and development of kinship ties, of transmission of names and possessions' (Foucault 1978: 106). In critical practice, Foucault envisaged a split between an *ars erotica* (the *plaisir* of the text) and a *scientia sexualis* (towards a sociological understanding of the economic and cultural forces that produce notions of sex). This virtuoso historiography advanced on at least two fronts, yet both confronted the central proposition: how and why could sexual pleasure be converted into a moral issue? (See Foucault 1988: 252–85.) For Foucault, from as early in his work as *L'Archéologie de savoir* (1969, trans. as *The Archaeology of Knowledge and the Discourse on Language* (1972)), this was due to the 'historical a priori', less a 'condition of validity for judgements' than a 'condition of reality for statements' – a smuggling into discourse of preconceptions (Foucault 1972: 127).

It should be clear from the above why those critics interested in exposing this deep structure of prejudice should be 'perverse'. As Jonathan Dollimore and Alan Sinfield have noted, this is nothing less than the discovery of alternative modes of defining the 'sexual' and also the 'historical' (see Dollimore and Sinfield 1990: 91–100), and, for Dollimore, the correct and liberating gesture is towards the 'transgressive reinscription' of gender and erotic models for conduct (Dollimore 1991: 279–325), a using of the rules of discourse to unstructured ends.

In his *Homosexual Desire in Shakespeare's England*, Bruce R. Smith regards works of fiction as privileged arenas that give us 'intimate access to [the] scripts of sexual desire' (Bruce Smith 1991: 16), which, while paying lip-service to extant cultural formations, actually subvert them. The result is a varied and often contentious array of alternatives, which achieve shape only through the promptings of literary models and genres. These topoi give shape and so promote recognition of typical *literary* characters (see also Smith's 'Making a Difference: Male/male "Desire" in Tragedy, Comedy, and Tragi-comedy', in Zimmerman 1992: 127–49). For Gregory W. Bredbeck, in his *Sodomy and Interpretation* (1991), Shakespeare's references to male relationship, especially in his *Sonnets*, were ways of achieving insights into the poet's 'subjectivity at the expense of sexual meaning' (Bredbeck 1991: 169), a linguistic experiment, not covert testament to homosocial aspirations. In both these studies, the point is to examine the particular freedoms granted by literature by the lack of direct reference – to a perverse degree. Both these studies draw on Alan Bray's seminal *Homosexuality in Renaissance England* (1982) – see also his study of male friendship in Bray (1990) – where the division between fictional type and historical reality proves surprisingly permeable, and where there is no clear line to be drawn between actual sodomy and general 'debauchery', the projection of a general moral distaste for all forms of abnormality (Bray 1982: 13–32).

In these recent investigations of the forbidden and taboo, there is also a comprehensive reassessment of the normal masculine roles. To some degree, this emphasis has been on the agenda with particular power since Coppélia Kahn's *Man's Estate* (1981), which dealt with the threat to male identity from the strong, and therefore disobedient, woman. Using several psychoanalytical approaches, Kahn also gets to the root of strict gender differentiation: the male had to secure separation from the female in the early stages of maturation, and accept the mantle of patriarchal power. This sphere was, ironically enough, not fully separate because underpinned by necessary female approval (Kahn 1981: 8–20 and, on Hal, 68–81). This insight has been given a stronger Lacanian/feminist slant in the work of Valerie Traub, who has stressed the varieties of psychic exchange in the relationship between Hal and Falstaff (Traub 1989; reprinted in Traub 1992: 50–70) – see also Simmons (1993); David Kuchta's 'The Semiotics of Masculinity in Renaissance England' (Turner 1993: 233–46); and Juliet Fleming's 'The Ladies' Man and the Age of Elizabeth' (Turner 1993: 158–81). What is clear is that the 'unbuttoned' behaviour associated with Eastcheap was tainted with 'effeminacy', so that the dividing line between madcap immaturity and constitutional 'unmanliness' went unregistered – see Sinfield (1992: 131–8); and Goldberg's own call for a criticism that resists heterosexual normality in Goldberg (1992b: 145–75).]

NIGEL WOOD

The *Henry IV* plays are, no doubt, history plays, yet their relationship to at least one kind of history – the history of sexuality – has gone largely unexamined.[1] The reasons for this are not all that difficult to understand. Sexuality is often thought to be nothing other than heterosexuality, and there is, especially in relationship to the central drama of these plays – the prince's ascendance to the throne – little to be said on that score. The fact that women seem exiguous in this political plot could make the plays available to the kind of gender analysis that takes as foundational and virtually transhistorical the exclusion and subordination of women (assumptions that shape the argument of Phyllis Rackin's *Stages of History* (1990)); such analyses often assume as well that gender relations are always already structured invidiously by an equally transhistorical heterosexuality. Thus, to raise, as I will be doing here, questions around the history of sexuality might have consequences for how one understands the historicity of gender, and might lead, even by way of such unpromising texts as the *Henry IV* plays, to the prospect of a more fully inflected reading of gendered difference.

The history of sexuality is by no means a field that is so established that one can refer to it in an offhand fashion, however. For my purposes here, since it is his title that I am using, the name of Michel Foucault might be invoked (along with other historians who advocate social constructionist views, among whom Jeffrey Weeks (1981; 1990) might be cited as of particular importance), especially for a set of pronouncements in *The History of Sexuality* (Foucault 1978) which I take as guiding assumptions: that the regime of heterosexuality is a modern one, that it came into existence at the same time as (if not slightly later than) the identification of a sexual identity formation called homosexuality, and that the early modern period in which Shakespeare wrote did not know such distinctions. Rather, Foucault audaciously argues that sexuality *per se* is a modern phenomenon (the argument may be familiar by now, but it remains remarkably counter-intuitive to many); while the Renaissance and ages before had managed marriage relations between men and women as a means of conveying property, title, privilege – a host of social relations that Foucault calls *alliance* in *The History of Sexuality* – these sociolegal ties are not the site for sexuality if by that term one means a supposed personal core that defines individual desire and structures identity as a consequence of such desires. In the nineteenth century, Foucault argues, a vast sexual science was developed; from its panoply of sexual possibilities (masturbators, zoophiles, sadists, masochists and fetishists of every imaginable variety) emerged the dichotomy in which everyone is presumably straight or gay, and in which object choice alone defines sexuality. (The confusions around these suppositions, and the reasons to be sceptical about them, are a central subject of Eve Kosofsky Sedgwick's recent and immensely powerful *Epistemology of the Closet* (1990).)

What Foucault's argument implies in terms of a reading of the *Henry IV* plays within the history of sexuality is that the absence of women from the central drama of the play – which might, now, be recast as Hal's desire to arrive in his father's place – does not make the plays simply available for a reading of homosexuality in them. Such an alternative reading would be as deeply anachronistic as any that mistakes the management of gender relations in Shakespeare for an account of heterosexuality in the Elizabethan age. Gay readings of Shakespeare have been made, of course, particularly in relation to the sonnets, from Oscar Wilde's *Portrait of Mr. W.H.* (1889) on; however, the history of criticism on the sonnets (the academic formation being, as it happens, virtually coincident with the history we are considering here) has in large measure been characterized by massive evasions of the erotics of the poems or, more recently, as in Joseph Pequigney's *Such Is My Love* (1985), by dehistoricized banalizations of them. (Pequigney is to be credited, however, with pointing out that the ways in which the sonnets have been 'universalized' has involved treating them as the repository for timeless wisdom about love, the timeless and the universal always turning out to be nothing other than the heterosexual.) In reading male–male relations in the *Henry IV* plays I will be arguing that the syntax of relations mapped in the sonnets also can be found in the plays, not to argue (as Wilde does in *The Portrait of Mr. W.H.*) that these texts participate in some transhistorical homosexuality, but to seek to understand how male–male relations in the plays – relations which are or which *could be* construed as sexual – are to be read before the modern regimes of sexual identities can be presumed as reference points.

Luckily, powerfully suggestive ways to address such questions have been provided before. Alan Bray's *Homosexuality in Renaissance England* (1982) and the reading of Shakespeare's sonnets in Eve Kosofsky Sedgwick's *Between Men: English Literature and Male Homosocial Desire* (Sedgwick 1985) provide necessary analytic tools for this enterprise. Sedgwick's importation of the social scientists' term *homosocial* provides literary critics with a crucial lexical item to describe male–male social relations that can, but need not, be sexual. Bray's book is keenly attuned to the fact that its title advances an anachronism that its every page seeks to address. 'To talk of an individual in this period as being or not being "a homosexual" is an anachronism and ruinously misleading', Bray writes (Bray 1982: 16); rather, he focuses on terms available in the period, particularly on *sodomy* as the nearest word in the Renaissance lexicon for what moderns might call homosexuality. In doing so, he agrees with Foucault, who points to sodomy as that which ruins alliance, sodomy thereby comprising a range of sexual practices all bent on frustrating the marital tie and the presumption that marriage exists only to ensure legitimate sexual acts – those leading to procreation. Memorably, Foucault labels sodomy an 'utterly confused category' (Foucault 1978: 101), and one of Bray's aims is to show that the term includes a wide range of sexual practices. It would limit and confuse things to assume that the modern homo–hetero distinction gives one much analytic purchase in dealing with a socio-sexual order that found *sodomy* a term capacious enough to include bestiality, adultery, rape and prostitution, to name only some of the possible kinds of debaucheries that are not organized in terms of the distinction of gendered object choices. (This is not to imply that sodomy occupies an archaic register utterly unavailable to us now (the term and some of its ancient confusions survive into modernity in US law); nor is it to imply that something like an archaeology of the homo–hetero distinction cannot be traced in the Renaissance, a point to which I will be returning.) Even more to the point of a reading of the *Henry IV* plays – indeed, this is crucial – is Bray's insistence (fully congruent with Foucault's pitting of sodomy against alliance) that these sexual possibilities register only in particular social circumstances: sodomy names a crime, not a behaviour, and sodomites were those as likely to be accused as well of treason, atheism (or Roman Catholicism, virtually the same thing in Renaissance England), sedition and the like. If alliance is part of a social fabric, sodomy destroys it.

As Bray argues in the crucial third chapter of *Homosexuality in Renaissance England*, because sodomy was demonized it necessarily existed at some distance from actual socio-sexual relations (think of the work the word *communists* used to do, or that *terrorists* does). There is every reason to suppose that those accused of being sodomites did what others did as well. For, as Bray suggests, in a world that has not assumed that people make sexual choices on the basis of excluding one gender or the other, it seems likely that members of the same sex will be having sex with each other, and in ways so ordinary as to be virtually unperceived – necessarily unperceived, if the only label for such relations was sodomy and if sodomy was a world-destroying practice. Bray assumes, in fact, that the very structures that assured order and provided conduits for power in the Elizabethan age were the sites for practices that might be called sexual, that hierarchies and social differences were maintained or created by sexual relations. It is, to complicate Bray's point, perhaps more accurate to say that upon these sites something that retrospectively would be called sexuality fastened. In this culture, servants regularly slept together or with their masters, as did pupils with their teachers. Indeed, Bray argues, the hierarchies of public life (which, in effect, almost always means male–male relations of the sort featured in the *Henry IV* plays) were oiled with such sexual possibilities if not virtually requiring them as part of relationships of patronage; in fact, in a recent essay on 'Homosexuality and the Signs of Male Friendship in Elizabethan England' (Bray 1990), Bray claims that as the social order swerved farther from the social ties summarized under the word *friendship* (ties that could include patronage relations, diplomatic bargaining, influence trading of all sorts), the acts that constituted evidence for sodomy came to be increasingly indistinguishable from those that maintained the normative ties. Bray argues that changes in the social structure in sixteenth-century England that marked the breakdown of an older social order are the largest context in which this crisis of definition occurred. The ties of friendship were no longer those uniting gentlemen. Thus, whereas Henry VIII had instituted the Gentlemen of the Privy Chamber as his bedfellows, and his companions were nominally aristocratic, by the end of the century, in *The Arte of English Poesie* (1589), Puttenham could imagine that a social climbing poet might claim such a position too. Henry VIII, he reports in the eighth chapter of the first book of that volume, made Sternhold groom of the Privy Chamber for versifying the Psalms, and what the king did, Puttenham holds up as an example for Queen Elizabeth I.[2]

It is in such a context that one can see how euphemized it is to speak of the sonnets to the young man as bids for patronage – as Arthur Marotti (1982) does – as if a desire for favours meant only money or position. One can also see that however sexualizable these social relations are – and the language of the sonnets is hardly desexualized – these are not poems about homosexual relations; nor are they about sodomy. The poems are not written with any assumption about exclusive identities, and in that respect it is useful to recall that the first group urges the young man to marry, an injunction that is not seen as an alternative to the young man's relations with the speaker of the poems. Nowhere are the suggestions of sexual relations between men taken to constitute the antisocial behaviour of the sodomite. If anything like sodomy does appear in the sonnets, it is in relation to the so-called dark lady of the final poems, a woman with whom promiscuous, non-marital sex occurs; this is seen as debauched and transgressive sex, not least because it threatens to destroy the relation between the sonneteer and his beloved young man. That conflict, seen in these terms, is not one between homo- and heterosexuality.

Sedgwick's reading of the sonnets, which seeks to vacate the modern lexicon of homo–hetero difference to describe far more labile desires that cannot be captured by those labels, begins to offer tools for further differentiating and relating male–male and male–female sexual relations. Like Bray, she sees that male–male sexual relations need not be read as outside the normative systems that promote male interests at the expense of women (the homosocial order can be the patriarchal one and can seek to erase women, allowing them no function beyond serving as conduits for relations between men); tellingly, she argues that as homosexuality becomes more visible and differentiated in the modern period, men who choose other men as sexual partners become subject to annihilative pressures congruent with those placed upon women. Misogyny and homophobia, while hardly reducible to each other, are also inevitably intertangled. But these relations will not be the same in different historical periods, nor is there an easy calculus to map these volatile relations; the history of sexuality provides necessary leverage for any understanding of the historicity of gender and of gender relations.

It is from this cautionary position that I would mention one final frame for reading the *Henry IV* plays, one way Renaissance critics recently have adduced 'homosexuality' in Shakespeare. I have in mind arguments about cross-dressing, where the presence of the boy actor beneath the woman's clothes has been taken to mean that the only sexual desire that exists in Shakespeare is homosexual desire. Despite major differences in their arguments and approaches, for instance, this is a point of agreement between Stephen Greenblatt, especially in the final pages of 'Fiction and Friction' (Greenblatt 1988: 66–93) and Lisa Jardine in *Still Harping on Daughters* (1989). When Jardine conveniently forgets that women formed a considerable portion of the audience for plays, she leaves out something that must complicate the circulation of desire in the theatre (antitheatricalists, in fact, worry more about promiscuous debauch among men and women than anything else). An account like Greenblatt's betrays a complicity between misogyny and male–male desire, since it assumes that male–male desire can only batten on, even as it opposes, male–female desire. In these accounts (and others as well), transvestism is taken to reveal a homosexuality that is claimed really to be a hetero-sexuality *manqué*; the assumption made (even by feminist and gay affirm-ative critics, who should have no interest in making such arguments) is that the only difference upon which desire moves is gender difference, a position ably dismantled in Michael Warner's 'Homo-Narcissism; or, Heterosexuality' (in Boone and Cadden 1990: 190–206). Against such claims, one would want to argue that in a culture like Shakespeare's that did not make the homo–hetero distinction, the availability of either gender as a sexual partner cannot be understood through our modern categories (themselves, it hardly needs to be said, suspect). Valuable at a theoretical level would be the point that Marjorie Garber argues in *Vested Interests* (1992), that the transvestite is a necessary and founda-tional third term – or third sex – that disrupts the more usual plotting of sexual difference in terms of binaries and dichotomies. (Their bankruptcy is further suggested by the structuring contradiction that treats men and women both as opposites and yet as 'made for each other'.) Although Garber's third term may be questioned for its own normalizing and stabilizing effects – she allies it, for example, with the Lacanian Symbolic and, thus, implicitly with the law – she nevertheless points to a highly impoverished way of thinking about gender that is a consequence arguably of the simplification that the hetero–homo distinction makes. In the Elizabethan period, it is, I believe, arguable, just for starters, that boys are a different sex – neither men nor women – that there are at least three genders in the period, and a corresponding geometrically increased number of sexualities. These cut across the binarism of gender, but they also are structured by (or violate) other boundaries – of age and status, most notably. It is these crossings that provide much of the excitement in the sonnets, when the older, often abject sonneteer addresses the young man, whose youth may place him in the position of his pupil, but whose money and social status make him the older man's master; make him that unless, of course, the young man is, as Oscar Wilde in *The Portrait of Mr. W.H.* and others since have sometimes thought, a boy actor, pretending to more than he has – and also possessed of a beauty that seems to feminize him, casting him as the cross-dressed master-mistress; this is a cross-dressing that he seems virtually to embody, though one, as Sedgwick argues, which, however much it makes him a 'dumb blonde', also renders him 'exaggeratedly phallic . . . He represents the masculine as pure object' (Sedgwick 1985: 44). From such observations, Sedgwick delivers a sweeping summary that points the path for the enquiry that follows. 'Gender and genitals we have always with us,' she writes (perhaps a bit overconfidently, but one has to start somewhere), 'but "family," "sexuality," "masculine," "feminine," "power," "career," "privacy," "desire," the meanings and substance of gender and genitals, are embodied in times and institutions, literature among them' (Sedgwick 1985: 47).[3]

The opening scenes of *1 Henry IV* locate Hal's career – his desire for the throne – in the context of others' desires for his arrival there. First, we catch the king in a narcoleptic moment, having virtually forgotten his wayward son and recalling him only as he spins out the fantasy of the son he desires – Hotspur. The king's wish – that 'some night-tripping fairy had exchanged' (I.i.86) children, so that Hotspur might be his Harry – conditions the plot of replacement brought to a close at Shrewsbury, when Hal steps into the place of this desired *alter ego*. How fantasmatic this desire is, both on the part of the king and his son – and therefore how much it might exceed the requirements of paternal succession and royal inheritance and bring the homosocial distribution of power between men on to a sexualizable terrain – is suggested by the degree to which the king's wish resonates with another royal plot of desire, the one in *A Midsummer Night's Dream*; there,

Oberon defeats Titania in order to possess the Indian boy, a changeling like the desired son in Henry IV's fantasy; the fairy king desires him as a companion, not as a successor, however, and this begins to suggest that the paternal fantasy of producing mirror children (the imaginary terrain described by Theseus in *A Midsummer Night's Dream* as the paternal power of duplication, the ability to figure or disfigure the wax impression of the child[4]) may be as opposed to the maternal and to procreation within marriage as Oberon is. Such image production also conditions the reproduction of the figure of the fair young man in the sonnets from the moment when the possibility that the young man will marry and reproduce is abandoned.

In the second scene of *1 Henry IV*, another voice is heard yearning for Hal's arrival, and it, too, offers a model for the legitimate heir based in a rebellious – and self-duplicating – *alter ego*. Falstaff, like the king, desires the prince's arrival, perhaps even more insistently, as is suggested by the refrain that punctuates the first words he addresses to Hal in the play: 'I prithee sweet wag, when thou art king . . . Marry then sweet wag, when thou art king' (I.ii.14–15, 22). Falstaff's desire for Hal to be a king of thieves is only a hair's breadth from the king's desire for his son to equal or to replace the rebel Hotspur, for him to legitimize the king's desire by being illegitimate, indeed for Hal to arrive in his father's place by being as illegitimate as his father, a usurper and a rebel himself, once was. Falstaff's longing and its echo of the royal desire baffles the commonplace critical distinction between good and bad fathers in the *Henry IV* plays, complexly intertwining legitimate and illegitimate desires – paternities and surrogate sonships, heirs and rebels. The territory of desire does not seem safely contained by the homosocial and patriarchal orders.

Not that Falstaff is presented in any direct way as a sexual partner for Hal. It remained for Gus Van Sant, in his cinematic translation of the relation between Hal and Falstaff into modern terms in *My Own Private Idaho* (1991), to realize these possibilities. There, Falstaff, now called Bob, is the leader of a gang of street kids, many of them hustlers, and including Scott, the mayor's son. This latter-day Hal affirms the supposition of his companion – his Poins, the narcoleptic Mike – that he has had a 'thing' with Bob; Bob, he says, loved him. Van Sant's film does not present this unequivocally as a sign of a homosexual relationship; rather, he explores the permeable borders between homo- and heterosexuality, and in ways that are suggestive for reading Shakespeare and the cultural situation in which he writes, one that has yet to invent these supposedly opposing forms of love and desire. While, to follow Bray, in Elizabethan culture sex could maintain male–male hierarchies and function as a site of exchange, in the film the cash nexus that defines prostitution allows for sexual crossings that need not testify to choices of identity. Thus, although Mike is a hustler, he also loves Scott and wants to have sex with him for that reason, while Scott claims that he only sleeps with men for money. Indeed, Scott's use of this claim functions as a site of refusal of homosexual identity even as it allows him to have homosexual sex. In this context, Scott's conversion to 'normalcy' is markedly different from Hal's in one respect: it involves the assumption of heterosexuality, acquiring a wife, and renouncing not merely Mike and Bob's company, but also, indeed more importantly, sex with men. It remains like Hal's conversion, however, in one respect: it is a site of betrayal.

No such renunciation, in fact, marks Hal's arrival, and no wife appears at the end of *2 Henry IV*. This suggests that the *Henry IV* plays are far less direct in their depiction of sex and sexuality than Van Sant's film is, in part because the sexual domains that characterize modernity have yet to come into existence, and therefore will not define the transformation or self-realization of the prince. This means that what could be called sexual in the plays will not be represented along axes that correspond to modern definitions. It helps to recall Bray's argument at this point: that sodomy in the period always will be voiced through or alongside other charges, and that the possibility of making sodomy visible depends upon its being attached to a social disruption that cannot be ignored. The king sees 'riot and dishonour stain' (I.i.84) his son's face, sees Falstaff as the blot on his character, the mark made where the paternal impression should be. One sign of the ways in which this illegitimate mark gets connected to the paternal impression can be found in Hal's lines spoken at the moment of his arrival into his father's place, at the end of Part 2, for he can see no difference between the dead father and the companion he is about to cast off (Van Sant goes even further, allowing Scott to declare his Falstaff a better and more beloved father even as he rejects him, a declaration that therefore functions to mark Scott's 'conversion' to heterosexuality as a self-betrayal motivated by social regulation):

My father is gone wild into his grave,
For in his tomb lie my affections.
And with his spirits sadly I survive
To mock the expectation of the world,
To frustrate prophecies, and to raze out
Rotten opinion, who hath writ me down
After my seeming.

(*2 Henry IV*, V.ii.122–8)

Harry replaces Harry here (V.ii.49) as he had replaced another Harry at the end of Part 1 ('Harry to Harry shall, hot horse to horse,/Meet' (IV.i.123–4)), and the Lord Chief Justice, *chosen* as father now in place of both the king and Falstaff, is the father only of the newest self-simulation, the artificial paternity that the king first dreamed, the position that Falstaff assumed. Hal is still bent, as he was in his first soliloquy in Part 1, on the mockery of expectation and the falsifications that are coincident with his truth, and this double erasure and the announcement of a new father figure is one more suspect legitimizing gesture. The parallel between this moment of arrival and the defeat of Hotspur at the end of Part 1 is another. All of these suggest that the plays continually negotiate Hal's career in terms of relations between men.

In his first soliloquy in *1 Henry IV*, and in the fulfilment of his promise to the king that he will prove himself the king's true son by taking upon himself the form of Hotspur's honour, Hal composes an image of himself in which he is at once both Harrys – Hotspur and his father, legitimate and illegitimate at the same time. Doing so, he makes himself the very simulacrum that the king sees in Act III, scene ii, when he reflects on how much alike they are (144–52). Hal's offer to redeem himself and prove himself the king's true son involves taking the form of Hotspur, the very shape of a royal desire that is all too like Falstaff's illegitimate desire for Hal. (In *My Own Private Idaho*, one further way in which such complexities are translated comes by having Scott appear for the reconciliation scene with his father dressed in his most outrageous street hustler guise – denim jacket, naked chest, slave collar. When he goes down on his knees and buries his head in his father's lap momentarily it looks as if a blow job is about to occur, thereby recalling the first scene in the film after the opening title sequence, which begins with Mike receiving a blow job and ends with him telling lies about his father.) Indeed, Hal's description of how he will replace Hotspur offers another version of the razing and replacement imaged when dead king and boon companion stand in for and erase one another to produce the final Harry at the end of the pair of plays:

> I will redeem all this on Percy's head,
> And in the closing of some glorious day
> Be bold to tell you that I am your son,
> When I will wear a garment all of blood,
> And stain my favours in a bloody mask,
> Which, washed away, shall scour my shame with it.
>
> (*1 Henry IV*, III.ii.132–7)

Hal's promised redemption involves a restaining and scouring that produces not exactly himself but, as he goes on to say, an exchange like the one his father dreamed: 'I shall make this northern youth exchange/ His glorious deeds for my indignities' (145–6). This shameless deed rewrites Harry's brow as unspotted only by casting the northern youth as the locus of his glory; that the lines also promise to 'engross' (148) these deeds further implicates this rewriting in the one that Part 2 brings to a close, when Hal's gross companion is cast off, leaving engrossing Hal once again supposedly unstained.

The rewriting here – the staining and erasing – aims at legitimizing the illegitimate. This is a political project, to be sure, but that in no way guarantees – the opposite, in fact – that it will not be played out in a bodily register. Hal can engross, but unlike his fat companion, his body fails to serve as the register of what he has done. Falstaff's *gross* body is not Hal's *engrossed* one, and the 'base contagious clouds' (*1 Henry IV*, I.ii.186), 'the foul and ugly mists/Of vapours' (190–1) which figure Falstaff's flatulent body[5] suggest a form of anality – sodomy – that Hal's anal economies seek to overcome.

Hal's arrival – easily exposed as calculating, and involving the defeat of Hotspur and, even more insupportably, the casting off of Falstaff – remains, for all that, something readers of the play may be expected to desire. How this is so depends on recognizing the mechanism the play produces to engage such desires, the way that the desire for arrival serves as an endless dissimulation of legitimate and illegitimate desires. In this context it is worth recalling arguments made by William Empson, some fifty years ago, in a few pages in *Some Versions of Pastoral* that have never received the critical attention that they deserve.[6] Empson forthrightly notes the register of desire that I believe must be taken into account. The prince has been cast in the part of the fair young man of the sonnets, he writes, and 'Harry has no qualities that are obviously not W.H.'s' (Empson 1950: 108). Falstaff's desire, even what is made of the father's desire, is, in this light, not to be distinguished from the desire of the sonneteer, always ready to take upon himself the faults of the faultless young man.

> Henry's soliloquy [at the end of Act I, scene ii] demands from us just the sonnets' mood of bitter complaisance; the young man must still be praised and loved, however he betrays his intimates, because we see him all shining with the virtues of success.
>
> (Empson 1950: 104)

In his soliloquy Hal makes up to the audience by promising to cast off his bad company (by the end of Part 2, as we have seen, his father makes up part of that disreputable crew). As Empson observes, Hal gives one twist further to the dynamics upon which the male–male relations in the sonnets depend: it is the prince, speaking in the position of the young man, who proclaims his own perfection and dumps his faults upon those who love and desire him. Empson concludes: 'We have the central theme of all the sonnets of apology; the only difference, though it is a big one, is that this man says it about himself' (1950: 105).

How Hal's self-love and corruption get a saving translation is suggested, for instance, in Falstaff's repeated claims that the prince has corrupted him. For the truth he points to is that no one in these plays is innocent, that predation is endemic, increasingly and overtly so in Part 2. From the first scene in Part 1 in which they are together to the final repudiation, Falstaff stands to be abused. It is often said that we desire Falstaff's resurgence (given in his resurrection at the end of Part 1, half promised in the epilogue to Part 2), but, if so, it is because that is his condition throughout the plays; comebacks are his forte. Falstaff teaches us to see the prince as a sweet wag as well as a thousand ways to prevaricate, to keep believing in the prince as he keeps letting Falstaff down. Somewhere along the line, the abuse of Falstaff becomes the lure of the prince – or, at least, that is what the plays count on, and numerous readers who acclaim the prince's arrival in his father's place attest to this effect; the equation of good and bad fathers at the end of 2 Henry IV is supposed to work to secure our love for Hal. Ideally – ideologically – at least, that is how desire is being channelled to fulfil the play's legitimizing political project. This is more or less what Hal declares in his first soliloquy, positioning the audience to assume the stance of the sonneteer, to love him despite his faults. If this makes us Falstaff, it is the Falstaff of an exchange like this one:

> PRINCE HENRY: Sirrah, do I owe you a thousand pound?
> FALSTAFF: A thousand pound, Hal? A million. Thy love is worth
> a million; thou owest me thy love.
>
> (1 Henry IV, III.iii.130–2)

This declaration of love is protected from being read at face value: Falstaff is once again being shamed, caught out this time lying to the Hostess and defrauding her (Hal can even, for a moment, appear to be the protector of women, a stance given the lie in 2 Henry IV, Act V, scene iv, when the Hostess and Doll Tearsheet are sent off to prison). As Empson says, 'the more serious Falstaff's expression of love becomes the more comic it is, whether as hopeless or as hypocrisy' (1950: 109); his love can always look like a form of rapacity. Nevertheless, the complex trajectories of Falstaff's declaration of love cannot fail to remind one of the structure of the sonnets. Indeed, as I remarked earlier, the royal desire for simulation participates in that project too. For, from the moment (at sonnet 17) that the possibility is abandoned that the young man might, through marriage, be the source of an ever fresh supply of duplicate young men, the sonnets seek to propagate the young man through the writing of his perfected image – the image declared perfect despite all the faults and failures revealed. Henry IV never specifies what stains his son's brow; although he characterizes him as a 'young, wanton and effeminate boy' in *Richard II* (V.iii.10), little afterwards would suggest that Hal is spending himself in the company of women (no bawdy houses for him, nor does the king ever think about a marriage for his son). Hal's 'loose companions' (V.iii.7) even in *Richard II* are highway robbers and tavern companions, a lowlife that appears as exclusively male as the public world of court and battlefield. These are the sites of struggle for Hal and in them the plays seem to occupy the terrain of sonnets 18–126, with their production of an image of perfection and the tainted rebounds of that desire – the desire that I have suggested rebounds upon king, rebel, and tavern companion.

That criticism has not followed Empson is thus perfectly understandable, since it would require seeing how its celebrations of Prince Hal might come close to a love only Empson seems to have had no trouble naming. If one follows Empson and historicizes the connection he makes between the prince and the fair young man, one must see that what keeps the play from making more overt the love relation between Hal and his fat companion is the proximity of their relation to sodomy: the terms *stain*, *riot* and *rebellion* suggest as much. The scandal of the play lies in suggesting how close that illegitimate desire might be to the usual workings of male–male relations, patriarchy in the play written, as we have seen, within the register of the sonnets' fantasies of duplicative inscription.[7] Hal, we know, is stained with riot, and the king fears he might join the rebels. His blot is embodied in Falstaff, his rebellion in Hotspur: they wear two of the faces of what the period calls sodomy. The very fact that Hal's misdeeds are never specified, and that his riots are allied to Hotspur's rebellion but supposed to be enacted in his relations with Falstaff, places his 'shame' on that unspeakable terrain. It is arguably that 'shame' that Hal scours when he dispatches Hotspur. Yet the defeat of Hotspur at the end of Part 1 importantly marks Hal's path towards becoming the son the king desires; it even points ahead to the end of *Henry V*, for it is a Hotspur-like Hal who woos a wife (like

Hotspur's, named Kate) in the voice of a plain soldier. Around Hotspur the plays negotiate an image of masculinity that serves to define the boundaries of what is allowable in relationships between men and between men and women. Hotspur, I would argue, serves as the site for the production of a misogyny and an incipient homophobia – an incipient heterosexuality – that serves both purposes.

In this context, it is important to note the purposes that Lady Percy serves in the *Henry IV* plays. If she appears in Part 1 largely to be abused, and in Part 2 to memorialize her dead husband, she none the less functions between men, in Part 1 thereby legitimizing Hotspur's alliance with the rebel Mortimer by making it a family affair. (In Part 2 she is so much a part of the political atmosphere of the play that her fiction of an ideal Hotspur serves to encourage his father once again to betray the rebel cause.) Under the modern regimes of the supposed exclusiveness of male–male and male–female desire, it would seem as if Hotspur's wife guarantees his heterosexuality. Yet what she guarantees is alliance, and the figure of Hotspur is troubled – in his relations with women and with men – with the spectre of effeminization.

This is explicit in the narrative that Hotspur offers to explain his refusal to behave as a vassal should, why he has not given up his prisoners to the king; in making his excuse, Hotspur fastens on a courtier who arrived on the battlefield speaking 'holiday and lady terms' (I.iii.46), talking 'like a waiting-gentlewoman' (55), perfumed and taking snuff. Hotspur reports himself 'pestered with a popinjay' (50). How threateningly reversible this might be is suggested when Lady Percy calls her husband a paraquito (II.iii.82) when he refuses her embraces in the name of his love for his horse and the masculine camaraderie of the battlefield. This is Hotspur's relation to Kate throughout Part 1; his exactions rebound, however, echoing his father's when Northumberland chastens the ranting Hotspur for what he calls his 'woman's mood' (I.iii.236). In that mood Hotspur is as impoverished in his vocabulary as the Welsh woman Hotspur would have his wife echo; he would train a bird – a starling – to parrot nothing more than 'Mortimer' (I.iii.223–4); the Welsh woman, Owen Glendower's daughter, can presumably say no more English. What Hotspur's father attempts with his son, Hotspur exacts with his wife in that scene among the rebels in Wales. When she calls him a paraquito she speaks with his father's voice.

These representations of Hotspur serve at least two functions in *1 Henry IV*. As the site of a contradiction in the production of 'proper' masculinity, Hotspur is, on the one hand, the locus of a normative misogyny defended against women and effeminization (a masculinity linked to that older order of aristocratic arms-bearing, founded in the exchange of women that solidifies ties between men); but, on the other hand, Hotspur also is a rebel; hence, the contradictory nature of the site he occupies, for what he achieves as a normative image is subject to the rebound accorded to him as rebel; thus, rebellion wears the face of femininity and theatricality. Hotspur's masculinity – emblematized by his devotion to his horse – is secured by the supplementary addition of a wife that assures that the all-male rebel world in which he thrives could not be tainted by the effeminacy of a perfumed courtier or of a man like Mortimer who loves his wife too much. But what secures him is also what threatens to make his heroism a sham and his masculinity a performance guarding against what it is always in danger of revealing.

In *My Own Private Idaho*, Van Sant translates the Welsh scene of *1 Henry IV* and the wooing scene at the end of *Henry V* to Italy,[8] and has Scott fall in love with a woman whose native language is not English. Carmela has been taught English by Mike's mother – the figure he seeks and never finds in the movie. This suggests that Scott replaces Mike by way of the mother and the mother tongue. The heterosexual object has been produced for him by the woman responsible for Mike's existence, too. At this juncture in Van Sant's film, Mike is as much Hotspur as he is Poins, and the killing of Hotspur, robbing him of his youth, is here, as it is with Falstaff/Bob, a matter of breaking a heart; in both cases, with Mike and with Bob, this is accomplished by making a heterosexual choice. (The conflation of Bob and Mike is suggested by our first glimpse of Mike in the film, wearing a shirt that has the name *Bob* on it, a crossing of identities that suggests how Shakespearian Van Sant's film is even when its text is not.) Carmela, like the Welsh woman Hotspur would have his wife be and yet whom he fears will emasculate him as she has Mortimer, further troubles Scott's assumption of heterosexual masculinity. Produced by Mike's mother and as a kind of Mike substitute, she suggests that Scott's assumption of heterosexuality obeys cultural compulsions, not necessarily incompatible desires. (The English in which they communicate is not Carmela's mother tongue.) This is conveyed, too, by the fact that the scene in which Carmela and Scott are shown having sex is shot in the same way as the earlier scene in which Scott and Mike have sex with Hans. By shooting these scenes as a series of stills, Van Sant refuses either of them the teleological narrativity associated with sexual identity as culminating in the 'mature' form of heterosexuality. It also suggests that the threeway – for money, supposedly – is another opportunity for Mike and Scott to have sex with each other, Scott having only once agreed to sleep with Mike without money being in question. But money is also in question with Carmela; when she appears with Scott in the funeral scene at the end of the movie, she forms part of his retinue as she had in the restaurant scene in which Scott finally rejects Bob. Carmela functions as an acquisition and as part of Scott's inheritance, a guarantee of his new-found respectability like the three-piece suit he wears; she has cash value. The film thereby suggests that compulsory heterosexuality is a form of self-prostitution for the sake of 'normalcy'.

In the film Scott is not, as Hal is in Shakespeare's play, at the centre; Mike is, and what is plotted is not his arrival. Rather, this is a road movie whose path is recursive, a journey backwards to a mother who is never found, and forwards to a future that remains indefinite. Although Mike hopes to find his mother working at a hotel aptly named 'The Family Tree', the movie relentlessly works against the patriarchal plot; Mike's brother is also his father, and the incest relationship is thus as recursive as his journey on a road that he continually revisits and which has no end. That Mike is a narcoleptic has its Shakespearian resonances, for Van Sant is remembering what Shakespeare forgets, the mother of course, but also Poins, one of those Shakespeare characters who simply disappear; the movie remembers him, prompted, in part, by Orson Welles's *Chimes at Midnight* (1966), to which Van Sant pays continual homage, and in which Hal is positioned repeatedly between Poins and Falstaff; if part of Van Sant's rewriting of Welles involves making explicit homosexual relations – which Welles tends to represent either phobically (for example, he represents Henry IV's desire for Hotspur as son as part of his 'sick' behaviour) or in euphemized ways (as free-for-all polymorphous perversity or as filial relationship) – through Mike, Van Sant offers a figure that holds up for scrutiny the lie that men cannot love men – a line Scott delivers – or that heterosexuality and homosexuality are necessarily mutually exclusive identities. Van Sant's 'Poins' thus also rewrites Welles's, who is cast as a dark angel and a rival to Falstaff; Welles 'remembers' him by having him point, at the end of *Chimes*, to the casket containing the body of Falstaff and to utter his name with utter indifference to his fate.

In his remembering, Van Sant recasts Mike/Poins as the good angel Scott abandons (another Bob, as the name on his shirt testifies); this rewriting of Welles insists on the homo-erotics that bind Scott and Mike, Hal and Poins/Hotspur. If we return now to the *Henry IV* plays and their plots of replacement to consider how Harry reproduces Harry – how Hal replaces Hotspur – we might note that the point of crossing is erotic attraction and rivalry. While Hotspur, in his woman's mood – playing out in the sexual sphere what counts as rebellion in the political sphere – suffers no womanish man to compromise his masculinity, it is in the throes of such hypermasculinity that he wishes to meet Harry on the battlefield, Harry to Harry, hot horse to horse (the slight asymmetry in Hotspur's phrase perhaps registers his attempt to maintain his advantage in the relation):

> Come, let me taste my horse,
> Who is to bear me like a thunderbolt
> Against the bosom of the Prince of Wales.
> Harry to Harry shall, hot horse to horse,
> Meet and ne'er part till one drop down a corse.
>
> (1 Henry IV, IV.i.120–4)

Hotspur responds here to Vernon's heavily eroticized depiction of Hal, vaulting 'like feathered Mercury' (107), his thighs tightly clenching the horse beneath, throned as Hotspur would be on his roan, the male horse he straddles. This is an image of Harry-as-Hotspur fully to be achieved when his rival lies dead at his feet. From Hotspur, Hal seeks a proper masculinity, a sexuality that will permit relations with men not tainted with effeminacy. But, as Empson suggests, some of this supposed achievement is marred immediately when Falstaff wounds the dead Hotspur in his thigh, delivering a counterfeit death blow that suggests that Hal cannot take from Hotspur what he most desires. The thigh wound is a sexual wound, Empson suggests, no doubt with a handbook like Jessie Weston's in mind, and that Falstaff can deliver it suggests what defeating Hotspur entails – and what was being resisted – and where the charge of male–male erotics lies. If in his defeat of Hotspur Hal becomes the Phallus, it is, to quote Judith Butler, to reveal that 'the Phallus is always already plastic and transferable' (Butler 1992: 164), which is to say that it is not in any way the natural consequence of having a penis, is no one's (and no one gender's) property, that as a construct it is movable and thereby contestable. How Hotspur's relation with Kate might redound upon Hal is suggested finally when he woos his Kate in Henry V; within the Henry IV plays, in which Hal is never seen involved with women, the moment closest to these occurs in an exchange with Poins in Part 2, the only other scene in the tetralogy in which a marriage is proposed for Hal, with Poins's sister, or so Falstaff claims. Hal's rejection of Nell constitutes a refusal to legitimize his relation with Poins through marriage with his sister: 'Do you use me thus, Ned? Must I marry your sister?' (II.ii.105–6) – such is the rebuff Hal delivers to the man he knows down to the peach stockings he wears.

The refusal to legitimize his male companion along the axis of alliance is not the same thing as the supposed differentiation of hetero- and homosexual object choice enacted when Scott chooses Carmela instead of Mike, although it is very likely that the scene between Hal and Poins conditions Van Sant's understanding of the relationship between Scott and Mike. In the *Henry IV* plays, the regimes of homo- and heterosexuality are only incipient, and more to the point is the remark the Hostess makes about Falstaff in *2 Henry IV*, that 'he will spare neither man, woman, nor child' (II.i.12–13), that he is 'a man-queller, and a woman-queller' (39–40) hence Hal's gift to him of the page-boy who presciently promises to 'tickle [the Hostess's] catastrophe' (45–6 – but hence, too, Falstaff's relations with Doll and the Hostess). Falstaff's sexual tastes are those possible for any man.[9] Yet that these possibilities are not necessarily indifferent, but can be threatening, is suggested both by Hotspur's relation to his wife and the effeminate courtier, or by Hal's negotiation of his relations with men, particularly with Hotspur and with Falstaff. One place this is especially clear is a theatrical scene that Hal imagines in *1 Henry IV*, in which his 'damned brawn shall play Dame Mortimer' (II.iv.106–7). Dame Mortimer is Hotspur's wife, but also the effeminized Mortimer, and for a moment Hal entertains the possibility that Falstaff might play Dame Mortimer, the woman, the feminized man to Hal's Hotspur. Hal imagines Hotspur and his wife in the same reductive mode that he does in his savage baiting of Francis – the show he does stage while awaiting Falstaff's arrival – all of them reduced to a trim reckoning. The scene participates in complex routings of identification and difference that exceed Hal's economizing, however, and we should note that Falstaff is made into a trial Kate only *after* Hal has (parrot-like) imitated her voice.

> 'O my sweet Harry,' says she, 'how many hast thou killed today?' 'Give my roan horse a drench,' says he, and answers, 'Some fourteen,' an hour after, 'a trifle, a trifle.' I prithee call in Falstaff. I'll play Percy, and that damned brawn shall play Dame Mortimer his wife.
>
> (II.iv.102–7)

This deflection of cross-gender identification has not been noticed by critics who have all too easily read Falstaff *as* a woman – on the basis of his 'gross' body, his corpulence, a reading first offered by W.H. Auden[10] and more recently by Patricia Parker[11]. Not only would one want to caution against the potential misogyny and homophobia of this connection, one would also want to add that the size of the body is as much an index to class negotiations as it might be to gender and sexuality.[12] Here it would be worth mentioning, of course, that the ambivalences around Hotspur as chivalric and effeminate mark a crucial moment in bourgeoisification. Hal's new regime of trim reckonings (the predations of the engrossing *arriviste* that write themselves as civilized restraint) would cut the body down to size; it is mobilized against decaying aristocratic corpulence – the fat body that will come to be the body of the malnourished poor – and the woman's body. As Empson brilliantly noted, the point at which the eulogies for Falstaff and Hotspur cross comes when Hal summons up the *weight* of their bodies. Critics who repeat Hal's agendas in Act II, scene iv, as the truth of Falstaff's 'female' body – rather than seeing it as a reflex against his own identification as a woman – or who associate Falstaff's loquacity with the female tongue, are like Hotspur in Act III, scene i, policing Kate's language and sexuality. Hal's imagined scenario with Falstaff is no more benign; he recoils from the possibility of crossing gender, and attempts to put Falstaff where he was a moment before. That recoil must be read if we are to interrupt the route from such grossness to femininity that has been understood as a 'normal' connection or even as one that psychoanalysis makes available as the truth (infantile Falstaff now seems to be the mother's body).[13] It is true that Falstaff claims his womb undoes him, that he compares himself to a sow that has overwhelmed her children; true, too, that Falstaff is the sole adult male in any Shakespeare play to don drag. Feminization, as in Hal's fantasy play with the brawn as Dame Mortimer, may be part of the casting off of the character, the slurring together of an abjected femininity whether male or female, but it also represents the attempt to distinguish male and female as sexual objects. It is just that distinction belied by Falstaff when he fails to know the difference between men and women. Falstaff's 'femininity' is not written within the misogynist masculinity of a proto-heterosexuality and homophobia. I do not mean to idealize Falstaff's sexual capacities or to suggest that his relations to women can be shielded from misogyny – he makes both Doll and the Hostess sites of continued demands and repeated frauds. Only to be noted is that unlike Hotspur (or the 'ideal' Hal), Falstaff is no supporter of rigidified gender exclusivity. It is the presumed difference between sexualities that Falstaff's body breaches.

Hal first casts Falstaff as Dame Mortimer as part of his attempt to cast him off. When Falstaff arrives, Hal attempts to shame the cowardly liar, the monstrous bedpresser. Falstaff catches Hal out – his truth that he robbed Falstaff makes the difference between lying and truth-telling moot. And to the charge of bedpressing, the fat knight has a devastating response, pointing to skinny Hal's pitiful endowment: 'you starveling, you eel-skin, you dried neat's tongue, you bull's pizzle, you stock-fish! . . . you tailor's yard, you sheath, you bow-case, you vile standing tuck' (II.iv.237–40). His thinness, in these charges, as David Bevington (1987: 190) glosses these lines, carries the accusation of 'genital emaciation'. Falstaff points to the phallus Hal lacks just as at the end of the play he will mock the one Hal has from Hotspur. The old bedpresser knows where to get the prince.

So much Hal all but testifies to in his first exchange with him. To Falstaff's irrelevant question about the time of day, Hal replies that the time would be of interest to his fat companion only were the 'blessed sun himself' to appear like a 'fair hot wench in flame-coloured taffeta' (I.ii.9–10). Hal, we know, thinks *he* is the blessed sun, and in this line the sun is male; Hal imagines himself as cross-dressed.[14] Hal places this imaginary woman between himself and Falstaff, this imaginary locus of self-identification between them. It looks as if the only desire Hal can acknowledge is male–female desire. It looks as if that is how he acknowledges his relation with Falstaff. Yet the lines intimate the kind of sexual pleasure Hal does have, just as they further suggest why Hal's other *alter ego*, Hotspur, has a wife *and* protests against feminization. As with the master-mistress of Sonnet 20,[15] this initial exchange with Falstaff suggests that the prince can be used elsewhere and otherwise, that if his prick is of no concern (as the sonneteer says of the fair young man in that sonnet), this does not exhaust the sexual possibilities. If this seems too crude a supposition, one can point to the ways in which their status difference, which should place Hal on top, is crossed by the age difference that has made Falstaff Hal's tutor and mentor. These crossings of age and status are the sexual locus for the rebound that Hal attempted in his reduction of Francis to a single parrot-like word ('Anon, Anon,' Hal's line too, in his economizing). In Part 2, Hal and Poins appear *as* Francis, and Falstaff has no trouble recognizing the two serving lads, and this is the last we see of Poins. When Gus Van Sant rewrites the taffeta wench into a hustler in black leather he is not very far, after all, from Shakespeare.

Are Hal and Falstaff bed companions? It is perfectly clear why the plays can never answer that question directly. For while the king could sleep with men, he could not be a sodomite. Hence, in *Henry V* when one of the king's betrayers turns out also to have been his bedfellow it was their physical intimacy that was supposed to have kept Scroop ever from turning traitor to the king. His crime is not what he did in bed. Although

Hal is forever casting off his companions, it is not bedfellows *per se* that are called into question. There is no reason, therefore, not to suppose that Hal and Falstaff were bedfellows, too. In what situation, after all, does Falstaff ask his first question – 'Now, Hal, what time of day is it, lad?' (1 Henry IV, I.ii.1)? If he is just waking up, what is Hal doing? What should be made of the fact that the next time we see Falstaff asleep (at the end of II.iv), Hal is in . . . his pockets? What *is* Hal talking about when he charges Falstaff with being an exorbitant 'bed-presser' (II.iv.235)?

There is no absolutely definitive way to answer such questions, but not because the plays give evidence for the modern supposition that a line can be drawn between homosocial and homosexual relations. That Hal has a bedfellow in *Henry V* is publicly announced as the scene opens (II.ii.8); with whom a man sleeps in the climb for power is not private knowledge, nor has sex been cordoned to the area of the private as in the modern fantasmatic.[16] We do not know whether Hal sleeps with Falstaff, though, and this points to one way in which the plays police male–male sexual behaviour. For if, on the one hand, it would be unremarkable for men to be sleeping with each other, it would be unspeakable if the wrong men were, if the sex between men was not conducive to maintaining social hierarchies and distinctions. What is at stake comes as close to being made explicit as is possible in that scene in which Hal confronts Scroop as he casts off the treasonous 'English monsters' (*Henry V*, II.ii.85); the monstrosity of the treasonous bedfellow is a way of naming sodomy, and it must be to the point that in the next scene of *Henry V* Falstaff's death will be described in lines in which the Hostess has pilfered the final page of the *Phaedo* for her account of how Falstaff's body, like Socrates's, grew colder and colder as she moved her hand up his legs;[17] the corrupter of Harry's youth is also the father of philosophy. What Hal's sexual relation with his bedfellows was is all but spelled out when Henry V declares that Scroop knew 'the very bottom of my soul' (97), and held the 'key' to Hal's treasure, 'almost might have coin'd me into gold/Would'st thou have practis'd on me for thy use' (98–9). The description returns us once more to the sonnets –

So am I as the rich whose blessèd key
Can bring him to his sweet up-lockèd treasure,
The which he will not every hour survey,
For blunting the fine point of seldom pleasure.
Therefore are feasts so solemn and so rare,
Since, seldom coming, in the long year set

(sonnet 52, ll.1–6)

– to the very lines that echo Hal's first soliloquy or his father's later ministrations on the economies of royal image production. In *Henry V* Hal attempts, Hotspur-like, to cast off the revolting male lover who makes the king a queen. One inheritance that critics and readers have from such moments is a resistance to seeing any possibility of male–male sexual relations in Shakespeare plays unless one man is wearing a dress. But what this account of the *Henry IV* plays might suggest is that, rather than continuing what is by now a zero-sum game of looking at cross-dressing in the comedies as the sole locus of male–male sex in Shakespeare, it is about time to follow the historical paths opened by Foucault and by Bray and the critical paths enunciated by Sedgwick and by Empson. There is no way of knowing in advance where they might lead.

Nor do I mean to suggest that such work has not begun; I would instance Joseph A. Porter's recent book on Mercutio (Porter 1988);[18] it, along with Bray's recent essay, suggests that the representation of friendship in Shakespeare (Hamlet and Horatio, Macbeth and Banquo, Brutus and Cassius, and the list goes on) would be one site that needs to be rethought. One might look again at Antonio and Bassanio, and begin to take stock of how Portia's assumption of masculinity might be read as a response to the threat that relation poses rather than as a further instance of the slide from the homosocial into sexual territory (as if only a woman or femininity could guarantee the slide). One would want, in a similar vein, to look again at Sebastian and Antonio in *Twelfth Night*, and have more to say about the end of the play than Stephen Greenblatt does in *Shakespearean Negotiations* when he expresses pity for 'poor Antonio . . . left out in the cold', and to contemplate under what guise and at what cost 'Orsino does in a sense get his Cesario' (Greenblatt 1988: 93). It is a pleasure to record that such thoughts are now thinkable – I would instance Valerie Traub's 'Desire and the Difference It Makes' (in Traub 1992: 91–116), which articulates female desires in Shakespeare plays that cannot be read within the matrices of the compulsory heterosexuality that conditions much feminist Shakespeare criticism, as well as Elizabeth Pittenger's 'Dispatch Quickly: The Mechanical Reproduction of Pages' (Pittenger 1991), which allies the unruly woman – Quickly in *Merry Wives* – with the scandalous mating of males that ends that play.

The *Henry IV* plays are, undeniably, history plays, but mixed genre plays, too, and the lines of similarity to the comedies are not surprising. But it is not just the histories and comedies that require further investigation. One might want to think about the substitutive logic of a play about lieutenants that lands Cassio in bed with Iago, his leg flung across him; or about Shakespeare's play about the economies of empire and gender, to ponder not only Prospero's relation to the transvestite Ariel, but also his horror at, and inability to punish that conspiratorial pair separated in *Twelfth Night* but rejoined in *The Tempest*, Antonio and Sebastian. These are characters Shakespeare could not let go of – Antonio is a byword for the sonneteer. Male–male sexual relations were not an early phase in the playwright's development which he outgrew, nor were such relations the marginal tastes of his culture. Students of Shakespeare – at all levels – have to be reminded continually of ways in which Shakespeare is not our contemporary. In this context, it is important not to enlist him as an unquestioned supporter of the modern regimes – themselves highly imaginary – of hetero- and homosexual difference.

SUPPLEMENT

NIGEL WOOD: You suggest that Hal sacrifices the sexual or libidinal side of his character to assume the necessary public image of king. Hal is, though, a fictional construct. Could you summarize the general problematic about the economies of power and desire that you find in *Henry IV*, and the part that the representation of Hal plays in it?

JONATHAN GOLDBERG: This question has two parts, and I would want first to say that its initial premise is not, in fact, quite what my essay argues. Rather, the question implies a familiar humanist reading of the plays (it can be found, for example, in Derek Traversi's *Shakespeare from Richard II to Henry V* (1957) or in Norman Rabkin's essay on *Henry V* in *Shakespeare and the Problem of Meaning* (1981)) that understands them within a modern liberal framework. In such readings, there is the supposition that a personal, private self is the locus of a privileged and valued realm of freedom secured against the impositions of the social, that the drama portrayed in Hal's development represents the sacrifice of that interiority for the necessary impoverishments of the assumption of a public personality. (It is this view, incidentally, that governs the strategies of representations of the king in Kenneth Branagh's film of *Henry V* (1989).) My essay seeks to discover where the sexual inheres, what its inevitable entanglements with power are: that is, it does not regard the sexual as separable from the social, nor does it imagine that the regimes of privacy assumed in your question have much purchase in the plays (privacy, rather, is a construct, a site for performances that serve eminently political purposes, as can be seen in Henry IV's soliloquy about sleeplessness in *2 Henry IV*, Act III, scene i, for instance, or even in his opening display of guilt and the desire for a pilgrimage to Jerusalem in *1 Henry IV*, a desire voiced to mobilize a project of national unity and cancelled by the end of the speech). As Foucault details in the introductory volume of his *History of Sexuality* (Foucault 1978), sexuality is, within the modern constructions of the individual, a privileged locus for the personal, private, and deepest truths about the self. These are the regimes of sexuality that Foucault aligns with modernity, and my essay follows his arguments in exploring the historicity of sexuality; in effect, this entails both a tracing of some of the paths to modernity, while also noting the differences that obtain in a period yet to organize itself through the modern distinction between hetero- and homosexualities. For the fact that modern regimes of sexuality cannot be found in Shakespearian texts does not mean that the topic cannot be broached, or that representations of sexual behaviour will not be entangled with and function across a range of public and political axes. Thus, sex between men will not be represented as sex *per se* but within various normative bounds that secure the social. One would be the emulation between Hal and Hotspur in Part 1, a desire for there to be one Harry who serves as the site both for the image of chivalric accomplishment and as the rightful heir to the throne. This identificatory drive carries with it a strong sexual charge as well as contributing to the production of gender in the play, to discriminations between masculinity and femininity. It is, of course, more familiar to modern readers to recognize that relations between men and women are to be read politically; Hal's career in the *Henry IV* plays is largely imagined in terms of male–male relations, but Hotspur's relations with his wife (who is related by blood to Mortimer, the supposed legitimate claimant to the throne) are a site for the management of women, their subordination to the masculine designs of power. Thus, if there is some 'sacrifice' performed in the plays, it has to do with the attempted consignment of a figure like Kate to the spheres of domesticity (a parallel to this would be the baiting of Francis the tapster that Hal performs in Part 1, and the attempts through him to manage unruly underclass desires), a carving out of public space as an exclusive aristocratic or, at the most, proto-bourgeois masculine preserve. *Henry V* in a number of ways – given that the claims to France rest on female inheritance and are secured by marriage – makes it clear that women play a part in public life and that marriage is a public and political sphere. This raises some possibilities for female empowerment in the plays as I discuss in the version of this argument that appears in *Sodometries* (Goldberg 1992b), although the energies of the plays – especially the *Henry IV* set – attempt to discount them. And the plays, in continuing to have their focus on male–male relations, open those relations as the most complete sphere for male self-realization. Since, as I suggested above, the modern division between hetero- and homosexuality cannot easily be read into the plays, one task of the essay is to see to what extent male homosocial relations can be construed as (potentially) sexual, where sexuality between men can be admitted (e.g., Henry V's bedfellow), where it must be occulted or recoded (Hal's relations with Falstaff and Hotspur, whose riot and rebellion, were they to be made explicit as sexual behaviour, would produce the image of sodomy, an impossible conjunction given the legitimating processes of the play, but one that none the less haunts Hal's career). The focus of my essay is thus on the imbrications of a legitimating process that has not ruled out spheres of desire but seeks to manage them. It thus seeks to read even in Henry IV's desire to reproduce himself in his heir a ground that is potentially a sexual one (indeed, in Orson Welles's *Chimes at Midnight* (1966), a major source for Van Sant's Shakespearian representations in *My Own Private Idaho* (1991), the king's desire for Hotspur-as-heir is cast in a strongly erotic mode, in part to deflect the possibility that Hal's relationship with his surrogate father might also be read this way; Van Sant 'misreads' Welles in order to make such relations explicitly sexual).

NW: It is a fairly universal conclusion that Parts 1 and 2 of *Henry IV* were probably conceived as different kinds of play, and not as a compact unit. Does this not question the validity of a reading that regards them both as figuring a single process?

JG: This question supposes that a critic's loyalties must be first and foremost to the integral formal qualities of a work of art; it is, of course, true that the two parts of *Henry IV* are two different plays, though it seems equally clear to me that Part 2 represents a sequel to Part 1 that serves a number of different functions, not least the exposing of some of the mechanisms of ideological production in Part 1, the failures of a supposed benign theatricality. (For a breathtaking argument along these lines, see Crewe 1990.) It seems clear, too, however different the four plays that comprise the second tetralogy are, that they are also committed to a historical narrative. This need not be regarded as seamless, of course, and the plays, as they succeed each other, no doubt are filled with a variety of *arrière-pensées* and retrospective rewritings (indeed, that process seems to me to be insistently thematized, as when Hotspur misquotes *Richard II* in *1 Henry IV*, Act I, scene iii, when Falstaff labels all of Justice Shallow's memories lies in *2 Henry IV*, Act III, scene ii, when Hal tells the unabashed lie that he does not know Falstaff as he falls on his knees before him at his coronation). Some of this process of self-censorship and forgetting no doubt arises from the textual history of the plays and the fact that the version of *1 Henry IV* that survives has been obliged to 'forget' Oldcastle in order to satisfy the mechanisms of censorship – and yet continually reminds us of the name it has been refused (as I argue further in Goldberg 1992a). So, one answer to the question, within the formal terms proposed, would be the appeal I have been making to the fact that the plays, if not in prospect, at least in retrospect are conceived of as a unit, if not quite as a formal unity. This is not to suggest, of course, that such retrospection would easily accommodate itself to the shibboleths of formalist criticism. In this respect, it is worth emphasizing the fact about the textual history of *1 Henry IV* glanced at above – there is equally telling evidence to adduce for *2 Henry IV* – which makes it difficult (to say the least) to maintain formalist notions of the integrity of *any* Shakespeare play given the multiplicity of Shakespearian texts and the history of revision that marks them. Indeed, the retrospection *in the plays* might be said to thematize their textual instability.

I could answer this question in opportunistic terms, that this essay was written for a volume on the *Henry IV* plays, and therefore was already assuming the possibility of writing about the plays without regard to formal differences. But to be more principled: the method of this essay, and, I would venture to say, of most work done since the heyday of formalist criticism, has other priorities than the so-called text itself, indeed regards the 'text itself' as a construct of critical procedures rather than an incontestable fact, and regards formalist criticism as itself devoted to and motivated by many other things besides its supposed object. That is to say, that agendas that seek to secure the literary against other supposedly extraneous questions are themselves as 'externally' motivated as any other form of criticism, motivated by political and institutional aims that need to be scrutinized, and that are imbricated in a history of the production of the 'intrinsic' literary object. Once such an argument is granted there is nothing more or less legitimate about considering the framework for posing the consideration of the text at an immanent or at a contextualizing level of inquiry.

NW: In Stephen Greenblatt's 'Invisible Bullets' essay (in Greenblatt 1988), the close of Part 2 is read as staging a disjunction between the perception of a royal authority based on stage-managed theatre and the inevitable obeisance it exacts by its power and our need for 'truth'. Some might miss a wider political perception in your piece. How would you claim a priority for your position?

JG: Like the first question, this one also seems to me to be asking more than one thing, since it seems to assume that Greenblatt's essay is *eo ipso* political while an essay located in the history of sexuality would not be and would need to defend its politics and 'priority' (thus, it seems to me that the question recirculates some of the assumptions I addressed in answering the first one, that sexuality would not be a political/social domain). I would have to say, too, in answer to the question, that the version of the political that Greenblatt offers is one that I would want to question, since its false dialectic of subversion and containment is, as is by now widely recognized, entirely committed only to the second of those terms and cannot imagine any site of subversion that is not produced and controlled by dominant forces. In Greenblatt's reading of *2 Henry IV* as a play that exposes the predations of power (a reading I find persuasive, though I am not moved to sympathize with those in power, as Greenblatt is, or to identify with them, as he does), what seems questionable to me is his belief that the exposure of the political and ideological serves to secure it. Greenblatt's essay thus posits, as your question nicely captures, something it constructs as 'our need' – a need to be bamboozled and mystified, to be placated and pleased, a need for what Greenblatt calls 'imaginary identification'. I take it, however, that the phrase is more exact than it might be meant, and that therefore it can be seen through as an ideological effect. Indeed, since I take the phrase also to expose an equally imaginary ego investment, a psychoanalytic argument also could be marshalled against it (i.e. a psychoanalytic argument that took seriously the imbrication of ego formations that take place under the aegis of an Other, and which granted a history to the unconscious and thereby recognized that the Other cannot be detached from sociohistorical loci of power).

The political impulses that might therefore be read in my piece start from the positions outlined in answer to the first question: the imbrication of sexuality and power, the multiple crossings of their paths, the impossibility of their full containment either by our modern (and themselves highly questionable) labels of hetero- and homosexuality or the equally imaginary spheres of private and public as absolutely sealed off one from the other. Rather, I take it, following Foucault, that they are produced by each other, and in ways that will not secure them. What I understand this to mean, to return to the topic at hand, is that containment is a dream of absolutist power (it is also the dream of formalist criticism), and while there are many mechanisms within the apparatuses of power that work towards closure and containment, a criticism that affirms those mechanisms *as the political* has sold short the possibilities of the political and of political criticism. Thus, while I am not interested in claiming *priority* for the position that I argue in my essay, I would want to say that its attempt to uncover the relationship of the plays to the history of sexuality means to redescribe the sphere of the political to include relations that many definitions of the political and many attempts at social theory ignore. It is, to say the least, a remarkable fact that a new historicism that claims major allegiances to Foucault operates as if his volumes on the history of sexuality were beside the point. And it is, by now, equally well understood that the non-relationship of much new historicist work to feminism also marks a serious historical liability in the approach.

NW: In the opening chapter in your *Voice – Terminal – Echo* (Goldberg 1986) you favour the resurrecting of the Renaissance idea of *copia* (as it was understood in Terence Cave's *The Cornucopian Text* (1979)) as an opening up of a text to multiple and fragmentary readings in order to replenish them and defer fixed meaning. Do you still find that approach appealing (post-Derrida?), and, if so, are there any limits on plurality you would observe?

JG: Oddly enough, then, some of the sentences towards the close of my answer to the last question lead to this methodological point. I would say that I remain a post-Derridean critic, though I would now be far more sceptical of the procedures of *Voice – Terminal – Echo* than I was able to be when I wrote the book. It now seems to me that to stay within a region of textuality, even if the aim is to expose a general economy of textuality, can look too much as if the textual is being secured against the historical, political and social. It was for that reason that in *Writing Matter* (1990), I sought to explore textual practices (specifically, handwriting) at a level of material production, and to position that activity within institutional sites and within a history of social transformation. I sought there to scrutinize the regulatory regimes of management of the hand and also to see what might escape them (thus, the argument was not on the side of containment, though it did not wish to ignore the massive forces involved in regulatory regimes). Elsewhere, for example in 'Dating Milton' (in Harvey and Maus 1990), I have tried to articulate a post-Derridean sense of the historical and political, one that might find in the non-self-presence of the historical moment possibilities of the sort that Raymond Williams offered when he saw that any moment is split among residual, dominant and emergent forces. While these seem to me rather overly tidy labels for forces that ought to be conceptualized relationally (viewed as discrete and separable, they can only be mobilized retroactively, and therefore seem to bear with them a teleology that one could easily question, especially if one were to note that emergents must therefore emerge into dominants and that residuals must once have been dominant), the terms, like the Derridean notion of the non-presence of presence, do divide the present and refuse to contain it (thus, the argument works against the new historicist paradigm of containment and its frequent recourse to empiricist evidence, the exact day and date of an event as some sort of guarantee of historicity). Having said all this, the main modification to my earlier work would certainly involve taking much more seriously the limits to what you call 'plurality'. I think I still believe in the utopian possibilities of deconstructive reading, that is, the ways in which such readings allow one to move beyond the impasses of ideological reinscription, but I also recognize the complicities between such 'Pluralism' and, as far as I am concerned, suspect political agendas that go under the same name (Derrida's recent work on Europe would be implicated in this statement, to take one example). Still, the work in this essay and in recent writing in the history of sexuality that I have been conducting, is everywhere enabled by deconstructive habits of reading and analysis, which still hold out for me vital tools for *contesting* hegemonic relations of power and the production of meaning.

CHAPTER 2

Uses of Diversity: Bakhtin's Theory of Utterance and Shakespeare's Second Tetralogy

RONALD R. MACDONALD

[Mikhail Bakhtin's unique contribution to literary study lies in his attempt to fuse historical and formalist interpretations of literature. Bakhtin's central concerns can be illustrated with reference to two associated ideas: first, that language is not solely a system of differences with no positive link to reality, but rather composed of historically specific speech acts that are only fully comprehensible given a particular social organization; and second, that literary work often provides an opportunity to play with orthodox social references by allusion or irony, a subversion of what exists to provide a glimpse of what could be.

The first idea emphasizes the 'dialogue' formed between a writer and her/his 'potential' audience (as opposed to what we can estimate statistically as the actual readers). This is always veiled when we view this speech act from a historical or social distance. Analysis of these 'dialogic' factors is a safeguard against the great sin of anachronism (see the four essays collected in Bakhtin 1981).

The second idea takes far more seriously than is the traditional case apparently fractured and perhaps 'unofficial' forms of writing (such as the Socratic dialogue or Menippean satire). *Because of* their close engagement with a particular historical period, they provide privileged access to social, and not just aesthetic, assumptions. Literary value, from this perspective, is never metaphysical, but always relative to our historical location. This process of literary expression Bakhtin (1984a) termed 'carnivalization', where the popular and communal forms of celebration associated with 'carnival' (fools becoming wise or beggars kings) invade the more acceptable, and so safer, genres.

Both of these perceptions promote literary forms that challenge the univocal and authoritative status of the 'author', manifest in 'monologic' work. In contrast, a 'dialogue' with the reader may employ several parodic or allusive borrowings from other kinds of writing and author, and 'carnivalization' supplies a 'polyphonic' or multiple-voiced account with little attempt at 'closure' that would derive from the placing of such varied accents in some hierarchy. This textual openness involves the reader in an active way. As Bakhtin put it in his *The Dialogical Imagination*: 'The word in living conversation is directly, blatantly oriented towards a future answer word. It provokes an answer, anticipates it and structures itself in the answer's direction' (Bakhtin 1981). 'Context' cannot be confined to verbal limits.

The forms of writing favoured by Bakhtin are dynamic (as opposed to monumental) and responsive or tactical (as opposed to polemical). They may not be idiomatic in form, but they still reach out to a local readership with a focused set of meanings, and, in so doing, often have to dismantle the canonical tastes that at any one time constitute 'literature'.

Thus far, I have perhaps construed Bakhtin's work merely as an aesthetics, which would be misleading. As Ronald Macdonald makes clear, the stylistic variety of both parts of *Henry IV* challenges criticism to discover in it a coherence or even secure 'intention'. What is often left out of the equation is the necessary part played in the work of interpretation by a third term between the writer and the intended readership: audience-as-writer or writer-as-own-reader (for there is very little to differentiate these concepts). If the 'author' is always a *relative* concept, and never an absolute, then texts never issue from the 'individual subject'. Meaning is always in process; indeed, it is often so multiple that it forms a 'heteroglossia' of social voices so numerous in origin that it would be fruitless to try to isolate them for analysis: 'all utterances are heteroglot in that they are functions of a matrix of forces practically impossible to recoup' (Bakhtin 1981: 428). 'Carnivalized' writing is thus merely an especially marked example of Bakhtin's perception of how literature is a *social* product.

In Carnival apparently familiar relations appear strange. It is therefore a means of displaying Otherness, i.e. an alien challenge to our accepted modes of perceiving the Real by suggesting all the alternatives not accounted for by and in our ideological grasp of the world. This has wide consequences and was hardly a safe compromise. In 1929, the year he published his *Problems of Dostoevsky's Poetics*, Bakhtin suffered arrest and internal exile in the Soviet Union because of its lack of Marxist rectitude. It is therefore entirely possible that Bakhtin issued some of his work under the names of his friends and colleagues: Valentin Voloshinov (*Marxism and the Philosophy of Language*, written in 1929) and Pavlev Medvedev (*The Formal Method in Literary Scholarship*, written in 1928). Voloshinov's writings on linguistics are relevant here, for he shows how linguistic choice could be regarded as social *interaction*. For Ferdinand de Saussure, the influential Swiss linguist, as represented in his collected lectures: *Course in General Linguistics* (written in 1915), the proper study for linguistics was the *general* system of language (*la langue*) which provides the grammar of rules that renders any particular speech act (*la parole*) intelligible. To take this model further, the speaker can be placed in the midst of inherited rules, rather than, as Voloshinov emphasized, a range of possibilities which exist always with reference to particular social contexts. For Voloshinov, the 'word' is never held in a consistent reference back to its grammatical or semantic position within its *langue*, but is 'dialogical', i.e. always exists as an actual or anticipated response to previous utterances and/or the responses it seeks to elicit. This forms a more precise and *historical* procedure by which there can be identified certain 'speech genres' (actual forms of social intercourse produced in literature), the most potent of which is the dramatic.

For Bakhtin (and contemporaries), therefore, 'literariness' ceases to be an end in itself, as literature is regarded as inescapably social *in composition* as well as consumption. For more on this, see Macdonald (1984).]

NIGEL WOOD

I

The eleventh chapter of Genesis tells of a time early in human history, doubtless more mythical than real, when 'the whole earth was of one language, and of one speech'. Now, with the solidarity and unity that such a uniform language created in the human community, the sons of men, as the author goes on to tell us, started to get some big ideas. Setting to work in concert, they began to build a city, the salient feature of which was a tower, whose top was to 'reach unto heaven'. This, together with perhaps even grander things promised by the perfect and effortless intelligibility among men, sufficiently alarmed the Lord that he took the radical and, in the event, wholly effective step of confounding the uniform language, to the end that men 'may not understand one another's speech'. A simple measure, carried out swiftly and easily by the Almighty: men ceased their building and were 'scattered . . . abroad from thence upon all the face of the earth'. What remained of the city and its tower was called, with an apparent appropriateness only tenuously rooted in etymological fact, Babel.[1]

Nothing, of course, could be clearer than that we continue to suffer the effects of this putative dispersion, though to a modern and secular sensibility the biblical narrative may seem more likely to be an *aetiological* fable or 'just-so story', deployed to explain causes, on the lines of Kipling's fanciful accounts of how the leopard acquired his spots or the rhinoceros his skin. The story of Babel purports to explain why it is that different groups of human beings speak in different, mutually unintelligible ways. But that there ever really was a time when language was one and perfectly intelligible to all human speakers comes to seem increasingly doubtful. To the author of Genesis 11, the plurality of tongues is a mark of our fallenness, a further baleful consequence of the original transgression in the Garden of Eden; to us, it is rather part and parcel of the way things are, have always been, and are altogether likely to remain, an aspect of what Gary Saul Morson and Caryl Emerson call, in a work to which we shall have occasion to return, the inescapable 'messiness' of the world (Morson and Emerson 1990: 139).

Still, the myth of a unitary language dies hard, if it dies at all, persisting in many guises, displaying varying degrees of formal rigour. The same Scripture, after all, that chronicles at its beginning the fragmentation and dispersion of language, tells toward its end of a miraculous restoration of mutual intelligibility in a moment of Pentecostal inspiration (Acts 2: 1–11). And, to descend to a decidedly more mundane level, we are perhaps all to some degree 'linguocentric', that is, some part of us (a large one in the case of the young and untutored, a proportionately smaller one in the case of the mature and educated) clings to the conviction that, whatever the demonstrable merits of other languages, our own mother tongue has the sole defensible claim to being the master language, the only one in which the truth can really be told in all its fullness.

The linguist, Roman Jakobson, tells the story of the provincial German Swiss woman who, when informed by a more widely travelled friend that people in the adjoining, French-speaking canton called cheese fromage, not Käse, responded, 'Käse ist doch viel natürlicher!' ('Surely it's more natural to say "cheese"!') (Jakobson 1962–85, 2: 349). We are perhaps not far here from an impression some small children harbour that their own mother tongue is the one *all* children around the world speak at first, the universal language that is gradually overlain by the acquisition of various ancillary 'foreign' tongues. And we touch the extreme in the caricature of the American abroad, convinced that the natives will understand English, if only he speaks loudly enough while prodding them with the point of his umbrella.

As long as we are dealing with the differences between recognized national languages, between French and Turkish, say, or Spanish and Japanese, it is relatively easy to dismiss the notion of a true 'master language' as a myth, as a kind of subconscious linguistic jingoism on a par with the tendency of many tribal societies to reserve the term in their languages equivalent to 'the people' for themselves. All outsiders become in this self-centring mode of thought an amorphous mass of inarticulate others, the *barbaroi* of the ancient Greeks (from which we derive our term 'barbarian'), meaning 'foreigners', 'those who do not speak Greek', and ultimately, perhaps, 'those who stammer'. It may be a bit more difficult to see that the notion of a unitary and homogeneous single national language, German or English, for instance, is just as much a construct, an ideological imposition, as the notion of a unified language for all humankind. For the Russian theorist and philosopher, Mikhail Bakhtin, in any case, the idea of a single, unified language is a proximate one, at best a convenient hypostasis which never entirely coincides with actual communicative practice, at worst a totalitarian tool for enforcing conformity. In Bakhtin's view, as in those of certain of his associates and collaborators, it is the essential and natural condition of a national language at any moment of its actual life to be heterogeneous, a collection of different modes of discourse, many voices, which are, to be sure, mutually intelligible in varying degrees by virtue of their common participation in the national language, but which are none the less distinctive and distinguishable. It was partly Bakhtin's long-standing interest in the novel as literary genre that led him to this view of language, a variousness which he called 'heteroglossia' ('different-tonguedness'):

> At any given moment of its evolution, language is stratified not only into linguistic dialects in the strict sense of the word (according to formal linguistic markers, especially phonetic), but also – and for us this is the essential point – into languages that are socio-ideological: languages of social groups, 'professional' and 'generic' languages, languages of generations, and so forth.
>
> (Bakhtin 1981: 272)

The affinity of the novel for social heteroglossia does not mean that the phenomenon is confined to that literary genre. It is simply that the novel is best suited to incorporating heteroglossia, which remains a general property of language as actually employed by a community of speakers on a day-to-day basis. The rich variety to be found within any living language, a variety that cannot be explained away by recourse to 'purely personal idiosyncrasy, to conscious or unconscious error, or to dialectology' (Morson and Emerson 1990: 139), is for Bakhtin a consequence of the ideological variety among speakers and groups of speakers, with their divergent attitudes, interests and agendas. It is the tendency of any living language left, as it were, to its own devices, to become multiplanar, to break down (or up, or apart) into separate modes of discourse, because a language is always pervaded by what Bakhtin liked to call 'centrifugal forces', forces not specifically linguistic, but more broadly social and ideological, the common cause around which a subgroup or faction forms, different from and not necessarily compatible with the common cause of another faction, conflicting positions, special interests that never entirely coincide. 'A unitary language is not something given [*dan*] but is always in essence posited [*zadan*] – and at every minute of its linguistic life it is opposed to the realities of heteroglossia' (Morson and Emerson 1990: 270).[2] 'The *realities* of heteroglossia': for Bakhtin, such unitariness that a language achieves is always the result of intervention and imposition, artful manipulation or wilful exclusion. A language, as a joke still current among linguists defines it, is a dialect with an army and a navy. Unitariness in living language is made, not found.

Much of Bakhtin's insistence on the essentially heteroglot character of a living language spoken day to day may be traced to his prolonged dissent from the assumptions of both traditional classical philology in the nineteenth century and of structural linguistics in the twentieth. It seemed to Bakhtin, as it did to his colleague, Valentin Voloshinov,[3] that classical philologists, with their concentration on the dead languages, chiefly Greek and Latin, had illegitimately generalized their assumptions about those particular languages to the study of language in general. Living languages, after all, are in constant flux. No living language ever entirely coincides with itself from one day to the next, for the simple reason that its speakers are always modifying it, extending it, encountering the challenge of using it in fresh and unique situations. The classical languages, in contrast, have been artificially, if permanently, arrested, fixed by historical contingency, limited to the record of surviving documents, which is unavoidably an abstracting selection from the plenum of a once living language. It is clearly a mistake to conflate this unimaginably skimpy record, what remains, with the complex reality of the classical languages as they were actually spoken, what must have been, given what we can observe about the linguistic behaviour of human beings in general. To make this conflation is to confer on living language a stability and orderliness that it simply does not have, to assume that when the student of living language returns after an interval to the object of his study he returns to the same object in the way that the philologist always returns to his unchanging documents. While insisting that the 'philological orientation has determined the whole course of linguistic thinking in the European world to a very considerable degree', Valentin Voloshinov made explicit the kind of abstraction philology entails:

> Guided by philological need, linguistics has always taken as its point of departure the finished monologic utterance – the ancient written monument, considering it the ultimate realium. All its methods and categories were elaborated in its work on this kind

of defunct, monologic utterance or, rather, on a series of such utterances constituting a corpus for linguistics by virtue of common language alone.

(Voloshinov 1986: 71–2)[4]

Clearly the written remnants of classical languages abstract from heteroglossia, for such a tiny fraction of the total linguistic output of a culture can only preserve a very narrow band of the complete spectrum of voices and accents a culture generates, a band, moreover, that will tend toward the formal and 'official' end of the scale by virtue of the fact that it comprises written language alone. But the object of philological scrutiny abstracts from context as well, for as the philologist studies ancient documentary monuments, he/she relates them, if at all, as examples of a common *language* alone, and suppresses the fact that they are also and crucially *utterances* and thus exist, or once existed, in what both Voloshinov and Bakhtin call 'dialogic' relations with other utterances, spoken or written. For all the ancient document's spurious look of authority and self-sufficiency, it must have constituted one link in a chain that had in principle no beginning, and only ended because the culture and its language ceased for historical reasons to be. For all that the isolated documentary monument seems to pronounce the first and final word, it is in fact a rejoinder and is itself formed in anticipation of further response. No one, presumably, in ancient times encountering the document for the first time was content simply to decode it, as the belated philologist does:

> The philologist-linguist tears the monument out of that real domain and views it as if it were a self-sufficient, isolated entity. He brings to bear on it not an active ideological understanding but a completely passive kind of understanding, in which there is not a flicker of response, as there would be in any authentic kind of understanding. The philologist takes the isolated monument as a document of language and places it in relation with other monuments on the general plane of the language in question. All the methods and categories of linguistic thought were formed in this process of comparing and correlating isolated monologic utterances on the plane of language.
>
> (Voloshinov 1986: 73)

The philologist simply forgets the fact that 'any utterance – the finished, written utterance not excepted – makes response to something and is calculated to be responded to in turn': 'Each monument carries on the work of its predecessors, polemicizing with them, expecting active, responsive understanding, and anticipating such understanding in return' (Voloshinov 1986: 72).

With the distinction between language, on the one hand, and utterance, on the other, we approach the heart of Voloshinov's and Bakhtin's objections not only to the ways of classical philology, but also to those of structural linguistics, particularly to that version of it founded by the great Genevan scholar, Ferdinand de Saussure. In his *Course in General Linguistics* (assembled from lecture notes and published posthumously in 1915 by two of his students), Saussure had insisted on a fundamental opposition in the study of language between what he called *la langue*, the abstract system of a language, the set of rules governing the production of discourse, and *la parole*, the speech that users of a given language actually produce by employing those rules. This distinction roughly corresponds with the Russians' opposition of language and utterance, but with the crucial difference that where Saussure proposes the system of language, which he saw as normative, orderly, and relatively stable over time, as the proper object of linguistic inquiry, Voloshinov and Bakhtin want to focus on utterances and the real relations between those who make them. For the structuralist, the study of language is a relatively disembodied affair. It deals with the conditions of and potentialities for utterance; but when we descend to the level of actual speech, to language incarnate in actual speakers, the structuralist loses interest and dismisses the utterance as idiosyncratic and isolated, unsystematic and therefore not susceptible to further inquiry. It is just at this threshold between the system of language and actual utterance, where the structuralist pauses and then turns back to the antechamber of abstract system, that Voloshinov and Bakhtin insist the real interest in thought about language begins.

For the Russians, thought about language is necessarily thought about speakers and their utterances, so from the Bakhtinian perspective, one unfortunate consequence of the structuralist approach is the promulgation of a misleading model of speech, speakers and the speech circuit. The structuralist views the speaker as absolutely constrained by the rules of *langue*, by means of which he/she forms utterances that are free, idiosyncratic, and determined by nothing save the combinatorial rules contained in the abstract system. The speaker's thought is his own, *sui generis* and independent; but the medium he uses to convey that thought is, as Saussure insisted, 'not a function of the speaker', but rather 'the social side of speech, outside the individual who can never create nor modify it by himself'. This abstract system of language is 'a well-defined object in the heterogeneous mass of speech facts' (Saussure 1959: 14).

Now, for Bakhtin and Voloshinov, the speaker and his utterance are at once less and more constrained than the structuralist allows. No speaker in practice consults the abstract system of language norms to encode her/his thoughts; even if we concede that such language norms exist, they do not exist *for the speaker* as he/she forms an utterance in response to an immediate situation:

> In point of fact, the speaker's focus of attention is brought about in line with the particular, concrete utterance he is making. What matters to him is applying a normatively identical form (let us grant there is such a thing for the time being) in some particular, concrete context. For him, the center of gravity lies not in the identity of the form but in that new and concrete meaning it acquires in the particular context. What the speaker values is not that aspect of the form which is invariably identical in all instances of its usage, despite the nature of those instances, but that aspect of the linguistic form because of which it can figure in the given, concrete context, because of which it becomes a sign adequate to the conditions of the given, concrete situation.
>
> (Voloshinov 1986: 67–8)

The real source of constraint on the speaker is precisely the context in which he/she forms an utterance, the fact that he/she is responding to the prior utterance of another and anticipating further rejoinder upon completion of his/her own utterance. We are no longer dealing with mere examples illustrative of general structural norms, specimens of language that belong in principle to no one in particular, but with 'authored' speech, speech with specific aims and speakers with specific stakes in saying what they say. When the object of scrutiny is a true speech unit, the utterance, and not a grammatical unit, the sentence, there is no such thing as a neutral word, as both Bakhtin and Voloshinov repeatedly stress. The word I actually utter is *my* word for the moment, though I utter it realizing that it has been someone else's word in the past and will soon be someone else's word again in the future. In either case, I realize, its inflection and accent will differ from my own – sentences can be repeated but each utterance is unique – and no small part of my energy in forming an utterance will go toward minimizing the possibility of such deflection. I will never succeed, however, in eliminating the possibility altogether: there are, for Bakhtin and Voloshinov no absolute first words, and for Bakhtin, at least, no absolute final words.[5] Communicative exchange is in principle endless.

It begins to emerge that the structuralist view implies a decidedly idealized and thinned-out version of the speech circuit as well. The structuralist's speaker is an encoder, who simply reads off his meanings (and they are not even really *his* meanings) from the abstract lexicon of language. By means of the code that is given to him, he imparts information to his listener, who passively absorbs it, reversing the encoding of the speaker. It is as if the whole purpose of the speaker were merely to duplicate his thought in the mind of the listener, the whole aspiration of the listener, even more improbably, merely to allow himself to be so imprinted. The possibility of an *active* response on the part of the listener is out of the question. As Bakhtin puts it in 'Discourse in the Novel', structuralists 'acknowledge only a passive understanding of discourse, and moreover this takes place by and large on the level of common language, that is, it is an understanding of an utterance's *neutral signification* and not its *actual meaning*' (Bakhtin 1981: 281; emphasis in original).

What Bakhtin intends here by 'neutral signification' is something like 'dictionary meaning', the property of the word as simple lexical item belonging to nobody in particular. What he intends by 'actual meaning' involves concrete use of the word by a specific speaker and carries with it that speaker's will and intention in speaking, the task he hopes to accomplish in the particular context in which he finds himself. Neutral signification is a property of sentences, actual meaning a property of utterances, and while the former may enable the latter, it is very far from exhausting it. Neutral signification is repeatable and relatively stable, actual meaning is unique and changes from context to context. The sentence, 'I am hungry', may be repeated indefinitely, always coinciding with itself *as* sentence. But this same sentence spoken by a starving child, on the one hand, and by a pampered child trying to postpone bedtime, on the other, yields two undeniably distinct utterances.

It follows that a word will have as many actual meanings as it has speakers in particular contexts, and yet any actual meaning, though radically contingent and unique, is scarcely unconditioned and free. Again, there are no neutral or first words on the plane of the utterance, and the spoken-about is always the *already*-spoken-about; the language that comes to us, as Bakhtin remarked, 'has been completely taken over, shot through with intentions and accents'. Because 'the word in language is half someone else's' (Bakhtin 1981: 293), every act of uttering is necessarily an act of appropriation, an infiltration of one's own intention into territory already occupied, however securely or uneasily, by an alien, opposing, in any case, an ineluctably *different* intention. 'Prior to this moment of appropriation, the word does not exist in a neutral and impersonal language' (it is not, after all, out of a dictionary that the speaker gets his words!), 'but rather it exists in other people's mouths, in other people's contexts, serving other people's intentions: it is from there that one must take the word, and make it one's own' (Bakhtin 1981: 293–4).

It should now be clear that, for Bakhtin, actual authentic meaning (the kind that is the property of utterances rather than mere words or sentences) is a process taking place between speakers, rather than a fixed set of correspondences to be read off from a language's abstract lexicon. After all, we not only take *in* the utterances of others, we take them *up* as well, entertain them as possibilities without necessarily acquiescing in them, agree or disagree with them (even agreement is already an active, properly dialogic response, a very different thing from mere passive acceptance). Above all, we try to fill them with our own wills and intentions. And this process, this linked series of appropriations, is in principle endless, 'unfinalizable', to use one of Bakhtin's key terms, because no utterance is entirely immune to rejoinder, no position or point of view contains all others, no appropriation of meaning is quite for keeps. Perhaps each of us shares to some degree the wish of Shakespeare's Macbeth that our actions might 'trammel up the consequence', that we might at last find the elusive final word that will act as 'the be-all and the end-all' (I.vii.3,5). But, as with a unitary, monoglot language, meaning is not given but posited, and the task of positing it can never really be completed.

II

Perhaps any dramatist working in Shakespeare's situation in the London public theatre of the late sixteenth century would have been something of a Bakhtinian dialogist *avant la lettre*. We are reasonably sure that Shakespeare pervaded all levels of the contemporary theatrical institution, wearing many hats, as sharer in a joint-stock company, as actor in a working troupe, and, of course, as playwright, the chief producer of the literary property of the company in which he was an active member. Accustomed as he must have been to seeing a theatrical script from both sides, first as its author, then as one of a group charged with giving the script body and voice before the public, it seems inevitable that Shakespeare would have meditated on the frequently problematic progress of a play from conception, through written script, to incarnation on a stage before an audience. And surely that moment, which the playwright shares with the orchestral composer, when he was obliged to surrender his work to a group of men, each with ideas, intentions, and a will of his own, must have had the potential for distress as well as fascination. For the playwright's medium is more than language, it is speakers, every one of whom must necessarily refract or deflect the author's intention in directions determined by his own particular, concrete, and unique situation in experience.[6] Artists, Jonas Barish reminds us, can force 'inert matter . . . to do their bidding; they can impose their shaping wills on it, stamp it with their signatures'. 'But how', he goes on to ask, 'subdue human beings in the same way, who have wills of their own? How control a medium recalcitrant not with the brute heaviness of inanimate matter but with the wild rebelliousness of flesh and blood?' Barish wryly concludes that 'Alice's croquet game with hedgehogs and flamingoes seems pedestrian and mechanical by comparison' (Barish 1981: 343).

The bare fact of the matter is that, while stone or bronze or paint can at best pose an inert and passive resistance to the artist's creative impositions, people can and will talk back. They do not constitute for the playwright a perfectly pliant medium which simply places itself at her/his disposal (and that they do not has been the source of a good deal of complaint from playwrights over the long history of the theatre); neither do they simply follow the playwright's text (whatever it might mean to do so), as if it were a recipe that, when faithfully followed, will always produce the identical performance from instance to instance. The playwright's yielding of her/his text for performance is neither a final nor a finalizing act: it is, rather, a ceding of monologic control, a renunciation of the kind of authorial privilege available, say, to a novelist when she/he speaks through an omniscient narrator. And it is the first move in a genuinely dialogic process which will never be in principle complete, as long as productions of the play are mounted and remounted, by the same company of actors, by different companies, in the short term, or into the distant future. If the relations between playwright and actors are dialogized, so, just as surely, are the relations between one performance and the next by the same company, as well as relations between the performances of a play by one company and those of the same play by another. Performances, like other kinds of utterance, are not repeatable, nor is the meaning of a play absolutely determined by the author's intention, which, after all, has met resistance and counter-intention from the very outset, from the time of her/his first, solitary encounter with a language already furrowed and creased with the intentions of others.

It should come as no surprise that the relations among characters within Shakespeare's plays reflect the relations among men in the theatrical institution in and for which those plays were conceived, if only because it seems to have been Shakespeare's way to thematize his medium, reflexively bending the focus of his drama back on itself.[7] A little consideration will turn up dozens of examples among Shakespearian characters of those who struggle to establish or maintain monoglot linguistic regimes, turning a deaf ear to the obstreperous and insistent heteroglossia in which they are in fact immersed. The obsessively precise and pedantic speech of *Twelfth Night*'s Malvolio, for instance, the social-climbing steward of the lady Olivia, is eloquent of nothing so much as his anxiety, lest his words and meanings be appropriated by his adversaries and turned against him. And the melancholy Jaques in *As You Like It* similarly aspires to control meaning, striking attitudes, delivering long set pieces in which he affects to dispose of questions before they can be posed, and in general attempting to be the only voice heard.

And it should come as no further surprise that it is Shakespeare's kings who are most concerned with enforcing monoglot regimes, none more so, though perhaps many are more forceful and effective, than Richard II. His play, the first in Shakespeare's second historical tetralogy, is notorious among actors, at least those who play supporting roles, for its long stretches in the middle acts, where Richard strikes a posture and speaks at great length, reducing his followers to one-sentence interjections and leaving the actors playing the parts of those followers with the considerable problem of how to comport their silent but highly visible selves while the king remains in full verbal spate. It sometimes seems as if Richard, having intuited the inherent heterogeneity of the dramatic medium in which he is embedded, would attempt to monologize that medium and thus banish the anxiety attendant on the realization that meaning is never the *exclusive* province of a sovereign self. His defeatist decision in Act III to disband such troops as he still commands tells this story succinctly: 'Let no man speak again/To alter this, for counsel is but vain.' And the response of the loyal, though thoroughly frustrated, Aumerle tells us even more: 'My liege, one word' (III.ii.213–15). We hardly need add that Aumerle's gentle request is denied.

Richard is haunted by the fact that, as Voloshinov observed, a '*word is a two-sided act* . . . determined equally by *whose* word it is and for *whom* it is meant . . . a territory shared by both addresser and addressee, by the speaker and his interlocutor' (Voloshinov 1986: 86; emphasis in original). As 'God's substitute,/His deputy anointed in His sight,' to use the traditional language with which John of Gaunt names the monarch (I.ii.37–8), Richard seems to think of himself as playing an almost priestly role, mediating to his subjects the word whose source is in God. As the top of the human portion of that hierarchy which has come to be called the Great Chain of Being, Richard behaves as if his pronouncements were immune from rejoinder, though there is much to suggest as well the nagging knowledge he sometimes succeeds in thrusting aside that they are nothing of the kind. 'Language', as Bakhtin insisted, 'is not a neutral medium that passes freely and easily into the private property of the speaker's intentions' (Bakhtin 1981: 294). To behave as if language really were perfectly obedient to one's intentions implies the conviction that one's own intentions are the only ones that matter, because they have the force of divine fiat. In short, such convictions betray a magical view of the self and its capacities quite at odds with any sober understanding of the compromising give and take characteristic of actual relations among politically organized human beings. Indeed, at the height of his hysterical reception of the news of Bullingbrook's return, Richard identifies his monarchical authority with natural process in a specious attempt to make it seem inevitable and irresistible:

> So when this thief, this traitor, Bullingbrook,
> Who all this while hath revelled in the night
> Whilst we were wandering with the antipodes
> Shall see us rising in our throne the east
> His treasons will sit blushing in his face,
> Not able to endure the sight of day,
> But self-affrighted tremble at his sin.
>
> (III.ii.47–53)

Here and elsewhere, Richard makes abundant use of a set of traditional analogies entailed by the hierarchical view of the cosmos which fifty years ago the Cambridge scholar, E.M.W. Tillyard, called the 'Elizabethan World Picture', stressing, however, the continuity of the cosmology with medieval modes of thinking (Tillyard 1943). As Tillyard's once highly influential study expounds this world picture, all of creation, from the angels at the top, through the sovereign and the various social classes ranged beneath him, right down to the brute animals and the vegetable and mineral kingdoms, is understood to be arranged in a series of subordinations forming a continuum from very top to very bottom, any point of which is thought to be under the immediate sway of the point directly above it. Not only does this Great Chain of Being as a whole suggest a universal order which is serene and secure, it also generates the opportunity for endless analogizing, and any section of it is seen as containing structures of relation similar to those in any other section. As God presides over the whole creation and the sun is pre-eminent in the physical heavens, so the sovereign is first among his subjects, the father first in his family, gold the noblest of minerals, and the lion the king of beasts. The last phrase reminds us that epithets appropriate to one section of the chain can be transferred by analogy to another section, and so not only does the lion become the king of beasts, but gold may be called the prince of metals and the king the sun of England (the analogy that Richard rather flat-footedly exploits in the passage above). This world view, as Tillyard asserted, was part of 'a mass of basic assumptions' which all Elizabethans 'had in common', and which, moreover, 'they never disputed and whose importance varied inversely with this very meagreness of controversy' (Tillyard 1943: 2).

There can be no doubt that the Elizabethan world picture makes some powerful claims, not the least of which lies in the way it treats all levels of the hierarchy and all prescribed relations within a given level as having exactly the same degree and kind of 'natural' inevitability. Thus it is in theory just as natural and fitting that some people are superior to and dominate others as it is that people in general are superior to and dominate domesticated animals, or that they till the earth and make it bring forth vegetable food. But a society's class structure is surely a cultural construct, not a fact of nature; to behave as if it were is, in Bakhtin's characteristic terms, to treat what is posited as if it were simply given, to conflate making with finding. The conflation will be a welcome and convenient one for the dominant classes, though the very insistence and frequency with which they reiterate it may render it suspect.[8] For the underclasses, it will clearly have less appeal.

If we have made any progress since Tillyard's work first appeared, surely part of it is expressed in a certain wariness about specifying just what it is everyone believes at any given time. Even if the people in question are available for polling, the best one can hope to do is establish what anyone says he/she believes or is willing to admit he/she believes, but that is a very different matter. Meanwhile, from the present perspective, Tillyard's assumption of a secure consensus among historical Elizabethans, on the one hand, and among the characters in Shakespeare's history plays, on the other, begins to look remarkably like an attempt to impose monoglossia on what is implicitly in *Richard II* and increasingly explicitly in the two parts of *Henry IV*, a various, heteroglot situation. What a view like Tillyard's elides is precisely the fact of different accentual possibilities, the deflections and refractions that take place as a way of speaking passes among actual speakers. Even Richard's allies, after all, will remind him with varying degrees of indirection that the analogies traditionally used to shore up and naturalize the monarch's authority are hardly written in stone. The language of sacred kingship is subject to dialogizing appropriation by other speakers with other ways of and other reasons for speaking. Multiple meanings, and not necessarily those the king sponsors, may be wrested from it. 'Rage must be withstood', Richard says in attempting to forestall physical conflict between Mowbray and Bullingbrook, 'Give me his gage. Lions make leopards tame.' But Mowbray, acutely, urgently aware of the threat to his honour posed by Bullingbrook's charges, has a telling reply: 'Yea, but not change his spots' (I.i.173–5). Two can play the game of finding analogies that will seem to naturalize the speaker's position, and even the king's most loyal followers will find that occasionally self-interested concerns will supersede duty and obedience.

The truth of the matter is, of course, that the language of sacred kingship, the language of the Elizabethan World Picture, is one discursive practice among others, one way of speaking rather than the master language which contains and interprets all the rest. It is not an 'indisputable language', fully unified and finished off. And though any single discursive practice may aspire to the status of privileged norm by turning a monologically deaf ear to the heterogeneous fragmentation that constitutes the true condition of a living language, such privileged status is never anything but a temporary illusion. Sooner or later the excluded languages of heteroglossia will return to assert their presence and rights. It is never the case that language really is monoglot: it is simply that certain speakers try to behave as if it were. As Clark and Holquist describe Bakhtin's general theory of discourse: 'I am never free to impose my unobstructed intention but must always mediate that intention through the intentions of others, beginning with the otherness of language itself in which I speak' (Clark and Holquist 1984: 245). But Richard behaves as if his word were the first and last, as if it did not admit of dispute or qualification. And he quickly and spectacularly discovers how very wrong he is in this matter.

By the time Henry Bullingbrook has installed himself, however uneasily, on the English throne, the shrewder speakers of English have become a good deal less magically naïve in their view of language as a means for implementing intent. There has been an implicit shift in the monarch's relation to the language he speaks, for that language no longer has the look of an exclusive royal preserve but is revealed for what it has in fact been all along, a heteroglot diversity in which no single speaker controls meaning exclusively or permanently. It turns out that the monarch, particularly one whose claim to the throne is suspect and whose means of attaining that throne highly dubious, is of all men the *most* constrained in speaking, not the least. Every claim he makes about his sovereignty is, after all, challengeable, and that because of the example he himself has set. 'If the man who believes himself a king is mad,' Jacques Lacan famously insisted, 'the king who believes himself a king is no less so."[9] This is a kind of wisdom Henry can scarcely afford to forget, for the minute he succumbs to the temptation to deploy the traditional language of sacred kingship in his own case, he reminds everyone who hears him that the power and authority that language claims for the sovereign have spectacularly failed in the case of Richard. Indeed, by seizing the throne Henry has demonstrated, willy-nilly, that the language of sacred kingship was never more than a way of speaking. And it is a way of speaking that he must exercise the utmost caution in using, if he uses it at all.

The return of heteroglossia is at best an inconvenience for the new monarch, at worst a genuine challenge to his power. It is not so much that he has lost divine sanction (divine sanction always being a matter of supposition in any case), but that he has lost the opportunity freely to speak as if he had divine sanction. Moreover, the emergence of heteroglossia reflects a world vastly expanded in social purview, when compared to the relatively narrow limits of *Richard II*, with its almost uniformly aristocratic group of characters, all of them speaking exclusively in the kind of theatrical verse that tends to smooth off the idiosyncratic corners and suppress individual accents. Even the menial supernumeraries of *Richard II*, after all, the Gardener in Act III, scene iv, or the Groom and Keeper in Act V, scene v, speak the same elegant poetry as their aristocratic overlords. With the second scene of *1 Henry IV*, however, we strike authentic prose for the first time in the tetralogy. And the flyting match of competitive rhetoric between Prince Hal and Falstaff is only the first indication of a thoroughly heteroglot world, which will finally comprise, without really containing, the accents of workers, countrymen, middle-class tradespeople, unlettered apprentices, northern lords as well as southern (the distinction is real and important in this play), speakers of Welsh and French, and many others. It is difficult to imagine a unitary, totalizing language that could possibly speak for each and every varied constituency, somehow providing a broad canopy under which every divergent point of view and set of interests might find satisfactory shelter. *1 Henry IV* reveals a world that seems to have many more meanings than any single, monoglot language can readily dispose of.

We have seen that even in the relatively homogeneous linguistic atmosphere of *Richard II*, the centrifugal tug of individual utterance can be felt. Mowbray can in a limited way appropriate the language of cosmologic and natural analogies and make it temporarily serve his own interests in the clash of wills between himself and the king. One suspects, further, that Mowbray's demurrer when Bullingbrook asks him to confess his treasons before going into exile – 'No, Bullingbrook. If ever I were traitor,/My name be blotted from the book of life' (I.iii.200–1) – is less a denial of his role in the Duke of Gloucester's murder (no one seriously doubts that he played one) than it is a denial that playing such a role was *in the circumstances* the action of a traitor, since it was done out of loyalty to his king. Now that same loyalty, born, no doubt, of an old-fashioned sense of fealty and obedience, keeps him silent on the subject of Richard's own complicity in the murder of Gloucester: 'Within my mouth you have engaoled my tongue' (I.iii.166), he says to Richard, and he is clearly alluding to more than the fact that Richard has just banished him to lands abroad where he will not be able to speak the language. But it will be Richard's mistake to behave at times as if Mowbray's silence were the result of the king's irresistible word and not, as it happens to be in fact, the result of Mowbray's loyal consent. What is at stake here is not only the meaning of the word 'traitor', but also the nature of the bond between the king and his subjects.

It is certainly to Bullingbrook's credit that as Henry IV he never makes a similar mistake about the nature and origin of meaning. But the usurpation has vastly complicated the king's relation to his subjects, for even as his seizure of power has restricted his own options for speaking in and of his new position, it appears to liberate the options of others in making claims for their various spheres of interest. Nor is this effect restricted to the obvious, to those fractious aristocrats who, having witnessed and abetted Bullingbrook's rise to power without incurring, at least in any unambiguous way, the divine wrath traditionally said to follow aggression directed at God's anointed, are now planning to seize power for themselves. For political opportunism seems to sanction other kinds, including linguistic; the appropriation of office with apparent impunity suggested the appropriation of meaning as well. Once it appears that God is either absent from or unwilling to become involved in the affairs of men, everything seems suddenly up for grabs, including the meanings of various common terms a society uses to set and stabilize its central values. The opportunities for the individual speaker to insinuate his own interests, to reaccentuate key terms, to play with and dialogize official discourse by suggesting its affinities with the less respectable discursive practices in the heteroglot ambience, are vastly expanded.

Consider Falstaff, taking his ease in his 'local' inn. His apparently casual and informal relations with Prince Hal are in reality a highly complex performance, a virtual demonstration of the power of utterance in context to appropriate and deflect meaning. Consider his response to Hal's mock virtuous refusal to be a party to highway robbery ('Who, I rob? I a thief? Not I, by my faith.'): 'There's neither honesty, manhood, nor good fellowship in thee, nor thou camest not of the blood royal, if thou darest not stand for ten shillings' (*1 Henry IV*, I.ii.130–3). A little reflection reveals a good deal more here than the merely sophistical play with value terms, the application of 'honesty', for instance, to an activity usually thought to be quintessentially *dis*honest. Let no one think that Falstaff has his eye only on the immediate context, for his purview is in fact considerably broader, silently encompassing the recent usurpation and the questions it raises about the legitimacy not only of the current monarch, but also of his son and heir, whom Falstaff currently addresses. It is mostly the punning play with coinage that enables Falstaff to dialogize authoritative official discourse. The true king must 'stand for ten shillings', that is, he must lend the authority he derives from being God's deputy to the coin of the realm by appearing in effigy on the coin known as a royal and worth ten shillings. If Henry's regime were less dubious, his act of seizing power of less recent memory, all might be well. But unfortunately, 'stand for' may also mean 'make a fight for', and even recalls the highwayman's order to 'stand and deliver'. By simultaneously invoking these two contexts, normally kept at a comfortable distance from one another, Falstaff manages to insinuate the very subversive suggestion that the new criterion for establishing 'the blood royal' is the willingness of the bearer of that blood to engage in acts of thievery, whether of petty sums from victims on the open highway or – and here the damage is done – of thrones and kingdoms and crowns. As Falstaff says a little later to Poins, hoping Poins will be able to persuade Hal to join the party of highwaymen at Gadshill and 'for recreation's sake, prove a false thief', 'the poor abuses of the time want countenance' (I.ii.146–7). He has only to stress 'poor' a shade more than 'abuses' to imply that the *great* abuses of the time already have all the countenance they need.

Clearly, in such a sensitive situation, where the possibilities for dialogizing the languages of a newly emergent heteroglossia are rich and abundant, the king must become the wariest of speakers, always on guard against the possibility that his meanings will be appropriated and deflected to serve speakers with intentions quite different, it may be, from his own. He will cultivate a certain distance from his own pronouncements, perhaps even treating them in private with a certain irony. And if he uses the traditional language of sacred kingship at all, he will certainly not fall prey to Richard's hysterical intensity with its tendency to plunge from metaphoric expression to literal assertion. He will use the traditional language without embracing as truths the things that language enables him to say.

III

With wariness in mind, let us turn briefly to an unobtrusive, though, as it turns out, rather telling moment at the very end of *1 Henry IV*, as the dust settles at Shrewsbury and Henry emerges, for the moment anyway, victorious. The king enters and speaks:

> Thus ever did rebellion find rebuke.
> Ill-spirited Worcester, did not we send grace,
> Pardon, and terms of love to all of you?
> And wouldst thou turn our offers contrary?

> (V.v.1–4)

This is extraordinary: Henry proclaims that the nemesis that in the traditional view inevitably dogs rebellion against the true sovereign has come to pass. His carefully impersonal construction, which reduces the recently completed action almost to an allegory (wherein Rebellion encounters Rebuke and is slain), suggests that the natural order has expelled a foreign body, cleansed itself, and once again informs and regulates the life of the state. He makes no mention of what many, very much including the condemned Worcester, might be pleased to call his *own* rebellion, staged not so very long ago and differing from the present instance most saliently in the fact that it achieved a measure of success. Nor does he flaunt the contradiction implicit in offering pardon to a rebel who, it is otherwise said, must inevitably find rebuke. Worcester, in any case, seems to have a pretty firm grasp of what Lancastrian offers of clemency to the likes of himself are worth, and if his scepticism, expressed earlier to Vernon (V.ii.3–25), seems cynical at that moment, it will scarcely continue to do so in the light of events in *2 Henry IV*, particularly the fate encountered by the Lord Mowbray and the Archbishop of York at Gaultree Forest (IV.i.229–351). Indeed, in the present instance, even as Worcester and Vernon are escorted off to execution, we learn of the capture of Douglas, Hal asks of his father the privilege of disposing of him, then immediately instructs Prince John to deliver the Scot 'Up to his pleasure, ransomless and free' (*1 Henry IV*, V.v.28). By this time, we are perhaps disposed to credit this piece of generosity not to Hal's inherently merciful nature, but to a shrewd calculation that an exotic outlander (who is not, incidentally, much of a politician), dramatically reprieved at the last moment, may lend considerable colour to the Lancastrian faction. Not so the wily old campaigner, steeped in *realpolitik*, who, granted his life, would be likely to go on causing trouble.

The little scene that concludes *1 Henry IV* turns out to contain something other than the usual clangour attendant upon the end of battle, when victors can safely detect the hand of providence now that the outcome is certain. But it would perhaps be a mistake to think that Henry here speaks naïvely, unaware of the dialogizing effect of the language of *realpolitik* on the more traditional language of providential history. Perhaps he merely seizes the opportunity, while followers recover breath, savour the triumph, and are little disposed to cavil, to deploy the brief romance of Rebellion and Rebuke. But he must be aware, after all, that most of the disaffected conspirators against his reign have not even put in an appearance at Shrewsbury, holding out, for various prudential reasons, for a more likely occasion. And he cannot have simply forgotten his own, successful rebellion, though, like Mowbray when confronted with the charge of treason, he would probably be disposed to argue that his deposition of Richard was *in the circumstances* a necessary redress of arrogant acts and fiscal mismanagement and not what we normally mean by rebellion at all.

What Henry's brief remark about rebellion and rebuke really points up is the unfinalized, open-ended character of events that have converged but briefly on the field of Shrewsbury. It is characteristic of Shakespearian endings, at least in the mature plays, that they conspicuously fail Macbeth's aim to trammel up consequences, and if Henry and Prince Hal choose to employ certain formulae of conclusion, they do so in full knowledge that their gestures are arbitrary, that, at bottom, they simply call a halt rather than effect a genuine resolution. Even the dead, after all, continue to demand a reckoning through their survivors and in the living memory of those who have opposed them; Falstaff's comic 'resurrection' after Hal has left him for dead (V.iv.110) is emblematic of this peculiar insistence of the deceased. Killing a man, as Bakhtin observed in a 1961 reconsideration of his own earlier work on Dostoevsky, is not the same as refuting him (Appendix to Bakhtin 1984b: 284).

After such knowledge, what forgiveness? Once the language of sacred kingship and divine right has been recognized as one way of speaking among others, there is no turning back. When a language, previously accepted as totalizing and complete, has been tested by the presence of other languages, 'it can never again', as Morson and Emerson observe, 'naively assume itself to be indisputable, because it has been disputed, may be disputed again, and is always guarding itself against possible disputes'. 'There is all the difference in the world', they conclude, 'between naive unself-consciousness and the polemical assertion of one's rights' (Morson and Emerson 1990: 311). One thing that may set Hal apart in *2 Henry IV* is his refusal to sink into nostalgia and sentimentality, the tendency that afflicts his father in moments of stress, under pressure of advancing illness, and a tendency that reaches a state of acute parody in Justice Shallow's delighted reminiscences of a youth that never was (Act III, scene ii). And it is perhaps not stretching concepts too far to assert that nostalgia in *2 Henry IV* is at bottom the longing for a simpler monoglot regime, where the king's word is once again (assuming it ever really was) current, final, the adequate expression of the views of his united subjects. Such nostalgia surfaces in Henry's recurrent, and recurrently frustrated, wish to lead a crusade against the infidel; in short, it is a longing for a world where lines are unambiguously drawn and that peculiarly athletic version of Christianity, last glimpsed in the description in *Richard II* of Mowbray's final days (IV.i.91–100), could claim to express God's will without fear of contestation. But Henry himself has moments when he recognizes that the idea of a crusade is itself a way of speaking not always and entirely separable from policy, a stratagem of distraction designed to divert the restlessness of his newly pacified subjects into channels less dangerous to his throne:

> [I] had a purpose now
> To lead out many to the Holy Land,
> Lest rest and lying still might make them look
> Too near unto my state.
>
> (*2 Henry IV*, IV.ii.337–40)

The days when one could unselfconsciously fight, as Mowbray is said to have done, 'For Jesu Christ in glorious Christian field' (*Richard II*, IV.i.93), are evidently long gone.

Nowhere is the continuing heteroglot character of the new regime clearer than in those moments when its monarch, no longer speaking as if his discourse were finished off and indisputable (and all the while reserving the knowledge to himself that it is anything but), lapses into a discursive mode that he appears to take perfectly seriously. We have such a moment in the king's soliloquy at the beginning of *2 Henry IV*, Act III, scene i, Henry's melancholy meditation on the burdens of high office, complete with an attendant sentimentalization of the putatively carefree lives of the lower orders (ll. 4–31). But it is a version of pastoral that seems highly doubtful in the light of what we have seen of the wakeful members of the underclass who have quarrelled and roistered in the scene immediately preceding. And, in a signal instance of what Stephen Greenblatt has called 'anticipatory, or proleptic, parody', as Henry enters and begins to intone the uneasiness of the head that wears a crown, we have just heard Falstaff, in what one supposes is a very different mood, call attention to 'how men of merit are sought after'. 'The undeserver may sleep when the man of action is called on' (II.iv.306–8).[10] There are no unbespoke words in a living language, though Henry appears, for the moment at least, to have forgotten that fact. Falstaff is in this instance a crucial step ahead of him.

But a still more telling exchange occurs in these central scenes as Henry is joined by Warwick, Surrey and Sir John Blunt, and the talk turns to the 'rank diseases' growing in the 'body of our kingdom' (III.i.37–8). For in his extremity of grief, fatigue, and ill health, Henry speaks of Richard as if he had well and truly possessed the gift of genuine prophecy, thus conferring on him in retrospect the mantle of sacred kingship which the Lancastrian usurpation has had the effect of denying:

> But which of you was by –
> [To Warwick.] You, cousin Nevil, as I may remember –
> When Richard, with his eye brimful of tears,
> Then checked and rated by Northumberland,
> Did speak these words, now proved a prophecy:
> 'Northumberland, thou ladder by the which
> My cousin Bullingbrook ascends my throne'? –
> Though then, God knows, I had no such intent
> But that necessity so bowed the state
> That I and greatness were compelled to kiss. –
> 'The time shall come', thus did he follow it,
> 'The time will come that foul sin, gathering head,
> Shall break into corruption.' So went on,
> Foretelling this same time's condition
> And the division of our amity.
>
> (III.i.64–78)

It is certainly no accident that Warwick is exceedingly quick to check this hagiographic tendency with a counter-explanation based on common sense and political shrewdness:

> There is a history in all men's lives
> Figuring the natures of the times deceased,
> The which observed, a man may prophesy,
> With a near aim, of the main chance of things
> As yet not come to life, who in their seeds
> And weak beginning lie intreasurèd.
> Such things become the hatch and brood of time,
> And by the necessary form of this
> King Richard might create a perfect guess

> That great Northumberland, then false to him,
> Would of that seed grow to a greater falseness,
> Which should not find a ground to root upon
> Unless on you.

(79–91)

'Near aim', 'the main chance of things', 'perfect guess': there is nothing inspired or magical about it. Where Henry speaks of the genuinely prophetic, Warwick counters with matters of prediction and informed conjecture.

And surely Warwick is right: England has become in the years since the usurpation what Bakhtin would call 'novelized'. It remains throughout the second tetralogy a collection of disparate voices, colliding, appropriating from one another, criticizing and parodying. Experience in this new world partakes of what Bakhtin identified as the novel's 'new and quite specific problematicalness: characteristic for it is an eternal re-thinking and re-evaluating'.[11] Events can no longer be ordered and foretold according to a providential pattern, for each step must be negotiated separately, according to its own concrete and specific context. Denied access to the transcendent, the monarch must rely on his knowledge of precedent and his experience with the ways of men to form educated guesses, some of which he may occasionally pass off as prophetic. But the prophet who believes himself a prophet is mad indeed.

Lest England were simply to return to a monoglot regime with the accession of Henry V and the spectacular success of his French campaign, apparently so much more finalizing than either Shrewsbury or Gaultree Forest, let us remember that even *Henry V* ends amid a language lesson, where the king confronts the alien and mostly unintelligible French of his newly affianced Katherine, and struggles to harmonize yet another voice with a distinct specificity of its own (Act V, scene ii). And the choric commentary with which Shakespeare concludes *Henry V* and the tetralogy as a whole serves to remind us of the fragility and transience of the order taking shape for the time being:

> Henry the Sixth, in infant bands crowned king
> Of France and England, did this king succeed,
> Whose state so many had the managing
> That they lost France and made his England bleed, . . .

(Epil., 9–12)

Henry V, for all its promise of peace and royal marriage and the uniting of kingdoms, is shadowed by the expectation of reversal and incompletion. There is no one in the second tetralogy to correspond with the saintly Richmond, the *deus ex machina* of *Richard III* at the end of the first tetralogy, the restorer, who, as Sigurd Burckhardt acutely observed, 'has no history; he is *only* the restorer, coming into the play by divine dispensation, from a realm beyond time' (Burckhardt 1968: 175). In the historical vision of the second tetralogy there are no guaranteed directions, no entirely foreseeable outcomes, no projected scenarios that can possibly contain all contingencies. There is only further contextualization and recontextualization in the interminable dialogic process of positing meaning.

SUPPLEMENT

NIGEL WOOD: Can you locate a 'dialogical' context for this essay, i.e. to what critical question or misapprehension is this an answer or corrective?

RONALD MACDONALD: In the most general terms, this essay might be thought of as a nominalist retort to realist approaches of all kinds, ranging from Tillyard, of course, with his presumption of homogeneous thinking, both among characters in Shakespeare's history plays and among the people of his contemporary England, to the pervasive assumption, very difficult to combat, that the plays somehow contain Shakespeare's 'philosophy', or that they offer a distillation of his mature wisdom. For me, this latter assumption is fundamentally undramatic. It leads to arbitrary decisions about what is authoritative, decontextualizes speeches (typically the longer ones tending towards the orotund and aphoristic), and generally ignores what I take to be Shakespeare's careful juxtapositions, wherein he contrives the questioning of one speech by another. The life of drama is in dialogic exchange, not monologic pronouncement on the part of characters awarded the status of author's representative by critical fiat. If an author's commitment to the dramatic medium is genuine, as I believe Shakespeare's was, he will certainly forgo opportunities to speak *in propria persona*, choosing, rather, to let his play arise from the collision of subjectivities within it, each with a distinct and distinctly partial 'take' on the dramatic world in which it finds itself embedded. A playwright *creates* his characters, to be sure; but I do not take that to mean that he therefore *coincides* with any one of them.

A few years ago, Malcolm Evans, in his incisive and very witty book *Signifying Nothing: Truth's True Contents in Shakespeare's Text* (1986), discussed a remarkable commercial item he had unearthed, *A Shakespeare Birthday Book*, compiled by the Reverend A.E. Sims. The book provides a quotation from Shakespeare for each day in the year, every one shorn of context and skewed in the direction of an improving sentiment. Lady Macbeth's incitement to regicide, for instance, becomes a version of 'he who hesitates is lost'. Sims, along with Evans, makes sobering reading for those in search of Shakespeare's essential wisdom.

NW: Bakhtin has been used to sanction a return to 'History' in that he seems always to direct our attention to any utterance's immediate context, both its 'official' and its 'unofficial' or carnivalistic aspects. Alternatively, you could claim that the most pressing result of any 'dialogical' consideration is not to recapture the past, but rather to become insistently aware of the dialogue with other discursive forms that influences each subsequent critical reading. Is it a case of 'either/or', or do historical considerations in your view incorporate present responsibilities?

RM: Not a case of 'either/or', I think. It is certainly true that dialogism directs our attention to specific context, which, it insists, is unique and unrepeatable. But the spoken-about is always the already-spoken-about, and the speaker will always frame his utterance in the awareness of previous utterances. The reach of such awareness will surely vary from speaker to speaker, one taking into consideration only the immediately preceding utterance of an interlocutor, another broadening the purview to previous conversations, remembered or read about, and so on. There are, after all, no free-standing utterances; each is a link in a chain, taking account of what precedes it, anticipating what will follow it, and for me, such looking-behind-and-ahead constitutes a genuinely historical awareness.

This is, in fact, one of the consequences of a linguistics based on the utterance rather than the sentence. As long as you concentrate on the system of language, the history of that system matters little. Somewhere in the *Course in General Linguistics*, Saussure compares a contemporary, synchronic system of language to the positions of chessmen on a board at the midpoint, say, of a game. What matters is the set of current relations among those men, not how they came to be where they are currently situated. A competent player might replace one of the original players and complete the game without having to know the antecedents of the current positions. So a speaker needs only to know the current rules for combining the elements of his speech into sentences. But to form a meaningful *utterance*, he must bring historical awareness into play.

NW: Falstaff's dramatic function is often a central topic of debate (and quite understandably so) where the Henriad is concerned. One of the possible effects of emphasizing his role as Hal's worldly guardian (instead of the more idealistic focus on the blood tie with Henry IV), is that he helps Hal avoid Hotspur's fatal fault of believing in his own rhetoric, that is, it is rarely performative: for example, 'Honour' is less a transcendental ideal than an expensive commodity. At *2 Henry IV*, IV.iii.18–19, Falstaff proclaims that he has 'a whole school of tongues in this belly of [his], and not a tongue of them all speaks any other word but my name'. How does he disturb a royalist's faith in a monoglot language?

RM: A good deal of Falstaff's power to disturb rests on his spectacular display of virtuosity. The speed and ease with which he changes role or voice, now speaking as a young man ('They hate us youth!'), now of himself as a man in advanced years ('That he is old, the more the pity, his white hairs do witness it'), suggest that an identity is not something inherited or conferred, but enacted, an option rather than an assignment. If a royalist can be said to have faith in a monoglot language, surely that means he has faith in that language as inevitable and indisputable, at least when it is uttered by the sovereign. For Falstaff, it is not so much that a man speaks like a king because he is one, but that he is a king, or can persuade people that he is, because he speaks like one. Once 'king' is recognized as naming a role rather than an essence, as something contingent rather than intrinsic, the possibilities for 'doing' the king (there is putatively only one way to *be* a king) begin to multiply. In the play *ex tempore* in *1 Henry IV*, Act II, scene iv, Falstaff begins by announcing he will do the king 'in King Cambyses vein' and then proceeds to perform in something like the euphuistic prose of John Lyly. Either style is calculated to make the sovereign look slightly ridiculous, but further, the very presence of multiple styles suggests that whatever the king's style, it is one of many and always in principle susceptible of appropriation. It is not, unfortunately, the case that the king's style emanates from his intrinsic dignity, but that the king's dignity emanates from his contingent style.

NW: Do you feel that some of the plays' more parodic elements (Bakhtin's emphasis on the medieval *parodia sacra*) challenge the need for some form of narrative closure to the cycle?

RM: I do think so, yes, and that partly because I have become increasingly sceptical about the 'safety valve' theory of parody and carnival, the notion that parodic occasions are part of the state's means for stabilizing itself, cathartic occasions where potentially subversive energies are safely bled off and done away with. It seems to me that for the mature Shakespeare, at least, closure is always premature, consequences never entirely trammelled up. Stability and stasis are stability and stasis *for now*, and there is always the possibility, indeed, given sufficient time, the inevitability of destabilization and further developments. Surely most in Shakespeare's audience must have realized that what they were seeing represented in the last scene of *Henry V* was not the end of English history but in fact the prologue to one of the bloodiest and most chaotic periods England had ever known. I have often wondered if what I take to be Shakespeare's fondness for open-endedness was not related to certain aspects of the theatrical institution in which he worked, the fact, for instance, that a play is never over in the sense that in principle it may always be, and very frequently will be, performed again. Any performance is thus a performance for now and may well be modified or amended in future performances.

CHAPTER 3

The Future of History
in *Henry IV*

KIERNAN RYAN

[Kiernan Ryan's reading of *1* and *2 Henry IV* draws on (while not wholly adopting) the Hegelian Marxist positions offered by Fredric Jameson's *The Political Unconscious*. Marxist theories of literature are varied in detail, but stem more or less directly from the view that, while art may seem to be produced just by individuals, we might learn much more about their work if we identify two things: first, the artist's 'ideology', i.e. not a set of codified beliefs, but rather an unphilosophical reflection of how individuals see their roles in class society and the values, symbols and ideas that help explain those roles to such individuals and which therefore ties them all the more securely to their inherited context; and second, the basic conditions under which such art can be produced (e.g. conditions of patronage, growth of the mass market, availability of new technologies of production) which establish inexorable limits to the apparent freedoms of artistic activity.

Marx's (and Engels's) terms still provide the original inspiration for Marx*ist* interpretation. In Marx and Engels's *The German Ideology* (1845–6) the 'production of ideas, of conceptions, of consciousness is at first directly interwoven with the material activity and the material intercourse of men'. Thus, thought is the 'direct efflux' of this 'material behaviour', and individuals must be brought to realize that they in fact have a hand in the production of their own conceptions, 'real, active men, as they are conditioned by a definite development of their productive forces . . .'. The conclusion is inescapable that 'life is not determined by consciousness, but consciousness by life' (Marx and Engels 1959: 287–8). This is given more specific focus in the Preface to *A Contribution to the Critique of Political Economy* (1859), where it is held as a condition of the 'social production' of one's own life that one enters 'into definite relations that are indispensable and independent of [one's] will, *relations of production* which correspond to a definite stage of development of [one's] material productive *forces*'. This forms 'the economic structure of society, the real foundation, on which rises a legal and political superstructure and to which correspond definite forms of social consciousness' (1959: 84). This model seems particularly deterministic, and most recent Marxist analysis regards this 'base–superstructure' divide as a preliminary move, one which, if carried through without extra sophistication, reduces all art to its modes of production, a position that makes it particularly difficult to account for individual variations.

The 'definite forms of social consciousness' group themselves in analysis as *ideology*. In order to render such awareness as narrow and partisan (i.e. stemming from a class identity, not 'nature' or 'common sense'), there is a need to compare it with some greater entity or notion that proceeds from a more 'scientific' grasp of the total system of social relationships. 'Ideology' was often, then, equated with 'false consciousness'. More recently, 'ideology' has come to be associated with *all* forms of social perception, without which we could not function as members of society. In the work of Louis Althusser the role assigned to art is a major one, for he claims that it is only through the depiction of a process of thought in literary form that the work of ideology can be inspected with sufficient detachment. In his essay 'Ideology and Ideological State Apparatuses' (1969), Althusser finds ideology integral to *all* thought processes. It supplies a focus for definitions, even if actually based on biased premises. The state apparatuses (e.g. the Church, political party, university and the legal system) 'interpellate' us (encourage us to believe) that we are free individuals, and therein lies their attraction and power (see Althusser 1977: 123–73).

This tendency to differentiate literary from non-literary expression is obviously fraught with the difficulty of defining just what the 'literary' might be, but it also creates a system of evaluation as well as of analysis. For Pierre Macherey, in *A Theory of Literary Production*, literary form was capable of showing up the internal incoherences and multiple contradictions of ideology. The apparent coherence of ideology can only be maintained by a process of repression and economies with the truth. By dwelling on the 'silences' that come to be implied by the work of art, Macherey reveals the way that ideology operates and, implicitly, how we can question its hold over us (see especially Macherey 1978: 61–101; Eagleton 1991: 136–51).

Jameson's great popularity stems from his ability to accommodate the private with the public sphere of analysis. History is not merely 'context' or 'background', but rather something far less unitary; it is perceived in 'ideologies' and several alternative points of access for the researcher. Hegel argued in his *Philosophy of Fine Art* (1835) that there was a very gradual unfolding in particular events of a History which was seen as stages in the development of a 'World-Spirit' or an 'Idea' or 'Absolute', an idealist concept which pointed towards a time (post-capitalist) when form and content might eventually form an harmonious unity. In the work of Georg Lukács and Lucien Goldmann there is an attempt to breathe new life into this perspective, by regarding art as the production of a whole social group whose 'trans-individual mental structures' (Goldmann's term, indicating the group's aspirations and how it makes sense of them) are transposed by the most valuable artists into eventually unified and recurrent structures. For Goldmann, in studies such as *The Hidden God* (1964), structural relations are sought between the literary text, the 'world-view' of the artist's social grouping and its particular historical situation. The tendency is towards an achieved totality of view that can take in something wider than history is more traditionally taken to be. In *The Political Unconscious* Jameson emphasizes this concept of the 'totality' as a standard of judgement, not as a predicted future state (Jameson 1981: 50–7). Ideology confirms a constricted horizon by 'strategies of containment' where limits to reference created by mimetic means (e.g. Holinshed's *Chronicles* as apparent source, or, more generally, the sense of a faithful historical record) enforce an unnecessary frontier to discourse in the interests of 'coherence' or just simply intelligibility. Reading texts as 'symbolic acts' entails 'the will . . . [to] grasp them as resolutions of determinate contradictions'. Interpretation becomes a rewriting of the rhetorical text 'in such a way that the latter may itself be seen as the rewriting or restructuration of a prior historical or ideological *subtext*' which is only ever available by self-conscious analytical (re)construction (Jameson 1981: 80–1).

Ryan, however, takes issue with some of the negative aspects of this use of literature. Are literary texts destined to 'contain' (that is, limit) radical comment? Or do they imply, either by irony or staged contradiction, a specific value in literary communication, almost as a basic condition of their appeal to a specific audience, wherein there is the possibility of hopeful prediction rather than anxious suspicion (see Ryan 1989: 1–43)?

In short, for Jameson, texts never 'tell' us their history; they must be made to do this, and this involves breaking out of what Jameson in 1972 called the 'prison-house of language' (see Jameson, 1972: 195–216) and re-engaging with a history which contains several coexistent 'histories' and competing ideologies (see his 'Marxism and Historicism' (1979) in Jameson 1988, 2: 148–77). To place the text within the 'totality' is thus also to express what it cannot, to identify not merely its conscious bias but also its inevitably partial grasp of a large diversity of cultural practices. The point here explored by Ryan is that this need not be a negative activity, and, indeed, if literature were just trusted a little more to escape its historical context, then its textual and performative devices could be means for exploration not containment.]

NIGEL WOOD

I

As history plays engaged in dramatizing the fate of Crown and nation across a period two centuries before the time of Shakespeare and his audience, *1* and *2 Henry IV* pose fundamental questions for the literary theory and critical practice of the present. What is the relationship between the reality of history and its creative representation, between the world of the past and the work's account of it? What is the political role of the work in its own world: to shore up or shake the foundations of power? Can the literature of the past only speak of the past, or has it secrets to reveal to the present and appointments to keep with the future?

No attempt to answer these questions in recent years has been more ambitious or compelling than Fredric Jameson's *The Political Unconscious* (1981). Although the subtitle, *Narrative as a Socially Symbolic Act*, and the devotion of chapters to Balzac, Gissing and Conrad suggest a narrower relevance to the novel, the book as a whole seeks to construct nothing short of a new Marxist hermeneutics, a comprehensive political theory of interpretation. The essential arguments of *The Political Unconscious* are developed in Chapter 1, 'On Interpretation: Literature as a Socially Symbolic Act', and Chapter 6, 'Conclusion: The Dialectic of Utopia and Ideology'. It is from these chapters that I will draw the ideas that strike me as most illuminating for the study of *Henry IV*; but I will also refer to Jameson's closely related essay 'Marxism and Historicism' (1979, in Jameson 1988), which tackles some of the thorny issues subsequently explored at length in *The Political Unconscious*.

I hope to show that the fresh perspectives supplied by Jameson's theory of interpretation make possible a more searching account of the *Henry IV* plays than the most influential readings to date have delivered. But the pursuit of that account should also establish the power of these plays to expose the limits of Jameson's methodology through their superior imaginative grasp of the complex problems his theory addresses.

Let us begin with the claims of the literature of the past on the critical practice of the present. What is at stake in the encounter between the late sixteenth-century scripts of *1* and *2 Henry IV* and their late twentieth-century students? Contemporary criticism offers two main strategies for dealing with a work that confronts us from the temporally remote and culturally estranged past which first housed it. One is the retrospective route followed by both the traditional and the newer kinds of historicist response: the restoration of the work to some apposite original context, in which its meaning may be more authentically and so more securely moored. The other path leads in the opposite direction, towards the colonization of the past by modernity: the collapsing of historical distance, and hence the erasure of difference, by an act of appropriation which makes the author of the text our contemporary. At the extremes, the work is either embedded in a past world which excludes modern consequence, or absorbed into current categories from which historicity has been drained.

Jameson's answer to 'the question of the claims of monuments from distant and even archaic moments of the cultural past on a culturally different present' is to reject 'this unacceptable option, or ideological double bind, between antiquarianism and modernising "relevance" or projection'. Interpretation can be released from this disabling impasse only by implementing a view of history 'capable of respecting the specificity and radical difference of the social and cultural past while disclosing the solidarity of its polemics and passions, its forms, structures, experiences, and struggles, with those of the present day' (Jameson 1981: 18).

Jameson is confident that a Marxist philosophy of history alone

> can give us an adequate account of the essential *mystery* of the cultural past, which, like Tiresias drinking the blood, is momentarily returned to life and warmth and allowed once more to speak, and to deliver its long-forgotten message in surroundings utterly alien to it.
>
> (Jameson 1981: 19; emphasis in original)

For this revival of the past through the magic of the cultural documents it has bequeathed us cannot be accomplished except by a vision of history which grasps both past and present moments 'as vital episodes in a single vast unfinished plot' (Jameson 1981: 20): the epic tale of humanity's collective struggle to transform its enslavement to necessity into a shared freedom from the coercions of nature and history alike. By severing the ties binding then to now, critics engrossed in the past or constrained by the present have conspired, in effect, to obscure literature's involvement in the telling of that tale. Hence the most urgent task of the new hermeneutics Jameson proposes lies 'in detecting the traces of that uninterrupted narrative, in restoring to the surface of the text the repressed and buried reality of this fundamental history' (1981: 20), which constitutes the 'political unconscious' of the literary work.

This should not mean, however, merely a revamped, politicized historicism, which continues to submit texts to the superior gaze of belated comprehension. The ideal relationship is one of genuine dialogue rather than the simulated exchange contrived between a dummy version of the past and the modern critical ventriloquist. 'We must try to accustom ourselves', Jameson stresses, 'to a perspective in which every act of reading, every local interpretive practice, is grasped as the privileged vehicle through which two distinct modes of production confront and interrogate each other' (Jameson 1988: 175). For if we can do this,

> We will no longer tend to see the past as some inert and dead object which we are called upon to resurrect, or to preserve, or to sustain, in our own living freedom; rather, the past will itself become an active agent in this process and will begin to come before us as a radically different form of life which rises up to call our own form of life into question and to pass judgement on us and through us on the social formation in which we exist. At that point the very dynamics of the historical tribunal are unexpectedly and dialectically reversed: it is not we who sit in judgement on the past, but rather the past, the radical difference of other modes of production (and even of the immediate past of our own mode of production), which judges us, imposing the painful knowledge of what we are not, what we are no longer, what we are not yet.
>
> (Jameson 1988: 175)

It is in the sense implied in that last phrase that Jameson believes the past 'speaks to us about our own virtual and unrealised "human potentialities"' (Jameson 1988: 175). The attempt to initiate an authentic dialogue between history and modernity through literature is indivisible from the quest to restore to the process of aesthetic interpretation the dimension of futurity: 'the hermeneutic contact between past and present outlined here cannot fully be described without the articulation within it of what Ernst Bloch has called the Utopian impulse' (1988: 176). What distinguishes the Marxist vision for Jameson is its combination of a critique of previous and contemporary social formations with 'the anticipatory expression of a future society', with a 'partisan commitment to that future or Utopian mode of production which seeks to emerge from the hegemonic mode of production of our own present' (1988: 176). Thus the Marxist practice of literary interpretation he envisages should involve 'a hermeneutic relationship to the past which is able to grasp its own present as history only on condition it manages to keep the idea of the future, and of radical and utopian transformation, alive' (1988: 177).

Jameson proposes an equally invaluable revision of the ways in which the relationship between the world and the work, between literature and history, is commonly perceived. His reappraisal of this relationship makes it possible to break yet another basic critical deadlock, wrought once again by the antagonism of two powerful but lopsided positions. For to take the line toed by old-fashioned practical critic and daredevil deconstructionist alike, and treat the work as a largely autonomous textual event, whose point owes few debts to biographical and social fact, is plainly unsatisfactory. But to espouse the sort of approach that reduces the work to dancing attendance on a prior historical reality, which thus provides the gauge of the text's significance and worth, is scarcely less problematic. For the poem, play or novel dwindles into a mere symptom or suffix of its age, a more or less recognizable restatement in literary form of the primal, empirical narrative established by historians.

Jameson's thesis endeavours to do justice both to our sense of the text's aesthetic integrity, its seeming independence of history, and to our recognition of its power to animate through language and form a version of that lived world in which it is rooted, but to which it cannot be reduced. For Jameson the literary text, far from being a passive imprint of historical reality, 'always entertains some active relationship with the Real'. This allows it to 'draw the Real into its own texture', to select and incorporate its own indispensable contexts, and thus 'carry the Real within itself as its own intrinsic or immanent subtext' (Jameson 1981: 81). To the extent that literature may be viewed as a form of symbolic action, 'a way of doing something to the world',

> to that degree what we are calling 'world' must inhere within it, as the content it has to take up into itself in order to submit it to the transformations of form. The symbolic act therefore begins by generating and producing its own context in the same moment of emergence in which it steps back from it, taking its measure with a view toward its own projects of transformation. The whole paradox of what we have here called the subtext may be summed up in this, that the literary work or cultural object, as though for the first time, brings into being that very situation to which it is also, at one and the same time, a reaction. It articulates its own situation and textualizes it, thereby encouraging and perpetuating the illusion that the situation itself did not exist before it, that there is nothing but a text, that there never was any extra- or con-textual reality before the text itself generated it in the form of a mirage.
>
> (Jameson 1981: 81–2)

If Jameson is right about the way significant literature internalizes and transports whatever circumstances it requires to make sense to its readers, then the kind of historical criticism which labours to 'restore' text to context by excavating and reconstituting the world to which it refers is labouring to little purpose. For those who still regard literature as a special, privileged enterprise, not to be confused with or subordinated to history, there is no point turning the text into a pretext for exhuming and expanding backgrounds from which the work itself has already looted all it needs, or which it has ruled out in advance as irrelevant to its purpose. Indeed, the current drive to dissolve literary into cultural and historical studies might strike the cynic as the convenient resort of those who have failed to recognize the literature of the past as an imaginative historiography in its own right. Be that as it may, this part of Jameson's argument can be recruited to tighten the focus on 'the transformations of form' to which the work submits whatever materials it has chosen to translate from the discourse of history into the language of literature. For the vital task is surely to interpret the way the work portrays and persuades us to view its subject, rather than to trace that subject superfluously back to its roots in the conditions from which it sprang. The changing meaning and value of classic literature is more profitably sought in how it handles its material than in where it found it in the first place.

The trouble is that Jameson's lack of faith in literature's powers of vision and resistance scuppers the positive potential of his argument at the outset. No sooner has the work been sprung from its incarceration in mere subsequence than it is thrown back into the airless slammer of ideology with slim prospects of reprieve. What might have blossomed into a genuine hermeneutics of hope withers into the familiar hermeneutics of suspicion routinely practised by more disenchanted political critics. Thus Jameson allows literature the agency to submit reality to the transformations of form, but purely in the interests of the ruling account of that reality: 'the aesthetic act is itself ideological, and the production of aesthetic or narrative form is to be seen as an ideological act in its own right, with the function of inventing imaginary or formal "solutions" to unresolvable social contradictions' (Jameson 1981: 79).

Far from giving us enlightened access to the truths of human experience and social relations, the literary text contrives to mask them, or make them vanish through the trapdoor of rhetorical or formal illusion. The most sacred texts in the secular scripture are not those that scorn such duplicity, but those that have proved its most accomplished exponents. For, assuming the individual work to be 'a symbolic move in an essentially polemic and strategic ideological confrontation between

the classes', then 'by definition the cultural monuments and master-
works that have survived tend necessarily to perpetuate only a single
voice in this class dialogue, the voice of a hegemonic class' (Jameson
1981: 85). Jameson shares with most devotees of the new historicism
and cultural materialism what he himself terms 'a manipulatory theory
of culture' (1981: 287), a kind of cultural conspiracy theory which com-
pels them to treat the work of literature as a seductive technique of containment, genetically predisposed to buttress the status quo and delay
or disguise the advent of liberating change.

But how can such a craven tool of reaction be expected to speak so
trenchantly of its time as to rattle the complacency of the present and
unfold premonitions of an unfettered future? The answer for Jameson
is that it can be made to do so only in spite of itself. Once the text has
been lured on to the psychiatrist's couch to deliver an account of its
intent, the critical analyst's role is to tease from that account involuntary
clues to the undeluded understanding it has distorted and repressed, to
coax its political unconscious to the surface. The best a radical modern
critic can do with a past masterwork is to read it with hindsight against
its conservative grain, forcing its symptomatic slips and silences to
betray the secret truths of history it has connived so ingeniously to
efface. The utopian aspect of the work can likewise be wrested from its
reactionary grasp only by an act of hermeneutic violence determined to
construe the ideology of the text as a travesty of that ideal human condition to whose possibility it bears unwitting witness.

At one point Jameson announces encouragingly that Marxist criticism 'can no longer be content with its demystifying vocation to
unmask and to demonstrate the ways in which a cultural artifact fulfills
a specific ideological mission, in legitimating a given power structure'
(Jameson 1981: 291). And he proposes instead that 'a Marxist negative
hermeneutic must in the practical work of reading and interpretation be
exercised *simultaneously* with a Marxist positive hermeneutic, or a
decipherment of the Utopian impulses of these same still ideological
cultural texts' (1981: 296). That 'still ideological' shuts down the opportunities opened earlier in the sentence. Jameson is more alert than most
to the ways in which theorists like Bakhtin, Bloch, Adorno, Marcuse
and Benjamin 'hint at a variety of options for articulating a properly
Marxian version of meaning beyond the purely ideological' (1981: 285).
But his own 'positive hermeneutic' cannot take the hint, and settles
instead for 'the proposition that the effectively ideological is also, at the
same time, necessarily Utopian' (1981: 286).

How can a literary work whose resources are supposedly devoted to legitimizing class society simultaneously express a vision and values antithetical to those sponsoring its ideological vocation? The key to the paradox, according to Jameson, is that 'all ideology in the strongest sense, including the most exclusive forms of ruling-class consciousness just as much as that of oppositional or oppressed classes . . . is in its very nature Utopian' (Jameson 1981: 289). It is utopian inasmuch as it expresses the desired unity of a people, an intimation of realized community:

> The achieved collectivity or organic group of whatever kind – oppressors fully as much as oppressed – is Utopian not in itself, but only insofar as all such collectivities are themselves *figures* for the ultimate concrete collective life of an achieved Utopian or classless society. Now we are in a better position to understand how even hegemonic or ruling-class culture and ideology are Utopian, not in spite of their instrumental function to secure and perpetuate class privilege and power, but rather precisely because that function is also in and of itself the affirmation of collective solidarity.
>
> (Jameson 1981: 291; emphasis in original)

In other words, even the most powerful feats of the literary imagination are condemned to conceal the oppressive divisions and conflicts of their world behind façades of formal harmony and structural unity; but these fantasies of reconciliation and closure cannot help symbolizing the very dispensation whose arrival in reality they were expressly designed to forestall. This might well prove a fruitful way of tackling works plainly transfixed by the legitimating myths of their day. What is questionable is the need to stifle at birth the possibility that literature may not always be so completely beguiled by ideology as Jameson presumes, but may prove intent on exposing the current map of experience to critique from a utopian standpoint irreducible to ideology of any sort.

Henry IV provides an ideal opportunity to explore both the strengths and the drawbacks of Jameson's theory when it is put to the test of textual analysis. Both plays are directly engaged with history, politics and ideology. *1* and *2 Henry IV* are as preoccupied as Jameson with the relationship of the past to the present, with the implications of converting historical realities into verbal fictions, and with the role of language and representation in preserving and contesting power. To what extent do these history plays not only speak to us of what our world once was, but also challenge us to confront what it remains and what it has yet to become? If Jameson is right to regard writing's relation to reality as one of active formation rather than supplementary expression, then to answer that question we need to examine how the plays' formal strategies act to organize our perception of their version of history. This in turn will enable us to determine to what degree both parts of *Henry IV* collude in mystifying the power structures they portray, and in what ways they foreshadow the dissolution of hierarchy itself.

II

On the face of it, it might seem hard to imagine a drama more eager to comply with Jameson's expectations of literature than *Henry IV*. Here, surely, is a perfect instance of art in the frank service of the reigning ideology, dramatizing the central contradictions of society in order to forge their imaginary resolution in a vision of personal and political unity. Why else devote two plays to the triumphant defeat of rebel forces by the incumbent monarch, and the inseparable victory of Prince Hal over the mutinous impulses destroying his credibility as heir to the throne of England? The divisions in the kingdom parallel the divisions in its future king, and their reciprocal suppression allows Part 2 to culminate in the prospect of a renewed nation unified by a transfigured sovereign about to divert the collective aggression of his people upon the French. Jameson's notion of literature imposing a spurious harmony on intractable social conflicts, but projecting through that illusion the true reconciliation anticipated from a classless community, appears to fit *Henry IV* like a gauntlet. Even without Hal's subsequent consecration as glorious warrior-king in *Henry V*, *1* and *2 Henry IV* arguably achieve a sense of closure strong enough to invest their history of bloodshed and guilt with the retrospective sanction of providential design.

What binds both plays into this reading is, of course, the myth of the Prodigal Son. The opening scene of Part 1 reveals Hal's sire so ashamed of the 'riot and dishonour' visited upon the House of Lancaster by his offspring that he wishes himself the father of Northumberland's boy, Hotspur, instead: 'a son who is the theme of honour's tongue' (*1 Henry IV*, I.i.84, 80). Hal has betrayed his identity as Prince of Wales and heir to the realm by preferring the idle fellowship of thieves, drunkards and whores to the resolute pursuit of his royal vocation. As his father puts it in their taut confrontation in Act III, Hal has, like 'the skipping King' Richard, 'mingled his royalty with cap'ring fools', diluting his prospective sovereignty in wanton familiarity with his inferiors, whose vision of him is consequently 'sick and blunted with community', when it should be awestruck: 'For thou hast lost thy princely privilege/With vile participation' (III.ii.60, 63, 77, 86–7). The most scandalous effect of Prince Hal's delinquency is this erasure of the line dividing the ruler from the ruled, the ultimately metaphysical distinction on which not only his own right to rule but also the whole social hierarchy depends.

The conflict between 'vile participation' and the enforcing of regal distance is central to Hal's story and the shaping of both plays. It is vitally entwined with the concern to preserve the fragile difference between the regicidal usurper Henry IV and the rebellious lords who helped him seize the throne they now seek to hijack in their turn. It is to defend this discrimination, upon which the legitimacy of the Lancastrian line relies, that the climactic battle at Shrewsbury is fought in Part 1 and Prince John dupes the rebels at Gaultree at the end of Part 2. The twin peaks of Hal's personal battle with his own wayward drives coincide dramatically with these victories over insurgence on the national plane. That the prodigal prince will return to the royal fold seems, however, a cast-iron bet from the start. The soliloquy with which he concludes his first scene with Falstaff notoriously predicts exactly the course his life will follow over both parts of *Henry IV*. The manipulative ease with which he divorces himself from the alehouse intimates of a moment before, reduces them to terms of unequivocal contempt, and swaps spontaneous banter for the calculated scripting of his public image, proves his father's anxieties unfounded:

> Yet herein will I imitate the sun,
> Who doth permit the base contagious clouds
> To smother up his beauty from the world,
> That, when he please again to be himself,
> Being wanted he may be more wondered at
> By breaking through the foul and ugly mists
> Of vapours that did seem to strangle him. . . .
> So when this loose behaviour I throw off
> And pay the debt I never promisèd,
> By how much better than my word I am,
> By so much shall I falsify men's hopes;
> And like bright metal on a sullen ground,
> My reformation, glitt'ring o'er my fault,
> Shall show more goodly and attract more eyes
> Than that which hath no foil to set it off.
>
> (*1 Henry IV* I.ii.185–91, 196–203)

This prince needs no lessons from the king in impressing the singularity and exclusiveness of his identity upon his people.

The dramatic interest is created, therefore, not by a genuine, unpredictable conflict in the 'sword and buckler Prince of Wales' (I.iii.229), but by the suspense of his deferral of the inevitable. We are constantly reminded that we are dealing with a strategic postponement rather than a purely feckless refusal of his appointment with history. Hal's sobering assurance at the end of the 'play extempore' (II.iv.269–70) that one day he will indeed 'banish plump Jack, and banish all the world' (II.iv.461–2) already prefigures the chilling dismissal of Falstaff for real in the final scene of 2 Henry IV: 'I know thee not old man. Fall to thy prayers' (V.v.43). Sharply upbraided by the father Hotspur calls 'this king of smiles' (1 Henry IV, I.iii.245), Hal responds by reiterating the pledge framed in his earlier monologue and so reinstating the crucial disparity between himself and his future subjects which he has allowed to evaporate:

> I will redeem all this on Percy's head,
> And in the closing of some glorious day
> Be bold to tell you that I am your son,
> When I will wear a garment all of blood
> And stain my favours in a bloody mask,
> Which, washed away, shall scour my shame with it.
>
> (III.ii.132–7)

At the Battle of Shrewsbury with which Part 1 concludes, where he saves his father's life and defeats his extravagant rival, Hotspur, Hal heroically proves himself a man of his word and a monarch in the making. His lingering, affectionate indulgence of Falstaff on the battlefield nevertheless confirms that the narrative of redemption is still incomplete when the curtain falls on Act V. The story is therefore resumed in Part 2, which recycles the pattern of disaffection and delay finally expiated by the promise fulfilled, only this time with a resounding sense of sublime culmination:

> My father is gone wild into his grave,
> For in his tomb lie my affections,
> And with his spirits sadly I survive
> To mock the expectation of the world,
> To frustrate prophecies, and to raze out
> Rotten opinion, who hath writ me down
> After my seeming. The tide of blood in me

Hath proudly flowed in vanity till now;
Now doth it turn, and ebb back to the sea,
Where it shall mingle with the state of floods,
And flow henceforth in formal majesty.

(V.ii.122–32)

This elegant tailoring of history to fit the moral myth of the Prodigal Son, of the sinner's salvation, works powerfully in *Henry IV* to rationalize hierarchy, glorify royalty, and disguise contingency as destiny, eventuality as providence. From Jameson's point of view, the chief task of the interpreter would be to expose the plays' obfuscation of historical reality by reading them against the drift of their orthodox import, by deciphering the undoctored version of the situation secreted between their lines. Their conformity could then be turned inside out to disclose the prophecy of collective emancipation and true unity concealed in the instrument of divisive misprision. But to return to the texts of *Henry IV* with this dual objective in mind is to recognize its redundancy in the light of a closer reading. For the straightforward, conventional account of the plays I have given so far can only survive through the systematic neglect of formal techniques, structural implications and dramatic parentheses, whose realized import changes the meaning of the narrative they articulate. By abstracting the double tale of Hal's redemption and the royal victory over rebellion from the syntax of its dramatization, and thus from the way we are induced to perceive and judge it, *Henry IV* is reduced to the very ideology it is intent on unravelling. A refusal to sunder what the plays say from how they say it restores to us more fascinating texts, which do not need to be read against the grain in order to be saved from themselves.

Jameson is irresistibly right about the need to release past texts into dialogue with the present, enabling them both to undo the governing illusions of their day and to foreshadow more desirable routes history might yet take. But his unargued assumption that the significant literature of former times is invariably in cahoots with the dominant view of things leaves him, ironically, in collusion with traditional historicist criticism, which has always thought literature expresses the prevalent ideas and values of the age. Unlike the latter, of course, Jameson finds this an unfortunate circumstance, which the radical modern critic fortunately stands poised to rectify by pressing the work to confess to knowledge and aspirations it never knew it possessed. But if we entertain the opposite expectation of literature, we may well find that the finest works have already uncovered and incorporated the political unconscious of the governing consciousness, exposing ideology to critique and envisioning its obsolescence through techniques which need no lessons from Jameson's positive or negative hermeneutics.

Consider two of the many scenes and passages in 1 and 2 Henry IV normally skipped over or marginalized in critical accounts, but whose function is to punctuate and inflect what is said and done in ways which not only complicate but also transmute the meaning of the drama. Indeed, we could no more hope to apprehend that complex meaning without them than we would expect to grasp the import of an elaborate sentence by extracting the main clause from the qualifying clauses and parentheses, and ignoring the commas, colons, dashes and brackets which advise us how to combine the components of significance into a complete statement.

In 1 Henry IV, Act II, scene i, there is an intriguing exchange between Gadshill and the chamberlain of the inn near which the robbery involving Hal is to proceed. It is ushered in by the complaints of the two carriers preparing their day's labours. One observes: 'This house is turned upside-down since Robin ostler died' (II.i.9–10), suggesting perhaps a plebeian parallel with the state of the kingdom following the death of Richard: the previous scene has witnessed the conspiracy of the rebels. The other echoes his abuse of the flea-pit they have just slept in: 'there is ne'er a king christen could be better bit than I have been since the first cock' (II.i.15–17). Fleas observe no distinctions of rank. Gadshill's badinage with the crooked chamberlain amplifies the scene's heightened awareness of the play's key concerns. Chamberlain and pickpurse are interchangeable titles, quips Gadshill, 'for thou variest no more from picking of purses than giving direction doth from labouring; thou layest the plot how' (II.i.48–50). The collapsing of distinctions between those who give the orders and those who obey them supplies the logic governing Gadshill's assurance that the participation of the powerful makes their criminal enterprise impregnable:

> I am joined with no foot-land-rakers, no long-staff six-penny strikers, none of these mad mustachio purple-hued malt-worms, but with nobility and tranquillity, burgomasters and great oneyers, such as can hold in, such as will strike sooner than speak, and speak sooner than drink, and drink sooner than pray. And yet, zounds, I lie, for they pray continually to their saint, the commonwealth, or rather not pray to her but prey on her, for they ride up and down on her and make her their boots.

CHAMBERLAIN: What, the commonwealth their boots? Will she
  hold out water in foul way?
GADSHILL: She will, she will. Justice hath liquored her. We steal
  as in a castle, cocksure. We have the receipt of fern-seed, we
  walk invisible.

(II.i.70–84)

The passage conflates the common thieves with their more elevated
brethren, whose ransacking of the commonwealth differs only in the
legitimacy which renders its criminality 'invisible'. The prince's role in
the robbery creates the occasion for this illuminating identification,
which pivots in turn on the more fundamental reflection with which
Gadshill bows out of the scene: '*homo* is a common name to all men'
(II.i.92).

Comparable implications can be quarried from otherwise pointless
remarks made by Falstaff in Part 2. During his evasive encounter with
the Lord Chief Justice in the second scene of the play, Falstaff pleads
the malady of deafness as his reason for not responding to the Justice's
admonitions, and he attempts to distract the latter by snatching up the
topic of the king's ill health: 'And I hear moreover, his highness is fallen
into this same whoreson apoplexy' (I.ii.85–6). This apoplexy is 'a kind
of lethargy', Falstaff informs the exasperated magistrate, 'a kind of
sleeping in the blood'; in short, according to Galen, 'it is a kind of
deafness'. 'I think you are fallen into the disease,' retorts the Lord Chief
Justice, 'for you hear not what I say to you' (I.ii.88, 89, 92–5). The full
value of these lines, in which the lord of the land and the lord of misrule
are subject to the same affliction, becomes apparent if we turn to
Falstaff's meditation on the peculiar affinity between Shallow and his
servants:

It is a wonderful thing to see the semblable coherence of his men's
spirits and his: they by observing him do bear themselves like
foolish justices; he by conversing with them is turned into a
justice-like servingman. Their spirits are so married in conjunction, with the participation of society, that they flock together in
consent like so many wild geese. If I had a suit to Master Shallow,
I would humour his men with the imputation of being near their
master; if to his men, I would curry with Master Shallow, that
no man could better command his servants. It is certain that either
wise bearing or ignorant carriage is caught, as men take diseases,
one of another.

(V.i.51–61)

The revelation of consanguinity running beneath the threshold of social difference is conveyed this time by an appeal to the democratic impartiality of infection, which holds the privileges of birth and blood in contempt. But here there is a further glimpse of the utopian potential of such benign confoundings of rank through 'the participation of society' (what Henry IV in Part 1 denounced in Hal as 'vile participation'): an idyllic condition in which spirits normally segregated by the antagonistic principle of subordination become 'so married in conjunction . . . that they flock together in consent like so many wild geese'.

Such passages supply the keys to decode more sustained enactments of improvised irrelevance, whose liberty from the burden of advancing the historical plot permits them to explore the cost and consequences of that history, reinstating the exclusions and suppressions that made it possible. In Act II of Part 1 Hal confesses wryly to Poins: 'I have sounded the very bass string of humility. Sirrah, I am sworn brother to a leash of drawers, and can call them all by their Christian names, as Tom, Dick, and Francis' (II.iv.5–8). The witty substitution of the tapster's name for the expected 'Harry' invites the equation of the former's plight with the prince's in the practical joke which follows. Francis is torn between the temptation 'to play the coward with [his] indenture and show it a fair pair of heels' (II.iv.45–6) and the immediate obligation to answer the call of a customer, which he postpones with 'Anon, anon, sir', the parroted watchword of his trade. Simultaneously hailed by vocation and desire, '*the Drawer stands amazed, not knowing which way to go*' (s.d. 76), the plebeian epitome of the future king's suspension in a limbo of delay. Hal's jest fleetingly lifts the barrier between the destinies of both men and dissolves Hal's narrow aristocratic identity in the broad stream of diverse humanity through the ages: asked by Poins for the upshot of the gulling of Francis, he replies, 'I am now of all humours that have showed themselves humours since the old days of Goodman Adam to the pupil age of this present twelve o'clock at midnight' (II.iv.90–3).

The intensity of this compulsion to lose himself in the soul of a subordinate by projection or displacement is confirmed by Part 2's obsessive return to the theme. The price of the prince's elision of difference by deferment is anxiety, guilt and melancholy. 'Before God, I am exceeding weary' (II.ii.1), he laments to Poins at the opening of Act II, at once disenchanted with his royalty and ashamed of his abandonment of eminence: 'But indeed these humble considerations make me out of love with my greatness. What a disgrace is it to me to remember thy name – or to know thy face tomorrow' (II.ii.10–12). The sense of a character caged in his own myth, stranded in a trance of procrastination until the cue to pace the stage of history breaks the spell, is insistent. But the whole point of forcing open such lacunae, in which history is put on hold, is to create the space to demolish the foundations on which that reading of history is built.

The Prince of Wales strives stoutly to drive the wedge back between his heritage and the 'vile company' (II.ii.37) he blushes to acknowledge, appealing to his script for eventual vindication: 'Let the end try the man' (II.ii.35). It requires, however, rather less than the Page's 'crown's-worth of good interpretation' (II.ii.70) to see that separatist urge vanquished by the need for communion in the hoax that springs from this scene. The path to the jape is paved by quips haunted by more of the same demarcation disputes. Poins glances at those who 'never prick their finger but they say: "There's some of the king's blood spilt"' as a prelude to claiming themselves to be 'the king's poor cousin'. 'Nay,' Hal chimes in, 'they will be kin to us, or they will fetch it from Japhet' (II.ii.87–8, 90–1) – Japhet being the son of Noah from whom all gentiles were thought to be descended. The pressure to dilute the prince's blue blood likewise dictates the ironic speculation about Hal's marrying Poins's sister, Nell (II.ii.97–107). And by the end of the scene the frail dyke of convention dividing Hal from the common tide of humanity has been breached by his compliance with Poins's scheme to disguise themselves in the 'leathern jerkins and aprons' (II.ii.133) of Francis's calling: 'From a god to a bull: a heavy descension! It was Jove's case. From a prince to a prentice: a low transformation, that shall be mine' (II.ii.135–6). The reincarnation of the heir apparent is complete two scenes later, when the prince-prentice answers Falstaff's 'Some sack, Francis!' with his surrogate's remorseless 'Anon, anon, sir' (II.iv.229–30), directly echoing the corresponding scene in Part 1.

Nor is the razing of hierarchy the only effect sought by such confusions of identity. In the 'play extempore' of Part 1, Falstaff plays Henry IV, reproving Hal 'in King Cambyses' vein' (II.iv.373–4), then swaps places to play Hal to the prince's own impersonation of his father. The self-conscious theatricality of this parodic performance highlights both the rootlessness of the roles and the staged nature of the historical realities being burlesqued. The majesty of the English throne dwindles to a few tawdry props stripped of mystique: 'Thy state is taken for a joint-stool, thy golden sceptre for a leaden dagger, and thy precious rich crown for a pitiful bald crown' (II.iv.367–9). Falstaff's caricature of the admonishing monarch deploys an obsolete theatrical rhetoric persuasive enough to captivate his tavern audience: 'O Jesu, he doth it as like one of these harlotry players as ever I see!' (II.iv.382–3). But more important for the audience beyond the footlights is the scene's pre-emptive ironizing of the serious clash of royal father and reprobate son in Act III. Their characters and their dialogue are marked out in advance as scripted creations, the impassioned appeals and protestations shadowed by their imputed conformity to recognized postures and patterns of exchange.

The spectators are encouraged to recognize majesty as a rehearsed production and reminded of the gulf between the performed events before their eyes and the remote past realities they presuppose. Henry IV himself activates this awareness by his frank confessions of using theatrical simulation and diversion as instruments of power:

> And then I stole all courtesy from heaven,
> And dressed myself in such humility
> That I did pluck allegiance from men's hearts,
>
> (1 Henry IV, III.ii.50–2)

> For all my reign hath been but as a scene
> Acting that argument . . .
>   . . . Therefore, my Harry,
> Be it thy course to busy giddy minds
> With foreign quarrels, that action hence borne out
> May waste the memory of the former days.
>
> (2 Henry IV, IV.ii.325–6, 340–3)

Indeed, the very battle fought at Shrewsbury to bolster the sovereign's unique authority involves the telling subterfuge of fielding noblemen 'semblably furnished like the King himself' (1 Henry IV, V.iii.21). Advised by Hotspur that 'the King hath many marching in his coats', Douglas swears: 'Now, by my sword, I will kill all his coats!/I'll murder all his wardrobe, piece by piece,/Until I meet the King' (V.iii.25–8). But when he encounters the monarch in person, he remains understandably sceptical:

> DOUGLAS: Another king? They grow like Hydra's heads.
>   . . . What art thou
>   That counterfeit'st the person of a king?
> KING HENRY: The King himself, who, Douglas, grieves at heart
>   So many of his shadows thou hast met
>   And not the very King . . .
> DOUGLAS: I fear thou art another counterfeit;
>   And yet, in faith, thou bearest thee like a king.
>
> (V.iv.24, 26–30, 34–5)

The action contrived to clinch the exclusive legitimacy of Bulling-brook's claim to the throne breeds a multiplicity of sovereigns, dispersing Henry's singularity and flagrantly insinuating that to bear oneself like a monarch and don the robes of royalty may be all there is to being royal for real – as Sir Walter Blunt discovers to his mortal dismay.

Detail and structure collaborate throughout Parts 1 and 2 to dismantle the scaffolding of dominion and unmask the arbitrary status of authorized social distinctions and moral oppositions. The factual coincidence of king and prince sharing their Christian name with the rebel Earl and his son is played up to the full in Shakespeare's phrasing to stimulate our apprehension of their covert equivalence:

> O that it could be proved
> That some night-tripping fairy had exchanged
> In cradle-clothes our children where they lay,
> And called mine Percy, his Plantagenet!
> Then would I have his Harry, and he mine.
>
> (*1 Henry IV*, I.i.85–9)
>
> Harry to Harry shall, hot horse to horse
>
> (IV.i.123)
>
> Two stars keep not their motion in one sphere,
> Nor can one England brook a double reign
> Of Harry Percy and the Prince of Wales.
>
> (V.iv.64–6)

Like Hal and Francis, or Hal and Falstaff when the latter takes the prince's part in the tavern, or ironically appropriates his promise of eventual contrition, the royal and the regicidal turn out to be Siamese twins. Indeed, as John Kerrigan has shown in an illuminating essay (Kerrigan 1990), both plays are obsessed with doubling and replication at every turn: from Falstaff with the dead Hotspur on his back, denying himself to be the 'double man' he seems, or Shallow's cryptic query 'And is old Dooble dead?' (III.ii.43: the Folio reads 'Double'), down to the fine grain of speech rhythms, where duplication reigns in the mouths of foolish judge ('Certain, 'tis certain, very sure, very sure' (III.ii.29)) and majesty alike: 'Not Amurath an Amurath succeeds,/ But Harry Harry' (V.ii.48–9). The rhetorical term for this figure of speech is *geminatio* or 'twinning'; and, as Kerrigan points out, quoting Thomas Wilson's definition in *The Arte of Rhetorique* (1553), 'In Tudor rhetoric, "doublet" translates *geminatio*: "when we rehearse one and the same word twice together", as in "Anon, Anon, sir!" ' (Kerrigan 1990: 41).

This constant local instruction in the art of gemination finds its global counterpart in the scenic composition of the plays. The structural principle of switching to and fro between king and conspirators, and from both to the Eastcheap empire of Falstaff, or the rural domain of Shallow and Silence, and back again, begins by obeying a logic of contrast and discrimination; but its cumulative impact transforms our initial acceptance of disparity into a dawning realization of resemblance. The ceaseless commuting between diverse ranks and value systems discloses an urgent appetite for consensus eating away at the ideology of difference and duality. The official scale of social worth, so graphically codified in the descending list of *dramatis personae* still fronting modern texts, is scrambled by these oscillations of perspective as surely as shuffling a new deck of cards confounds the fastidious decorum of each suit. The kaleidoscopic vision of *Henry IV* helps forge a prospect of egalitarian community which exposes the national and royal principles of union as frauds.

Nor can the teleological view of history conscripted by those principles survive the repeated sabotaging of inevitability and completion to which Part 2, as the expected resolution of questions left dangling in Part 1, is especially subject. A stubborn refusal of deterministic historiography is declared at the outset in the extraordinary Induction and opening scene of the play. In a direct address to the audience the allegorical personification of Rumour introduces himself as one upon whose tongues 'continual slanders ride,/The which in every language I pronounce,/Stuffing the ears of men with false reports' (*2 Henry IV*, Ind. 6–8). His present purpose, as he stands before the castle of Northumberland, is

> To noise abroad that Harry Monmouth fell
> Under the wrath of noble Hotspur's sword,
> And that the king before the Douglas' rage
> Stooped his anointed head as low as death.
>
> (Ind. 29–32)

The first scene then thrusts us into the midst of enacted history as Lord Bardolph repeats Rumour's false account to Northumberland as 'certain news from Shrewsbury' (I.i.12). Northumberland needs convincing: 'How is this derived?' (I.i.23). But the 'certain news' is rapidly unseated by Travers's revised report, which Morton's no less breathless arrival confirms: young Harry Percy's spur is cold indeed, and

The sum of all
Is that the king hath won, and hath sent out
A speedy power to encounter you, my lord,

(I.i.131-3)

For a moment the closed book of historical fact is reopened and rewritten. The fixity of the past surrenders to the flickering supposition that all might have been otherwise, that the chronicles could quite plausibly have been obliged to tell another tale. We are forewarned that this rival version is unfounded, and the upstart is of course swiftly deposed; but it is entertained and elaborated for long enough to stake its claim to likelihood and thus restore the original fluidity of ostensibly deep-frozen events. History is rewound and replayed with the subjunctive scenes spliced back in. We are called upon to witness the translation of once vital experience into a vulnerable narrative, refracted through this dramatic reconstruction in the lived present of performance: 'Open your ears; for which of you will stop/The vent of hearing when loud Rumour speaks?' (Ind. 1-2). History, it is plain, is not simply what happened, but what gets made, misconstrued, disputed and remodelled.

Part 2 is riddled with double-takes, false starts and stops, rewrites and reversals of expectation: all of them calculated to resist, and thereby transform, the ultimate course things must take to climax in the defeat of the rebels and the coronation of the prodigal redeemed. The infectious doubling of identities discussed above is matched by a doubling of incidents, in which the actual occurrence is unsettled by the sustained imagination of another possibility. Thus the achievement at Gaultree of a bloodless and just resolution, whereby the rebels' grievances will find redress and both sides enjoy the concord of 'restorèd love and amity' (IV.i.293), is acted out convincingly up to the very last moment, at which the apparent meaning of events is abruptly turned on its head by Prince John's brutal duplicity. A similar effect is produced when King Henry envisions a persuasive future ruled by Hal's 'headstrong riot':

The blood weeps from my heart when I do shape
In forms imaginary th'unguided days
And rotten times that you shall look upon
When I am sleeping with my ancestors.

(IV.ii.58-61)

But these grim predictions prove as mistaken as the abandoned future under Hal which excites Falstaff's fantasies, or the prophecy of the king's death in a Jerusalem which turns out to be the name of a palace chamber far from the Holy Land he hoped to wrest from the infidel.

Most disconcerting of all, perhaps, is the way the play trips Hal up on the very threshold of his accession and moral resurrection. Having diagnosed his father's death with exemplary alacrity, he seizes the crown from the pillow and ceremoniously sets the 'polished perturbation' (IV.ii.153) on his own head:

> My due from thee is this imperial crown
> Which, as immediate from thy place and blood,
> Derives itself to me. Lo where it sits,
> Which God shall guard; and, put the world's whole strength
> Into one giant arm, it shall not force
> This lineal honour from me: this from thee
> Will I to mine leave, as 'tis left to me. *Exit.*
>
> (IV.ii.171–7)

Seconds later, the conclusive resonance of this speech is shattered as the king revives, denounces his son's precipitate, callous theft, and forces Hal to crawl back, crown in hand, to convince him of the innocence of his motives and the genuineness of 'the noble change that I have purposèd' (IV.ii.283). Shakespeare's dramatization of the episode exploits its disruptive impact to the full, compelling the denouement to double back and restart from revised assumptions about Hal, and with a refreshed feeling for the unpredictability of experience before the fact.

Such backtracking devices allow the blood to flow once more through the veins of chronicled history, flushing act and incident with the indeterminacy denied them by the Medusan gaze of providential narrative. It comes as no surprise to find the question of history on the overt agenda of *2 Henry IV*, with characters speculating continually on the relation of the past to the future and on the possibility of foreknowledge:

> KING: O God, that one might read the book of fate
> And see the revolution of the times . . .
> WARWICK: There is a history in all men's lives
> Figuring the natures of the times deceased,
> The which observed, a man may prophesy,
> With a near aim, of the main chance of things
> As yet not come to life, who in their seeds
> And weak beginning lie intreasurèd.
> Such things become the hatch and brood of time, . . .
>
> (III.i.44–5, 79–85)

'Jesus,' exclaims Shallow, 'the days that we have seen!', confirming in his nostalgia for 'the times deceased', when he heard 'the chimes at midnight' (III.ii.180, 177), that a predilection for edited highlights of the past is not the exclusive preserve of great lords. This gentle guying of selective retrospection ('Lord, Lord, how subject we old men are to this vice of lying!' (III.ii.246)) calls the whole project of the *Henry IV* plays to account. For it keeps alive in the spectator's mind the distortions inevitably entailed in the process of historiography, the gap which must always divorce long-gone realities from the discursive representations in which alone they become intelligible. Not the least virtue of the Epilogue's appearance at the close of Part 2, to promise that 'our humble author will continue the story' (Epil. 21), is its oblique insistence that *as* a story, to quote Samuel Daniel's *Defence of Rhyme* (1603),

> an Historie . . . is but a Mappe of Men, and dooth no otherwise acquaint us with the true Substance of Circumstances then a superficiall Card dooth the Seaman with a Coast never seene, which alwayes prooves other to the eye than the imagination forecast it . . .
>
> (Smith 1904, 2: 370)

Both power and history in *Henry IV* are demystified, even as the plays complete their putative contract with the dominant ideology. The prescribed royal reading of history dictates the narrative shape of Parts 1 and 2. But the strategies of disenchantment built into the dramatization rob that narrative of its supremacy, breaking its monopoly on what is thought to have happened. This critique of the approved account is anchored in the utopian assumptions of an anticipated world. At the end of *1* and *2 Henry IV* monarchy, hierarchy and the illusions that sustain them emerge intact, even strengthened, within the world of the plays; but our understanding and judgement of them has been changed completely by the way they have been presented. What the protagonists persist in believing, and what the spectators are encouraged to conclude from the standpoint they are obliged to adopt, are two quite different things. The perspectives of the denizens of *Henry IV* – high and low, urban and rural alike – must remain bound by the categories and limits of the imagined universe they inhabit; our assessment of them, however, is released from that bondage by our vantage point as audience or readers, whose vision of their universe is filtered through the warped lens of defamiliarization. As a result the plays liberate us to decipher 'the main chance of things/As yet not come to life' encoded in their depiction of 'the times deceased' (III.i.82–3, 80). They afford us a proleptic glimpse through their eyes of the future in the past.

III

Reading *Henry IV* in the light of Jameson's theory of interpretation explodes the reductive misconception of literary texts which prevents Jameson's most fertile insights from releasing the full potential of literature from the past. Jameson begins by blazing a trail towards viewing texts as active transfigurations of vanished realities, capable of vexing modern preconceptions and signposting the extinction of oppressive social divisions. But this admirable enterprise soon shrivels into the extortion of progressive significance from works whose instinctive commitment to the legitimation of class society is taken as read. *Henry IV* testifies, however, to the historically evolved capacity of poetic language and dramatic form to turn what would otherwise comply with Jameson's assumptions into an undoing of the ideology of division from a standpoint beyond the reach of subjection. Jameson remains trapped in the historicist hermeneutics of suspicion from which his own more attractive arguments offer the readiest escape route. To demonstrate this, moreover, is to pull the plug on a range of critical responses and a long tradition of theatrical productions, which have diminished or denied the power of *1* and *2 Henry IV* to undercut the ideological narratives they stage.

Scott McMillin has recently traced the British performance history of *Henry IV* from the 1945 Old Vic production starring Olivier and Richardson to the 1986 touring version by the English Shakespeare Company under the direction of Michael Bogdanov (McMillin 1991). His survey dwells on three bench-mark productions, all of which put the plays on as part of a cycle sequence: the staging by the Shakespeare Memorial Theatre Company in 1951, directed by Anthony Quayle, which established the cycle mode as the standard modern format for the Histories, and the RSC productions of 1964 and 1975, under the direction of Peter Hall and Terry Hands, respectively. McMillin discerns an uncomfortably direct relationship between the politics of the institutionalized theatre and the political message all too predictably read into Hal's reformation in *Henry IV*:

> The modern subsidised theatre helps cycles be staged and cycles make Falstaff a figure to be rejected. This is what happens to

1 Henry IV in its modern cycle-oriented treatments: the Prince grows into royal authority by turning aside the old fat man, and it is government subsidy that provides the wherewithal . . . to let this lesson be dramatised.

(McMillin 1991: 11–12)

These major productions seem to have swallowed whole the hier-archical assumptions and the teleological conflation of personal and national destiny which the plays are not fooled by for a moment. For Peter Hall, the world-view affirmed by *Henry IV* was plain: 'all Shakespeare's thinking, whether religious, political, or moral, is based on a complete acceptance of this concept of order. There is a just propor-tion in all things: man is above beast, king is above man, and God above king'; rebellion is monstrous because it 'destroys the order and leads to destructive anarchy' (quoted in McMillin 1991: 57). Terry Hands's pro-duction bent the drama into an ageless study in the growth of majesty, traced through the exemplary evolution of the adolescent male from callow disaffection to responsible maturity. For Hal, according to the programme note for the production, the stage 'is always the blank slate on which life writes its lessons', 'the bare metaphysical arena in which the soul of a royal Everyman discovers his destiny and true friends' (quoted in McMillin 1991: 83). As McMillin observes: 'So long as Prince Hal is said to be caught up in such timeless and essential experi-ence, his career will seem purified of the political and all the more agreeable to the managers of our affairs' (1991: 87).

Given the opportunities for inculcating conformity afforded by suit-ably slanted productions, it leaves one less than astounded to learn that 'More than any other play, *1 Henry IV* is swung into position on occa-sions of dignity and ceremony in Stratford' (McMillin 1991: 85). After baptizing the new Stratford Memorial Theatre in 1932 on the Bard's birthday, it was the birthday play during the History cycles of 1951, 1964 and 1975; and when the RSC opened at the Barbican in 1982 with another inevitable cycle of Histories, the birthday production was once more *1 Henry IV*. 'The thinking of the RSC', remarks McMillin wryly, 'had become so accustomed to taking the *Henrys* as curtain-raisers for occasions of wealth and power that the venture could be predicted before some of the actors in the eventual production were out of sec-ondary school' (1991: 86). It is the cultural centrality and enormous influence of these imaginatively stunted versions of the *Henry IV* plays that make the development of readings that can do them justice so important. And this endeavour demands an interpretative theory and practice fuelled by diametrically opposed ideas about the relation of poetic writing to the enthroned prescriptions and stereotypes of the age.

That E.M.W. Tillyard's study of *Shakespeare's History Plays* (1944) directly and indirectly shaped the 1951 and 1964 cycle productions of *1* and *2 Henry IV* is no surprise. Tillyard's work has remained the cornerstone of the conventional view of the Histories to this day, and the automatic antagonist of those seeking to contest the nationalistic and authoritarian attitudes he found ratified in these plays. According to Tillyard, Shakespeare

> expressed successfully a universally held and still comprehensible scheme of history: a scheme fundamentally religious, by which events evolve under a law of justice and under the ruling of God's Providence, and of which Elizabeth's England was the acknowledged outcome.
>
> (Tillyard 1944: 320–1)

For Tillyard, therefore, the two parts of *Henry IV* exemplify the ideal education of the Christian prince for the office destiny has prepared for him. Tillyard's Hal 'is a man of large powers, Olympian loftiness, and high sophistication, who has acquired a thorough knowledge of human nature both in himself and in others. He is Shakespeare's studied picture of the kingly type' (1944: 269). Hal's tormenting of Francis in Part 1 clouds Tillyard's admiration for a moment, but the perfection of Hal's portrait is swiftly restored by the historian's appeal to the principle of degree: 'The subhuman element in the population must have been considerable in Shakespeare's day; that it should be treated almost like beasts was taken for granted' (1944: 277). It is perhaps too easy to feel superior now to that telling rationalization, whose offhand inhumanity has been highlighted in a recent radical study of the histories (Holderness 1992: 27). But it gives the measure of Tillyard's commitment to reading Shakespeare in *1* and *2 Henry IV* as the unquestioning advocate of a rigidly stratified society.

Reinforced by similar views of the Histories promoted in John Dover Wilson's *The Fortunes of Falstaff* (1943), G. Wilson Knight's *The Olive and the Sword* (1944), and Lily B. Campbell's *Shakespeare's Histories: Mirrors of Elizabethan Policy* (1947), this conception of *Henry IV* as a defence of the divine necessity of order and authority controlled discussion of the plays for decades. Its survival, in a subtly adapted form, was guaranteed by C.L. Barber's classic study, *Shakespeare's Festive Comedy* (1959). Barber allows the saturnalian zest of Falstaff and the Eastcheap world much more play and purchase than most of the Tillyard camp are inclined to, but only because of its ulterior role as the negative pole in the moral schooling of the budding ruler. The temporary reign of misrule under Falstaff functions here as a kind of safety-valve, a cathartic release of anarchic energies and appetites, which Hal must finally reject to qualify as the governor of a stable, disciplined kingdom. The lawless threat to propriety is introduced in order to enhance the triumphant return of dutiful decorum with Hal's fulfilment of his royal vocation: 'the misrule works, through the whole dramatic rhythm, to consolidate rule' (Barber 1959: 226).

Thirty years on, this angle is still going strong: recycled in a still more sophisticated form and yoked now to a dissenting critical politics, but fundamentally unchanged. In his widely cited construction of a new-historicist Shakespeare, *Power on Display* (1986), Leonard Tennenhouse maintains that

> the various confrontations between licit and illicit authority com-prising the *Henriad* more firmly draw the distinction between aristocracy and populace even as they appear to overturn this primary categorical distinction ... Criminalizing the popular figures of inversion is as necessary to the poetics of power as incor-porating a certain popular vigor within the legitimate body of the state ... Legitimate order can come into being only through disruption according to this principle ...
>
> (Tennenhouse 1986: 83–4)

This is also the position endorsed by the founding father of new his-toricism, Stephen Greenblatt, whose celebrated essay 'Invisible Bullets' selects *1* and *2 Henry IV* as ideal texts with which to bolster his belief that 'Shakespeare's plays are centrally, repeatedly concerned with the production and containment of subversion and disorder' (Greenblatt 1988: 40). In Greenblatt's view, power feeds off the transgression and sedition it needs in order to define its identity and authority. And by inoculating itself with a controlled symbolic dose of realizations which could destroy it, the body politic helps preserve its immunity to genuine, full-strength subversion. Hence, as theatrical instruments of the power of the Elizabethan state, 'the Henry plays confirm the Machiavellian hypothesis that princely power originates in force and fraud even as they draw their audience toward an acceptance of that power' (1988: 65). Greenblatt's account of the relationship between drama and domination is incomparably more intricate than Tillyard's or Barber's, and its objective is demystification rather than occlusion, but the bottom line is the same: *Henry IV* is the voice of Elizabethan orthodoxy, and never more so than when it mimics the accents of dissent. This approach dovetails perfectly with Jameson's belief that the masterpieces of the past cannot earn political salvation by their own merits, but must depend for redemption on the grace of the modern critic.

In *Shakespeare Recycled: The Making of Historical Drama* (1992) the cultural materialist, Graham Holderness, has attempted to overturn conservative readings of *Henry IV* by tying Falstaff into Bakhtin's concept of the carnivalesque and stressing his substantive function as

> a constant focus of opposition to the official and serious tone of authority and power: his discourse confronts and challenges those of king and state. His attitude to authority is always parodic and satirical: he mocks authority, flouts power, responds to the pressures of social duty and civic obligation by retreating into Bacchanalian revelry. His world is a world of ease, moral licence, appetite and desire; of humour and ridicule, theatricals and satire, of community, freedom and abundance; a world created by inverting the abstract society, the oppression and the hierarchy of the official world.
>
> (Holderness 1992: 138)

But Falstaff can indeed merely invert; he cannot transcend that official world, which beholds in him its mirror image, its secret sharer, not its negation or displacement. Exhilarating as Holderness's sketch of him sounds, to champion the cause of Falstaff against the bleak disciplines of authority and historical necessity simply reverses the poles of the orthodox view. Defecting to Eastcheap and elevating a sentimental idealization of its ethos over the imperatives of duty and national destiny sells the plays short. For it leaves them caged within the system of social disparities and moral dichotomies they seek to dismantle. To privilege the liberties of 'headstrong riot' (*2 Henry IV*, IV.ii.62) over 'The majesty and power of law and justice' (V.ii.77) is to repress the covert reciprocity of the royal and plebeian realms, whose values are in practice identical, and so leave the entrenched divisions of the status quo intact. This strategy plays straight into the hands of the new-historicist paradox whereby the upshot of subversion is to consolidate dominion and the rule of law.

As long as criticism of *Henry IV* keeps shuttling between the claims of the Crown and the lure of the taproom, it remains tangled in the spurious dilemma forged by Hal himself as he hesitates between his father and plump Jack. Whether the rejection of Falstaff is applauded, regretted or safely construed as ambivalent, the critic accepts the characters' perception of their world and the alternatives they confront at face value, as the terms on which we are supposed to interpret and evaluate *Henry IV*. But such readings must block out all the devices deliberately constructed to colour our vision and complicate our judgement. For, as I have tried to show, the plays are designed to withdraw through formal implication what they avow through overt statement and action. Both parts of *Henry IV* mobilize techniques of framing, interruption and conflation, which weave a counterfactual perspective into their dramatization of history, investing it with a buoyancy it would otherwise lack. By preventing our submersion in the mentality of the cast, they unravel the rationale of the standard interpretations. Far from enclosing the spectator in an Elizabethan perception of late medieval England, the *Henry IV* plays create a prospective climate of understanding, which invalidates the hierarchical terms in which the problems of the protagonists are posed and solved, even as it concedes the factual force and historical triumph of subjugation.

The inhabitants of *Henry IV* are doomed to dwell for ever in 'the times deceased' (2 *Henry IV*, III.i.80) which, as one of them laments, 'Crowd us and crush us to this monstrous form' (IV.i.262). But the plays' perspective on their lives reaches forward 'to sound the bottom of the after-times' (IV.i.279) and anticipate the transfigured shape the 'hatch and brood' (III.i.85) of history might take. The opening speech of Part 1 tunes us subliminally to this dual vision informing both plays:

> Those opposèd eyes
> Which, like the meteors of a troubled heaven,
> All of one nature, of one substance bred,
> Did lately meet in the intestine shock
> And furious close of civil butchery,
> Shall now in mutual, well-beseeming ranks
> March all one way, and be no more opposed
> Against acquaintance, kindred, and allies.
>
> (I.i.9–16)

Henry IV is written in a way which allows us to behold a world ruled by brutal divisions through the eyes of a world which has surrendered such barbarism to the cooperative sway of human solidarity.

Old and newer forms of historicist criticism share a notion of literature as the incurably anterior expression of an extinct reality. They evince a chronic aversion to the conjecture that works like 1 and 2 *Henry IV* might be drawn as much towards a future beyond our own apprehension as back to their points of origin in the past. For all its shortcomings, it is the virtue of Jameson's theoretical stance that it argues so effectively against such sterile historicism and so passionately for the activation of the utopian dimension of literature. Jameson's error, however, is to arrogate to the interpretative act alone that potent blend of critique and prescience which, as *Henry IV* attests, the most demanding literature of the past has always possessed, but which will remain inert and ineffectual if the prevalent accounts of that literature go unchallenged.

It is an error which Ernst Bloch, one of the most crucial influences on Jameson's thinking, never made, mistaking as it does the power of the critic for the power of the work. For Bloch,

> Every great work of art, above and beyond its manifest content, is carried out according to a *latency of the page to come*, or in other words, in the light of the content of a future which has not yet come into being, and indeed of some ultimate resolution as yet unknown.
>
> (Quoted in Jameson 1971: 149; trans. from Bloch 1959: 110)

And what lifts a work 'above and beyond its manifest content' and into the light of the future is the lever of form. As Theodor Adorno puts it: 'Perspectives must be fashioned that displace and estrange the world, reveal it to be, with its rifts and crevices, as indigent and distorted as it will appear one day in the messianic light' (Adorno 1974: 247). It is precisely such distortion that *Henry IV* inflicts on its age, which we are invited to see not as it was, but as it one day *will have been* for those no longer walled up in that kind of world. In these works we perceive Elizabethan realities transposed into the history of *Henry IV*, then filtered through the lens of futurity, which twists the plays out of line with convention and into their proleptic form. Parts 1 and 2 of *Henry IV* afford us nothing less than a preview of the past. They project us forward to a point where we can grasp Shakespeare's anachronistic version of his times as the eventual past of a still unfolding future.

SUPPLEMENT

NIGEL WOOD: I sense a silence in your piece about the role of the critic in the manufacture of the history to which you refer. Jameson stresses how the critic intervenes to place what is perceived to be the text's ideology within a utopian (and more holistic) context. You seem to argue that this is not necessary, as the text of *Henry IV* is radical and prefigurative enough. Have I got this summary correct?

KIERNAN RYAN: What I'm after is a dialogue between history and modernity, between the text from the past and the critical practice of the present. The aim is to evolve a way of reading from an engaged modern viewpoint which can do justice to what is demonstrably inscribed in the form and phrasing of a work transmitted from an earlier epoch. The idea that the text's meaning is self-evident and free-standing is as unsatisfactory as the notion that it is purely the product of subsequent critical projections. I do not think that what a Shakespeare play has to say is unproblematically given and complete, since its import will grow and change as the perspective from which it is read changes, as new generations bring fresh expectations to bear on the words that compose it. But that is not to agree with those who hold that the play is the construction of its readers, and who would deny its capacity to determine which critical accounts it is disposed to confirm and which it must expose as unfounded.

The validity of a theory of literature or of an interpretation of a particular work must be tested through a detailed analysis of the text. My reason for parting company with Jameson is not that I wish to dismiss the role played by the critic in turning the work's potential import into actual significance; it is rather that a fundamental assumption of his hermeneutics founders on the textual evidence of works like *Henry IV*. It is not the fact that Jameson recommends radical critical intervention that bothers me; it is the misconception of literature on which that intervention is supposed to ride into battle with the text. Jameson proceeds on the assumption that literature can only be made to yield a progressive, utopian vision if it is deliberately read against the grain of its instinctive conservative intent. What I contend is that *Henry IV* provides a powerful example of literature readily yielding such a vision when read *with* the grain of its language and form. A work like *Henry IV* does not need the kind of reading Jameson's theory promotes in order to be saved from its supposedly reactionary self; but it does need the sort of approach I try to illustrate here if it is to be saved from the criticism which represses its radical potential.

NW: How would you account for the formal differences between the two plays? As Giorgio Melchiori (among others) has pointed out in his Introduction to the New Cambridge edition of *2 Henry IV* (1989), it is likely that Part 1 was conceived as self-sufficient. Why might (should?) we take them as a self-contained whole?

KR: I have no trouble accepting the proposition that Part 1 of *Henry IV* was originally meant as a complete play in its own right, but with an ending left sufficiently open to allow the production of a sequel if the public appetite demanded it. Likewise, as with any sequel, Part 2 can plainly be understood and enjoyed both as a finished drama on its own terms and as the development and conclusion of the narrative begun in the play which it expressly invokes and invites us to regard retrospectively as its 'prequel'. I have no desire to make a case for Part 2 being in effect the last five acts of a single ten-act play, and so see no obligation to treat them as if they formed a self-contained whole. (When I refer to the texts jointly as *Henry IV*, I am simply employing a routine critical shorthand.) At the same time, whatever their author originally had in mind, there is nothing to stop one hooking the plays together either, whether for the purpose of critical analysis or in the theatre as parts of a cycle sequence. The blunt fact that Part 2 completes the twinned tales of nation and prince left unresolved by Part 1 seems a reasonable argument in itself for writing about them in tandem, and one which the conspicuous structural and thematic parallels only reinforce. If I were dealing with either play on its own, I would still make the same basic points about it, so I do not think what I am claiming in this essay stands or falls by the validity of considering them together. My case is certainly enhanced by reading Part 1 and Part 2 in conjunction, but it does not require them to be indivisible.

NW: Back in 1943, John Dover Wilson inaugurated a set of formal analyses of the plays by dubbing them 'Shakespeare's great morality play'. Do you find the morality structure a salient feature of *1* and *2 Henry IV*, especially in view of your perception of them as an attempt to sabotage teleological notions of history?

KR: There is no doubt that both plays exploit the morality structure furnished by the story of the Prodigal Son: the debt is so patent and thoroughly documented by commentators as to demand no further corroboration here. What interests me is challenging the construction placed on Shakespeare's use of the myth by an influential strain in criticism of the plays. Critics of the persuasion Dover Wilson helped consolidate are content to take Hal's re-enactment of this narrative at face value, because the plays' alleged subscription to an idealized view of monarchy and a providential conception of history clearly depends on it. But the plausibility of Hal's portrayal as the wayward prince redeemed depends in turn on sustaining the normal distinctions between the ruler and the ruled, the royal and the plebeian, the makers and the breakers of the law. That is why I devote so much space to explaining how Shakespeare consistently dissolves these social and moral divisions by disclosing the scandalous analogies and identifications they strive to conceal. For if the moral opposition of the Court and Eastcheap, the polarized choice between the lord of the land and the lord of misrule, proves groundless, the morality structure of the drama collapses and the ideological orthodoxy ascribed to the plays by old and new historicist criticism caves in on top of it. Hence my contention towards the close of the essay that 'As long as criticism of *Henry IV* keeps shuttling between the claims of the Crown and the lure of the taproom, it remains tangled in the spurious dilemma forged by Hal himself as he hesitates between his father and plump Jack (p. 120). What makes

1 and *2 Henry IV* remarkable is their intent erosion of the hierarchical mentality that dictates both Hal's and his critics' misperception of his plight.

NW: I'd like you to expand on your call for 'an interpretative theory and practice fuelled by diametrically opposed ideas about the relation of poetic
writing to the enthroned prescriptions and stereotypes of the age'
(pp. 117–18). Could you suggest other Shakespeare plays that would
benefit from such reading against the grain?

KR: As I pointed out in my reply to your first question, my chief quarrel with
Jameson's theory stems from his taking for granted that the role of
imaginative literature is to defend the ideas and values that secure the
status quo. The same assumption unites many cultural materialists and new
historicists writing on Shakespeare with much of the traditional criticism
they commonly claim to have deposed. I prefer to throw my lot in with
those whose working expectations include the possibility that most of the
literature we study is less duped and deluded than the 'hermeneutics of
suspicion' supposes. Far from being the blind or witting accomplice of the
ruling ideology, caught up in the discursive webs woven by power,
literature at its strongest is actively disposed to dispute the conventional
wisdom of its day and even invent ways of seeing which are way ahead
of its world. But the corroboration of this theoretical postulate requires a
critical practice prepared to engage with the implications of language and
form in a way I have tried to demonstrate in my analysis of *Henry IV*. For
it is the decisions the author makes at the level of phrase and structure, the
techniques he/she deploys to govern our perception of the subject, that
determine whether the work remains in thrall to the orthodoxies of its age
or not.

As far as other plays are concerned, I've tried to show in my book
Shakespeare (Ryan 1989; 2nd edn 1995) that the comedies, tragedies and
romances can be reinterpreted from this perspective, too. My aim there,
as in the present essay, is to reveal how Shakespeare's plays possess the
power, historically invested in their strategies of representation, to
estrange and transcend not only Shakespeare's world but also our own. To
return once again, therefore, to a point made in my response to your opening question, I want to stress that 'reading against the grain' (which you ask
me about here) is the reverse of what I think Shakespeare deserves. On the
contrary, I think it is possible to redefine what is too often automatically
accepted as the grain of his drama by tackling it from a frankly modern
standpoint which turns out to be both textually founded and historically
valid. But, as I hope my account of *Henry IV* confirms, Shakespeare's plays
do benefit considerably from being read against the grain of the criticism
which has imposed its unwarranted preconceptions upon them, and
which has thereby obscured the far more valuable visions stored within
their pages.

CHAPTER 4

Henry IV and Epic Theatre

PETER WOMACK

[Walter Benjamin (1892–1940) was a heterodox Marxist thinker. It is possibly because of this stubborn resistance to formalized materialist terms and concepts that his work has recommended itself to a wide range of critical opinion. Often proceeding according to a 'logic' based more on an association of ideas than on strict dialectical reasoning, his work consistently exemplified how aesthetic criticism was not merely an option, but inescapable. Texts, indeed all artefacts, imply a reader, and this 'unfinished' aesthetic state is much like the critical positions one takes up on art in general: they seem to be moments of rest and synthesis, yet, as soon as they appear to be ritualized and ceremonious, such critical acts actually lose the name of criticism – see Jürgen Habermas, 'Consciousness-Raising or Rescuing Critique' (1972), in Gary Smith (1991: 90–128).

One could take several works to illustrate how this might be a practical undertaking. In his 'Die Kunstwerk im Zeitalter seiner technischen Reproduzierbarkeit' ('The Work of Art in the Age of Mechanical Reproduction' (1935)), Benjamin recognized a shift in how we regard an artefact in the modern age of mass reproduction and consumption. Such technical advances have robbed the work of art of its 'aura': 'its presence in time and space, its unique existence at the place where it happens to be' (Benjamin 1973a: 222). It is no longer 'authentic', and so its origin (provenance, authorial intention) cannot determine any future perspective on it, rather as a religious icon, which originally might have been designed to occupy a particular niche in consecrated ground, now hangs on a public gallery wall. This is not, however, a fearsome prospect. Such changes are actually emancipatory: 'for the first time in world history, mechanical reproduction emancipates the work of art from its parasitical dependence on ritual' (Benjamin 1973a: 226). In its place, there is inevitably a politics of understanding and contemplating the new context for the artefact. While Shakespeare antedates the advent of film or video, we mature in a culture where our 'Shakespeare' cannot be seen without weighing in the balance these later structural presuppositions as to how to regard art. Even if we have not seen *1 Henry IV* before, its unique qualities are no longer guaranteed by Shakespeare's original conceptions or their first conditions of performance.

In this essay, Peter Womack stresses how Benjamin's work on German baroque drama can open up new possibilities for working with Shakespeare's dramatic conventions. The *Trauerspiel* was found to challenge several basic assumptions behind theatrical narrative, and Benjamin found a revived significance in the allegorical separation of emblematic signifiers and the 'things' signified. This space between the symbol and reality is where criticism can start. As Terry Eagleton puts it:

> The blank, petrified objects of *Trauerspiel* have undergone a kind of leakage of meaning, an unhinging of signifier and signified, in a world which like that of commodity production knows only the empty, homogenous time of eternal repetition . . . But once all intrinsic meaning has haemorrhaged from the object, in a collapse of [an] expressive totality . . . any phenomenon can come by the wily resourcefulness of the allegorist to signify absolutely anything else, in a profane parody of the creative naming of God.
>
> (Eagleton 1990: 326)

The work on *Der Ursprung des deutschen Trauerspiels* (1928, published in English as *The Origin of German Tragic Drama* (1977)) and on epic theatre (*Understanding Brecht* (1973b)) pursued the radical possibilities in discontinuity, and the consequent discovery of an awakening of hidden meaning otherwise obscured by the 'common sense' of apparently natural surfaces. This disturbance of fantasy and wish fulfilment, which is actually an encouragement by the text not to think, is the peculiar significance of film, its rapid succession of scenes and camera angles a breaking up of an audience's 'process of association' (*Work of Art*, in Benjamin 1973a: 237–9).

To interrupt is to provoke, and to identify discontinuity is to foreground cracks in the façade of the 'Real'. What this might suggest is a writer committed to non-mimetic art, but this expressiveness is not a result of subjectivity. We may have lost those 'minimal residues of the magical correspondences and analogies that were familiar to ancient peoples', but we retain the ability to develop a recognition of 'nonsensuous similarity' in language:

> the mimetic element in language can, like a flame, manifest itself only through a kind of bearer. The bearer is the semiotic element [the facility to signify by use of linguistic signs]. Thus the coherence of words or sentences is the bearer through which, like a flash, similarity appears.
>
> ('On the Mimetic Faculty' (pub. 1955), in Benjamin 1978: 334–5)

Here there is both a nostalgic reverence for a past, almost atavistic, art of storytelling and a practical assessment of the needs of the present, which is condemned to repetition and thus devaluation. This crisis is also an opportunity. Storytelling, in an oral culture, presupposed a community of hearers and the instinctive talents of improvisation. Drama is the nearest re-creation of that state in the modern world, where the shock of new information is at the same time a recognition of something primeval that allows us to comprehend it as a radical departure, as shocking, something pre-psychological: 'the seeds of grain which have lain for centuries in the chambers of the pyramids shut up air-tight and have retained their germinative power to this day' ('The Storyteller' (1936), in Benjamin 1973a: 90).

For the present purposes of this volume, we need perhaps to be reminded of Benjamin's respect for historiography, the basis of all forms of epic. As a chronicle, History invites interpretation and involvement. Medieval chroniclers did not need to substantiate themselves as authors of the events they described, or look for deep motivation in their historical protagonists, for their faith in 'the divine plan of salvation . . . lifted the burden of demonstrable explanation from their own shoulders'. In its place there emerged 'interpretation, which is not concerned with an accurate concatenation of definite events' ('The Storyteller', in Benjamin 1973a: 95–6). One could claim that this new-found freedom to appropriate History – and rival God's authorship – is particularly pertinent to the writers of History plays of the 1590s.]

NIGEL WOOD

The Mule Track

Walter Benjamin never set out a theory of drama; we have to go into the labyrinth of his work and find it. The main texts are *The Origin of German Tragic Drama* (Benjamin 1977) and the writings on epic theatre collected and translated in *Understanding Brecht* (Benjamin 1973b). These two sources are very different in purpose and manner. The first was an academic treatise on the aesthetic problems raised by the baroque tragic drama of the German seventeenth century. It was completed in 1925 and submitted (unsuccessfully) for a university post-doctoral qualification. The pieces on Brecht, on the other hand, are public polemics produced between 1932 and 1938 to expound a contemporary theatrical project which they explicitly and unreservedly endorse. To derive a usable theoretical perspective from these distinctly located writings, we need to trace the threads which nevertheless connect them.

In both, Benjamin is consciously writing 'after the collapse of German classical culture' (Benjamin 1977: 55). The German *Trauerspiel* is a clumsy and bombastic dramatic form whose usual place in literary histories is a dismissive footnote.[1] Benjamin's study is addressed from its own moment – the disintegration of German culture and society after the First World War – to that of its object – the matching chaos and ambition of the age following the Thirty Years' War. One period of 'decadence' in the arts looks subtly for itself in another. These are times, Benjamin says, 'when the well-wrought work is only within reach of the epigone' (Benjamin 1977: 55); or when (to translate the idea into the idiom of Brecht), the good old things are no use, and it is necessary to start from the bad new ones (Benjamin 1973b: 121). Both of these formulations reverberate specifically for an English critic in 1995. The concept of the 'well-wrought' is, after all, conspicuous in one of the founding texts of Anglo-American literary criticism, as the mark of a version of seventeenth-century literature very different from Benjamin's,[2] and the slogan of an aesthetic of harmonious wholeness which is still powerful in literary education. And the injunction to start from the bad new things bears with ironic sharpness on a moment of the general political culture when the Marxism shared by Benjamin and Brecht appears itself to have become one of the good old things which are no longer usable, and Europe finds itself without a coherent revolutionary ideology for the first time in over two centuries. In this double context, we trace with particular interest Benjamin's complicated praise of a drama which like the baroque fails, or like epic theatre refuses, to achieve the status of the well-wrought.

Badness forms one link between the *Origin* and Brecht in a conversation noted by Benjamin in the summer of 1938:

> Brecht talks about epic theatre, and mentions plays acted by children in which faults of performance, operating as alienation effects, impart epic characteristics to the production. Something similar may occur in third-rate provincial theatre. I mention the Geneva production of *Le Cid* where the sight of the king's crown worn crookedly on his head gave me the first inkling of the ideas I eventually developed in the *Trauerspiel* book nine years later.
>
> (Benjamin 1973b: 115)

By not being on straight, the crown draws attention to the actor's (incompletely realized) intention as something separate from his visible presence. His crown fails to form a single composition with his head – on the contrary, it seems to be about to fall off. Sign and being have come apart in a way which is at once mournful and ludicrous: where the spectator is obviously meant to see one thing (the king in the play), he sees two (first that the man with the crown is meant to be a king, and second that he is not one).

For a modern reader, this reflection makes obvious sense in the context in which Benjamin recalled it in 1938, when it appeared as an instance of accidentally 'Brechtian' theatre. But the ideas it provoked in 1916 were not Brechtian at all; rather, what Benjamin is saying about the crooked crown is that it gave him the beginnings of an insight into the *baroque*. In baroque drama, as it is presented in the eventual '*Trauerspiel* book', the world of objects is a fallen world; things, lightless and insignificant in themselves, have constantly to be forced on to the eternal plane of meaning by the will of the artist. Dramatic form is thus an interminable struggle between the meaning-making energy of the iconographer and the inertia of his materials, and the name of this conflictual duality is allegory:

> The penchant of the baroque for apotheosis is a counterpart to its own particular way of looking at things. The authorization of their allegorical designations bears the seal of the all-too-earthly. Never does their transcendence come from within. Hence their illumination by the artificial light of apotheosis. Hardly ever has there been a literature whose illusionistic virtuosity has more radically eliminated from its works that radiance which has a transcendent effect, and which was at one time, rightly, used in an attempt to define the essence of artistry.
>
> (Benjamin 1977: 180)

Allegory is an eyesore to aesthetics in general, and to German Idealist aesthetics in particular, because of its crass splitting of the image into appearance and meaning, profane and sacred, body and spirit. It offends against the whole conception of art as that supremely human state in which the rational and the material are reconciled in beauty. Utterly failing to effect that creative union, it preserves both doctrine in all its bald didacticism and matter in all its recalcitrant grossness. So far from releasing its materials into the free space of imaginative play, it demarcates a realm where, as Benjamin graphically puts it, 'significance rules, like a stern sultan in the harem of objects' (Benjamin 1977: 184). Hence the pedantry and ostentation of *Trauerspiel*, its heavy-footed lack of mystery (for which it substitutes riddles). Fettering the means of expression to a mere concept, allegory is almost representatively what art is not: such was the drastic prevailing verdict on allegorical drama, and it was certainly part of Benjamin's programme in the *Origin* to challenge it. But he is not simply concerned with the judicious revision of a scholarly underestimate. The real point is: when the theorist under-takes that revision, and constructs a positive philosophical account of these bad old plays, what *else* shifts?

Allegory, according to Carl Horst, a neo-Kantian critic whom Ben-jamin quotes, represents a 'violation of the frontiers' in which the 'rhetorical' arts illicitly invade the territory of the 'plastic' arts:

> In the unemotional permeation of the most varied human forms of expression with autocratic ideas ... artistic feeling and understanding is diverted and violated. This is what allegory achieves in the field of the 'plastic' arts. Its intrusion could therefore be described as a harsh disturbance of the peace and a disruption of law and order in the arts.
>
> (Benjamin 1977: 177; quoted from Horst 1912: 39–40)

This extract is a devastating example of Benjamin's principle that 'Quotations in my work are like wayside robbers who leap out armed and relieve the stroller of his conviction' (Benjamin 1979: 95). Horst, whose work on baroque aesthetics appeared in 1912, is made in 1925 to set out, with an emphasis which is all the sharper for being negative, the programme of the early Weimar avant-garde: Dada, Expressionism, *neue Sachlichkeit* and epic theatre all enact just this 'disruption of law and order in the arts' by the unemotional but imperious intrusion of ideas, manifestos, slogans, information (see Willett 1978: 67–94). Moreover, Benjamin describes the effect of this impulse within baroque drama as one of fragmentation; the supervention of the idea upon the image is ruinous; 'it is as something incomplete and imperfect that objects stare out from the allegorical structure' (Benjamin 1977: 186). Baroque allegory, then, sacrifices not only the radiance of the object but also its organic unity, piling up fragmentary emblems in a manner which anticipates the key formal principle of 1920s experimentation in all the 'plastic' arts (including theatre): montage.

To generalize somewhat: in elaborating the theory of *Trauerspiel*, Benjamin develops the idea of a theatre of *signs*. The dramatic spectacle is not a form of life, but a form of writing; 'the image is only a signa-ture, only the monogram of essence, not the essence itself in a mask' (Benjamin 1977: 214); consequently, the activity of the spectator is not like experiencing something but like reading something:

> Basically, then, the *Trauerspiel*, ... which grew up in the sphere of the allegorical, is, in its form, a drama for the reader. Although this says nothing about the value or the possibility of its

stage-performance. But it does make it clear that the chosen spectator of such examples of the *Trauerspiel* concentrated on them
with at least the same thought and attentiveness as the reader; that
the situations did not change very frequently, but that when they
did, they did so in a flash, like the appearance of the print when
a page is turned.

(Benjamin 1977: 185)

Benjamin draws attention to different instances of this inorganic ascend-
ancy of script. The balletic design of the *Trauerspiel*, for example,
entirely ignores the neoclassical attempt to imitate natural time, placing
scenes instead in a pseudo-spatial relationship. The intrigue is presented
with so little illusionistic intention that it 'takes place like a change of
scenery on the open stage' (Benjamin 1977: 75); in at least one example,
a crucial motivation is explained in a footnote; nowhere is there a convincing attempt to naturalize the economy of the plotting. The dialogue
is addicted to *Denksprüche* (like the *sententiae* of English Jacobean
tragedy) which resemble captions to the stage picture, or those early
paintings in which the figures have scrolls attached to them to show
what they are saying; the speeches themselves are weighed down by
their rigid versification and the burden of emblematic metaphors they
have to carry. In some texts the action is complemented by upstage
allegorical interludes which dramatize *exempla* and metaphor directly
and spectacularly. In all these ways, the *Trauerspiel* offers itself to a
'chosen spectator' who is a reader, a melancholiac collector of fragments, a decipherer of signs.

From here, the route into the theatre of Piscator and Brecht is
straightforward. There, too, the action is harried, punctuated, robbed
of its air of spontaneity, by the incursions of the written – seen in
placards, back-projections, scene montage, songs. Later, the allegorical
interlude is directly appropriated in *Simone Machard*, *Schweik in the
Second World War*, and *The Good Person of Szechwan* – which also,
like the ballet of the *Seven Deadly Sins*, experiment with the arbitrary
splitting of the character. In the two versions of his essay 'What Is Epic
Theatre?' (Benjamin 1973b: 1–22), Benjamin constantly highlights
Brecht's deliberate 'literarizing' of the theatre: he makes the novel reader
the model for the epic theatre's spectator; he draws attention to the way
Brecht's designer, Caspar Neher, frames the action with posters rather
than decor; he requires the actor 'to space his gestures as the compositor
produces spaced type'. These marks of a 'drama for the reader' are not
reducible to the literal presence of written messages on and around the

stage; they are more inwardly a question of rhythm. Instead of the 'lifelike' flow of classical or realistic drama, the *Trauerspiel* is 'characterized . . . by the irregular rhythm of the constant pause, the sudden change of direction, and consolidation into new rigidity' (Benjamin 1977: 197), while 'the interrupting of the action is one of the principal concerns of epic theatre' (Benjamin 1973b: 3). Interruption – the device by which the theatre imitates, not the 'natural' transition of events, but the turning of a page to reveal new emblems, new typographical configurations – isolates the gesture, freeze-frames it, holds it still for a moment so that it can be *read*.

This arrested instant, when 'the stream of things breaks against this rock of astonishment' (Benjamin 1973b: 13), is central to Benjamin's understanding of epic theatre. In three of his attempts at a definition, the same fable recurs:

> a family row. The mother is just about to pick up a pillow to hurl at the daughter, the father is opening a window to call a policeman. At this moment a stranger appears at the door. 'Tableau', as they used to say around 1900. In other words: the stranger is suddenly confronted with certain conditions: rumpled bedclothes, open window, a devastated interior. But there exists a view in which even the more usual scenes of bourgeois life appear rather like this. The more far-reaching the devastations of our social order (the more these devastations undermine ourselves and our capacity to remain aware of them), the more marked must be the distance between the stranger and the events portrayed.
>
> (Benjamin 1973b: 5)[3]

The epic theatre is the stranger whose point of view, by virtue of distance and suddenness, reveals the 'devastated interior' which those who only inhabit it have made, and which they are too distraught and preoccupied to observe themselves. In one way this is a very faithful exposition of what Brecht says himself: the sudden opening of the door is *Verfremdung*, the act of making strange which shocks the (historical) 'conditions' of the gesture into visibility. But there is also a distinctly un-'Brechtian' note in the mysterious appearance of a stranger in the middle of such an intimate scene; and this enigma connects the fable with Benjamin's own more serpentine line of enquiry. Where has this stranger come from?

Benjamin names him in several linked ways. He is the 'thinking man', the sage, the figure who appears, not as the passionate subject of action, but as the dispassionate subject of pedagogy. He is therefore an 'undramatic' figure in an Aristotelian sense (he has no necessary role in the imitation of an action).[4] This fact can serve as a measure of how radically epic theatre opposes itself to dramatic theatre when it insists on placing him at the centre of the stage. But that is not to say that this move is an unprecedented twentieth-century innovation. On the contrary, Benjamin insists that the thinking man stands in a theatrical tradition which is as long as that of Aristotelian tragedy – precisely as long, in fact, since its founding text is firmly identified as the *Phaedo*, the Socratic dialogue in which Plato brings the 'undramatic' sage 'to the very threshold of drama' (Benjamin 1973b: 17). In 'a parody of tragedy' (Benjamin 1977: 113), Socrates meets his sacrificial end in a manner entirely devoid of the conflict, the *agon*, which tragic death requires. Dispersing the daemonic force of tragedy in an unflagging display of reason, he enacts the death of the *untragic hero*. The dramatic form which is all but discovered in this rejection of drama is the passion play:

> The medieval Christ, who also represented the wise man (we find this in the Early Fathers), is the untragic hero *par excellence*. But in the secular drama of the West, too, the search for the untragic hero has never ceased. . . . This important but poorly marked road, which may here serve as the image of a tradition, went via Roswitha and the mystery plays in the Middle Ages, via Gryphius and Calderón in the Baroque age; later we may trace it in Lenz and Grabbe, and finally in Strindberg. Scenes in Shakespeare are its roadside monuments, and Goethe crosses it in the second part of *Faust*. It is a European road, but a German one as well – provided that we may speak of a road and not of a secret smugglers' path by which the legacy of the medieval and the Baroque drama has reached us. It is this mule track, neglected and overgrown, which comes to light today in the dramas of Brecht.[5]

In this extravagant and tentative sketch (not a tradition but what 'may here serve as the image of' one; not a road but a mule track), Benjamin explicitly places baroque *Trauerspiel* and epic theatre on the same map. His imagery makes the connecting path sound unofficial, almost illicit; and the context explains what law is being evaded – elsewhere he speaks of it making its way over 'the sublime but barren massif of classicism' (Benjamin 1973b: 6). The apparently eccentric choice of its defining waymark – the untragic hero – makes sense in this context, since it is the gaze of the thinker that fragments the unity of the classical image into the fierce dualities of spirit and matter, picture and caption, process and interruption, and so is capable of generating the antithetic, dialectical structures of revolutionary art. The reason that it is almost paradoxical to speak of a tradition at all is that its formal principle is discontinuity; its kings have their crowns on crooked. It is the theatre of those figures – the sage, the saint, the melancholic, the communist – to whom the world looks discontinuous, too.

The presence of Shakespeare among the 'roadside monuments' of this twisting path is a kind of provocation. If, after all, Benjamin's critical project can be described as a dialectical recovery of 'bad' drama, no one could offer it less of a handle than Shakespeare, who stands at the apex of the European dramatic repertoire as a convenient epitome of what is 'good'. An aesthetic of shocks, of gaps, of divisive intellection, seems least of all applicable to that genius whose character, as it was bequeathed to the world by Romanticism, is that of an untrammelled and inexhaustible creativity. 'Shakespeare is, above all, an imagination',[6] 'the Spinosistic deity – an omnipresent creativeness';[7] everybody knows that his writing is 'an apparently unstaunchable flow of what modern theorists might call "textual productivity"'' (Eagleton 1986: 1). When critics reject philosophical dialogue as undramatic, or the baroque emblem as pedestrian, or the political prodding of Brechtian theatre as inartistic, it is surely with Shakespeare that they are ultimately implying a comparison. In his infinitely plastic and comprehensive medium, if in no other, everything is dramatized; the invading squads of 'autocratic ideas' are disarmed and become naturalized citizens of the aesthetic realm.

Under these circumstances, it is not surprising if theorists and practitioners in search of the mule track turn their backs on the 'sublime but barren massif' of Shakespeare and follow Benjamin into those neglected parts of the repertoire which have escaped Romantic apotheosis. That, for example, is what Brecht himself was doing at the precise moment when Benjamin was writing the *Origin*. For his debut as a director at the Munich Kammerspiele, he prepared *Macbeth*, and then changed his mind and did an adaptation of Marlowe's *Edward II* (see Hayman 1983: 98). The adaptation exaggerated all the respects – which are striking in any case – in which the play resembles Benjamin's model of *Trauerspiel*: its irregular chronicle form, its ambiguous monarch who is both indecisive tyrant and Christ-like martyr, its brutal atmosphere of frigid intrigue and rhetorical extravagance. It was on this show that Brecht felt his way towards the basic principles of epic theatre, which Benjamin was later in a position to set out with such lucidity: for both of them, separately but simultaneously, the way to make progress was a sideways move that circumvented the imposing and unusable grandeur of the theatrical classic. This charged coincidence enables me to put my question quite simply. If that sidestep had not been taken, and the Elizabethan chronicle playwright at Munich in 1924 had been Shakespeare instead of Marlowe, what possibilities would he have offered? In surveying the landscape of the *Henry IV* plays, extensively farmed as it is by a powerful theatrical and critical tradition, can we trace the mule track?

Shakespeare as a Bad Playwright

The two-hundred-year critical project which has bequeathed *Henry IV* to us as an expression of Shakespeare's genius is no stranger to the idea that it is also a badly made play. The rhetoric of critical appreciation presents it as a glowingly inclusive affirmation of life (Humphreys 1960: lv–lvi); but at the same time, the logic of scholarship exposes a geological ruin, shot through with 'unconformities' (Smidt 1982: 103–20; see also Jenkins 1956). We ask, for instance, why the play begins with the announcement of an immediate Crusade which has in fact already been cancelled; or why Edmund Mortimer, the principal royal pretender in the Percy–Glendower insurrection, vanishes without comment in the course of Act III; or why Falstaff is travelling through Gloucestershire on his way from London to Yorkshire. And so on – the full charge sheet extends to over a dozen major and minor absurdities in the plot. The critical tradition, then, paradoxically delivers a great historical drama which repeatedly if narrowly fails to make narrative sense.

As the geological metaphor suggests, the investigators who unearth these unconformities explain them as telltale flaws in the fit between successive layers of the text. The two parts of *Henry IV* did not spring fully armed from Shakespeare's head: there had been the chronicles, the narrative poem by Samuel Daniel, the popular play of *The Famous Victories of Henry the Fifth*, and also, according to a contested but plausible hypothesis, a five-act Shakespeare script (the 'ur-*Henry IV*', expounded by Melchiori 1989: 12–15), which was dilated into two plays after having already taken shape as one. Even when the two-part structure had been established, the process did not end: there are detectable gaps between the playhouse version, the first printed editions (1598 and 1600), and the 1623 Folio; and within a few years of Shakespeare's death there is a manuscript version, the Dering MS, which cuts the script down to one play, so initiating the stage tradition of adaptation which has continued ever since. Patches of incoherence in any one of these versions, then, can be read as traces of its imperfect transformation of the version before.

It seems, sometimes, as if the different sectors of the Shakespeare industry do not receive one another's memoranda. In the light of the labours of the textual archaeologists, *Henry IV* appears as a somewhat arbitrarily immortalized moment in a continuous process of adaptation; not so much a drama which has been created as a dramatization which has been constructed out of angular, unconformable materials. Rejected possibilities haunt the play in the form of textual spectres, disconcerting its artistic integrity. Yet the idea of *Henry IV* as an organically unified work of genius continues to thrive in critical discourse, as well as in the symphonic homogeneity of its most recent London production.[8] We go on elucidating themes and deducing artistic and political purposes, devising rationales to dispel the confusion which threatens us from the text. But what if the unconformities which resist our totalizations are intrinsic to this kind of theatre, just as, for Benjamin, the monstrosity of *Trauerspiel* is not a failure to achieve Aristotelian unity, but the mark of a different dramatic logic altogether? What, in other words, if we are trying to make the plays make the wrong kind of sense?

Time in the Scene

The first unconformity runs through the opening scene of Part 1.

The king makes a speech to his counsellors, declaring that the time of civil war is now ended, and that an army is to be raised 'Forthwith' (I.i.22) to fight the Turks in Palestine instead. The markers of time seem clear and specific, but before the end of the speech he admits that this purpose 'now is twelve month old' (I.i.28), and that the levying of the crusading force is not after all the purpose of the present meeting. The Earl of Westmoreland then makes a report from a Council meeting held the previous evening, at which discussion of the crusade had to be broken off because of two items of news: a menacing insurrection in Wales, and a battle at Holmedon, its outcome so far unconfirmed, between the Percys and the Scots. Only then does the king reveal, not only that he knows that the Percys won this battle, but also that he is already involved in a dispute with them about the prisoners from it. 'And for this cause', he adds, 'awhile we must neglect/Our holy purpose to Jerusalem' (I.i.100–1).

Again the time-frame is quite tight. The first, inconclusive news

from Holmedon arrived last night; the problem about the prisoners
blew up earlier today; it will be addressed at a Council meeting next
Wednesday. We seem to be in a monolinear, realistic temporality with
its own consistent clock. But by that clock, the king's behaviour is
unintelligible. Why does he announce as imminent a project which he
has already decided to postpone, and why does he attribute this
postponement to his Council's response to the Welsh crisis when it is
already his own response to the Scottish one?

This question is not so much answered as dissolved if we transfer our
attention from fictional time to stage time. The latter yields a very clear
sequence:

1 The king wishes to launch a crusade.
2 But there are domestic threats in Wales and Scotland.
3 But the Percys have successfully defeated the Scottish threat.
4 But the Percys' success constitutes a new threat.

The four phases, each negating the one before, are rhythmically spaced
across the scene: the first 'but' comes at line 28, the second at line 62,
and the third at line 90. Each phase has its own emotional attitude:
pious determination for the crusade, dismay at the insurrections, celebration of Percy's success, and anger at his presumption. These attitudes
are in conflict with each other, and can also contain their own internal
conflicts – for example, the celebration of Hotspur's victory switches,
in a subordinate 'but', to the king's chagrin that the champion is
Northumberland's son and not his own. The king's complex relationship with his realm is laid out, facet by facet, along the linear axis of
the scene in performance, each facet eliciting from the king a fresh
political and rhetorical action – what Brecht calls a *gest* (see Brecht
1964: 104).

The king's behaviour was unintelligible only if one assumed the
fiction of an unbroken inner consciousness underlying his actions (for
example, he knows that the Scots have been defeated at line 62, and
nobody has told him during the scene, so he must have known at the
beginning). But the sharply dialectical gestic grammar of the scene –
'the irregular rhythm of the constant pause, the sudden change of direction, and consolidation into a new rigidity' (Benjamin 1977: 197) – is
incompatible with such an inner continuity. The actor is asked – as, for
example, Brecht asked Peter Lorre in *Mann Ist Mann* (see Brecht
1964: 55–6) – not to 'live' an evolutionary flow of thought and feeling,
but to *show* the successive states of being which the action contains: pro-
claim, concede, exult, denounce. Consequently, there is no demand for

the scene's temporality to be homogeneous; it can move from one point in time to another as readily as it can move between different points on the stage. *Now* the unholy wars are over and the holy war can begin; *now* the travel-stained messenger has arrived and the Scots have been beaten; *now* Hotspur has denied his prisoners and is under the malign influence of one of the king's enemies. The idea is not to follow a monolinear track of time which moves at a constant speed, but to arrest the moment, dilate upon it, hold it until its various contradictory aspects have been displayed, and then to turn the page.

Time and Interruption

The heterogeneity of time is not only a matter of the internal dynamics of the scene. The temporality of the historical plot as a whole is disrupted by that of the sub-plot. In the first two acts of Part 1, for example, the sub-plot moves from the planning of the robbery at Gad's Hill through its execution to its aftermath in the pub – a total time-span which cannot be more than two days. But in the interstices of this action, Hotspur quarrels with the king at Windsor, withdraws to his castle in Northumberland, writes to his potential allies, receives their replies and sets out to join Glendower in Wales. These developments must be the business of several weeks; yet news of the insurrection reaches London before the long evening in the Boar's Head is over. The Falstaff scenes are time out from the crisis of state, mocking its coercive schedule with the unyoked humour of their idleness.

This structural unconformity is also thematized. Immediately after the tightly spaced *gests* of the first scene of Part 1, Falstaff appears and asks what time it is. As a way of starting a scene, it sounds like the most tame and casual kind of expository move; but then Hal responds with a speech whose virtuoso redundancy is itself an elaborate waste of time, and the question is never answered. This opening has the force of a manifesto: in the sub-plot, as in the Forest of Arden (see *As You Like It*, III.ii.291–2), there is no clock. Consistently throughout both plays, the Falstaff scenes happen in an open-ended suspension of temporal progression which is brought to an end only by the intervention of a messenger from that other world where they know what time it is. These messengers are exhausted, agitated, and almost farcically numerous:

> there are twenty weak and wearied posts
> Come from the North, and as I came along
> I met and overtook a dozen captains
> Bare-headed, sweating, knocking at the taverns,
> And asking everyone for Sir John Falstaff.
>
> (*2 Henry IV*, II.iv.289–93)

Their feverish anxiety is that of the main body of the play reacting to the alien time-world it uneasily hosts. The men of action are, as they say, 'Time's subjects' (*2 Henry IV*, I.iii.110), but a whole dimension of the play lies outside the jurisdiction they acknowledge. Reluctantly preparing to leave this sanctuary, Falstaff complains, 'Now comes in the sweetest morsel of the night, and we must hence and leave it unpicked' (II.iv.300–1) – this is the reveller's time, which is not to be obeyed, but to be consumed. He bids Doll Tearsheet a soldier's farewell, but then sends for her from off-stage: the play never compromises the barrier between time-worlds by showing Falstaff actually crossing it. Not, that is, until the end – then, at last, he becomes one of the messengers, 'to ride day and night, and not to deliberate, not to remember . . . stained with travel, and sweating with desire to see him' (V.v.18–22); and the effect of this violent precipitation into the urgencies of history is that the other time-world is brutally shut down, as absolute power proclaims a single temporality for all.

Until that closure – of which there is more to be said later – the dramatic times remain in a state of mutual interruption, each harassing and disconcerting the continuity of the other. The effect of this instability is to denaturalize both; the procession of scenes never appears to emerge naturally out of the logic of events, but has the character of an arbitrarily imposed design. This imprint of a willed, external agenda is not confined to the interface between plot and sub-plot, but penetrates deep into both. Take, for instance, the scene in Wales (*1 Henry IV*, Act III, scene i). It begins as an apparently businesslike conference about the division of the kingdom, but in fact this matter occupies only a fragment of the scene (67–136), and takes the form of an argument which flares up only to be dropped. What is actually happening, it seems, is that an off-stage scribe is drawing up a form of agreement between the conspirators, who are passing the time until it is ready to sign. They banter, compete for status, relax with their wives; relationships between the various participants are developed despite the fact that only Hotspur and Worcester will appear in the play again. Business, love, temperament, music – each of them runs for a few moments before being interrupted by one of the others. In this scene, typically, the action is not being determined by the plot, and the plot is not being advanced by the action; rather, the dramaturgy takes hold of a narrative moment, stops it, and expatiates in the stasis. The stage action does not embody the story, but illustrates it like a series of frames in a frieze; each scene stands independently in relation to a narrative which is not present on the stage but which lies beyond it, in the historical world.

The Quotable Gesture

Arresting, quoting, dilating – this is the procedure of epic theatre. As Benjamin puts it, quoting and interpreting Brecht:

> The relationship of epic theatre to its story, he says, is like that of a ballet teacher to his pupil; his first task is to loosen her joints as far as they will go ... The epic 'stretching' of ... events by the method of acting, by posters and by captions aims at exorcizing their sensationalism.
>
> (Benjamin 1973b: 16)

Exorcising sensationalism means dispelling the illusion of presence (for example, by ensuring that the spectators already know what happened) so as to break the grip of monolinear sequence, loosening the joints between events so that they can move freely and separately instead of all being locked in to the single knot of the story.

In the article by Brecht to which Benjamin is referring, there is an extended example of what this 'epic "stretching"' might entail. A girl leaves home in order to take a job in a fair-sized city. 'For the bourgeois theatre this is an insignificant affair, clearly the beginning of a story; it is what one has to have been told in order to understand what comes after, or to be keyed up for it' (Brecht 1964: 97–8). The questions lead out of the scene into others: was she happy at home, what will happen to her in the city? In the epic theatre, according to Brecht, the questions are different. 'Can't families keep a grip on their children any longer? Have they become (or remained) a burden? Is it like that with every family? Was it always like that?' And so on: is this event a natural, biological separation, like birth, or does it bear the traces of a historical force? A critical, opinionated intelligence infiltrates the action, spoiling its compactness, fingering and fraying its textures. The representation does not serve the story, but chivvies it, bothers it with 'points'; the analogy of the dance teacher suggests not only the new extensiveness which is supposed to result, but also the taxing, bullying quality of the process. Literally, the 'joints' of the story are to be stretched, its structures articulated by pressure and repetition. All this can only happen if the forward movement of the narrative is suspended, so that, as in a rehearsal, the *gest* can be dilated at leisure.

What happens if we play this light over the first scene of *2 Henry IV*? A great provincial magnate receives the news that his son has been defeated and killed by the forces of the state. The audience knows the facts, normally having seen the event at the end of the earlier play, and been reminded of it by the prologue to this one. But half the scene – over a hundred lines – is taken up with the breaking of the news. Three messengers come to the castle: the first with uncertain tidings of Hotspur's success, the second with uncertain tidings of his death, and the third with an authoritative report of his death and the rebels' utter defeat. Relieved of suspense, the sequence is free to expand the gesture (giving and hearing bad news), elaborating it with something like the epic theatre's questions. It is a moment of pathos: the old father, ill and anxious, receives the shock of his brilliant son's death. But 'is this event a natural, biological separation, like birth, or does it bear the traces of a historical force?'

> Every minute now
> Should be the father of some stratagem;
> The times are wild: contention, like a horse
> Full of high feeding, madly hath broke loose,
> And bears down all before him.
>
> (I.i.7–11)

The gesture is full of its historical moment: we are watching an event which is characteristic of the time. For example: the messengers buttress their stories by reference to the rank of their informants; the first one claims to have had his good news from 'a gentleman well bred, and of good name' (l.26), and pours scorn on the second one's contradictory information by suggesting that it comes from 'some hilding fellow that had stol'n/The horse he rode on' (ll.57–8) – that is, from someone who was only pretending to be a gentleman. As Rumour has already implied, filling the 'peasant towns' between Shrewsbury and Warkworth with false reports, the confusion of information is at the same time a confusion of social order. When eventually the eye-witness Morton resolves the conflict of messengers, Northumberland's hopeless desire that the news should be false is expressed in the conceit of a sort of happy *lèse-majesté*:

Tell thou an earl his divination lies,
And I will take it for a sweet disgrace,
And make thee rich for doing me such wrong.

(ll.88–90)

According to the code of honour, a nobleman is supposed to reward those who honour him and chastise those who dishonour him. The idea here is that Northumberland would, absurdly, reward anyone who could dishonour him by making him a liar. His passion is inverting his official values, undermining that rigid intolerance of 'disgrace' which is precisely what has brought his son to the death he is now trying to deny. But the great lord's power to control what his followers say to him encounters its limits in the fact of death. Besides, Northumberland's 'honour' has already been called into question, and will be again. So the scene enlarges, not just on a father's resisting the knowledge of his son's death, but at the same time on the twists and turns of a baron in rebellion, for whom this is also a political and dynastic disaster, and a crisis in the ethical code of his class.

The mechanism of this enlarging of the *gest* – the equivalent of Benjamin's posters and captions – is the vigorously generalizing, pattern-making verse. The scared face of the bringer of bad news speaks more readily than his tongue; fear finds its confirmation in the eyes of the other; the unlucky messenger sins by lying or offends by speaking the truth; the shock of grief, which would strike the healthy man down, imparts a sort of violent health to the invalid – the writing is an anthology of commonplaces and allusions around the topic of bad news. The words of the scene dictate and interpret the physical gestures: the messengers blench or shake their heads; the last, in pity, tries to find fragments of good news to postpone what he must say; at the onset of certainty, Northumberland throws away his crutch and coif, the emblems of sickness, and calls for a sword and helmet. This is, as Benjamin puts it, drama for the reader. The language is gestic, and the gestures are clear and quotable like linguistic signs.

The Crooked Crown

When the royal representative, Westmoreland, meets the rebels in Part 2, he upbraids the Archbishop of York for appearing in arms:

Wherefore do you so ill translate yourself
Out of the speech of peace, that bears such grace,

Into the harsh and boist'rous tongue of war –
Turning your books to graves, your ink to blood,
Your pens to lances and your tongue divine
To a loud trumpet and a point of war?

(IV.i.47–52)

Here, explicitly, the objects referred to are signs: in turning from pens
and ink to lances and blood, the Archbishop is translating himself from
one language into another. Every noun is emblematic: as Benjamin says
of a comparable speech in a *Trauerspiel*, 'the writer succeeds in signi-
ficantly dividing a living entity into the *disjecta membra* of allegory'
(Benjamin 1977: 198). But then what makes this dissection possible is
precisely the solecism of which the Archbishop is being accused. His
abandonment of his books separates them out from the 'living entity'
of his existence and makes them into a sign. It is in the act of 'ill translation' that objects disclose their linguistic character; their allegorical
potential is revealed by their being *misplaced*. This is the general condition of the allegorical logic which runs through the plays, and the
misplaced object at the centre of the whole divisive signifying system
is the crown.

Henry IV is clearly a usurper, responsible for the death of the rightful king. On the other hand, the plays' stress on his care of government accords him a *de facto* sovereignty:[9] he is not, like Richard III or
Macbeth, a monarchical antitype. His status is consequently ambiguous; the word used by both Hotspur and Henry himself is 'indirect'
(*1 Henry IV*, IV.iii.105; *2 Henry IV*, IV.ii.312). He is and is not the
true king. The effect of this incomplete identity is to rob the royal
image of its transcendence. Whereas the kingship of Richard II exists
in a sacred space because he is the Lord's anointed, and that of Richard
III also exists in a sacred space because he is diabolical, Henry's royalty
is contingent. His kingship represents the fall of the symbol into
history. His reign is literally unredeemed time – one long postponement of the journey to the Holy Land which was apparently promised
to him by a prophecy that he would die in Jerusalem. In the end,
'Jerusalem' turns out to be the name of a room in his own palace: when
he dies, he is still in the unholy land of allegory, where the sign 'is
prevented by guilt from finding fulfilment of its meaning in itself'
(Benjamin 1977: 224).

Henry reigns, therefore, over a baroque realm, where the signs
of sovereignty have no inner radiance, and every scenic element –
space, time, objects, words, persons – is fissured by translation and

misprision. 'Thy state is taken for a joint-stool, thy golden sceptre for a leaden dagger, and thy precious rich crown for a pitiful bald crown' (*1 Henry IV*, II.iv.367–9). At the climax of Part 1, in a darkly appropriate joke, the king himself splits into an indefinite number of counterfeits, and Douglas, like the crazed exegetist of a polysemous text, runs around the battlefield killing illusory kings in the hope of arriving at the true one by sheer aggregation.

Part 2 deploys a subtler representation of the king's self-divided state: his depression. Nowhere does *Henry IV* come closer to the principle of *Trauerspiel* – Benjamin's secret link between allegory and melancholy – than in the figure of the sleepless king:

> O Sleep! O gentle Sleep!
> Nature's soft nurse, how have I frighted thee,
> That thou no more wilt weigh my eye-lids down
> And steep my senses in forgetfulness?
> Why rather Sleep liest thou in smoky cribs,
> Upon uneasy pallets stretching thee
> And hushed with buzzing night-flies to thy slumber,
> Than in the perfumed chambers of the great, . . .?
>
> (III.i.5–12)

The inhabitants of the smoky cribs are visited by the gentle nurse because they are unaware of her; their days and nights, spent among common noises, are innocent of meaning. The king in the artificial stillness of his palace is kept awake by consciousness; just that consciousness which gives the pictures – the sleeping poor, the kindly but capricious goddess – their tormenting vividness. The verse derives its incomparable metaphoric power and precision from the absence of its object: what makes the allegorical components so distinct is the idea of the natural wholeness of which they are the sharp-edged fragments.

'Uneasy lies the head that wears a crown' (*2 Henry IV*, III.i.31) – the disharmony of the king's majesty is expressed in the denaturing violence of thought. As in the moment Benjamin describes in the production in Geneva, sign and body fall short of unitary being and are held in uncomfortable and precarious duality. Later in the play, Hal describes himself contemplating the literal visual image of that duality – the crown and the head that wears it, side by side on the pillow:

> I spake unto this crown as having sense,
> And thus upbraided it: 'The care on thee depending
> Hath fed upon the body of my father;

Therefore thou best of gold art worst than gold,
Other, less fine, in carat more precious,
Preserving life in med'cine potable;
But thou, most fine, most honoured, most renowned,
Hast eat thy bearer up.'

(IV.ii.286–93)

Here the duality intensifies into a murderous opposition: the sign, in its implacable, inorganic perfection, ruins the living body on which it feeds. The insistence of allegory is cruel, extracting significance from sensuous life only by shattering its healthful rhythms.

Allegory in *Henry IV*, then, as in Benjamin, is the discourse of a fallen nature, a failed transcendence. In that sense, the disintegral character of the plays' temporal and metaphoric structures is meant to be attributed to the original sin of Richard II's deposition. The analogy with epic theatre would on this view be a merely opportunistic one, because here the theatrical principle of discontinuity is not embraced as a form of technical progress, but suffered as a burden of guilt. But then on the other hand, the figure of the care-worn king is a commonplace: the crown in popular iconography is always this oxymoronic emblem of 'polished perturbation! Golden care!' (*2 Henry IV*, IV.ii.153).[10] So the dividedness of Henry's psychological and political state is not simply the effect of his happening to be a usurper; on the contrary, it is his being a usurper that enables him to serve as a universal representative of greatness. No sovereignty lies outside the doubling, translating processes of history: that this particular king is not the true king gives him a typicality of kings in general which is, itself, allegorical.

It is true that the play ends with an immensely ambitious attempt to transcend these conditions. Capitalizing on the fact that he is one generation away from the original transgression, Hal executes a miraculous self-transformation designed to merge his identity with that of the Crown and end the corroding antinomy which he saw on his father's pillow: 'Presume not that I am the thing I was' (V.v.52). But the success of this breathtaking leap into immanence is problematic. For one thing, the audience has watched him practising, which compromises the self-identity of the eventual performance: possibly, after all, 'This that you heard was but a colour' (V.v.79–80). For another, the divisions and deferrals of presence which he seeks sublimely to transcend have constituted the very substance and texture of the drama itself. What if the fallenness of the symbol was, all along, the theatre's opportunity – not only, as the providentialist reading would have it, the necessary breakdown of unity preparatory to its eventual reconstitution, but also the contradictory space in which the other, unofficial, 'unconformable' voices could make themselves heard? In that case, Hal's apotheosis is achieved at the cost of withering the plural, material life of the drama. Or to put it another way, he has to reject Falstaff.

The Character of Falstaff

> *All of them, the way they carry their bellies around*
> *You'd think it was swag with someone in pursuit of it*
> *But the great man Laughton performed his like a poem*
> *For his edification and nobody's discomfort.*
> *Here it was: not unexpected, but not usual either*
> *And built of foods which he*
> *At his leisure had selected, for his entertainment.*
> *And to a good plan, excellently carried out.*
>   (Bertolt Brecht, 'Laughton's Belly', in Brecht 1976: 393)

Nothing in *Henry IV* suggests an organic authorial creativity so compellingly as the figure of Falstaff. In his magnificent corporeality, and his endlessly teasing mixture of admirable and despicable qualities, he appears to transcend the condition of a mere textual function and acquire, as it were miraculously, the autonomy and substance of a real person. Surely here, if nowhere else, the Spinosistic deity sweeps aside the duality of meaning and substance and creates a fully realized presence – a rounded character in every sense.

In one sense, indeed, the *original* rounded character. Maurice Morgann's *Essay on the Dramatic Character of Sir John Falstaff* (1777) has a strong claim to be regarded as the founding document of English Shakespearian criticism (Morgann 1972: 143–215),[11] establishing, in its combination of close reading and non-technical moral philosophizing, a discourse about Shakespeare which is still pedagogically and theatrically dominant. If we accept this claim, then it is hardly an exaggeration to say that the originating question of the entire genre to which this book belongs was 'Is Falstaff a coward?' We all inhabit the space opened up by this innocent-sounding query.

It is the space of a half-hidden interiority. The assumption of the question is that what the character does and says is a set of traces of what he *is*; this unwritten essence is then considered as the origin of the written signs. Criticism comes into existence as that which shuttles between the visible surface and its invisible source. Its investment in this vertical distance is a contradictory one. On the one hand, it must be possible to grasp the essence of the character, because if it were not, the critical project would be going nowhere. But then, on the other hand, it is equally necessary that this essence – the answer to the question of the character – should never actually be grasped, because it is the ultimate elusiveness of the essence that constitutes the vitality of the representation. It is because the imaginary person cannot be pinned down that it lives; it is because its true nature is implied but never revealed that we perceive it as having one.

Falstaff generates exactly the right kind of not quite decidable question: he is not only witty in himself, but the cause that wit is in Shakespearian critics. Is he a coward? Yes: because he runs away at Gad's Hill. No: because of his imperturbable self-possession on battlefields. Is he a liar? Yes: because he makes a whole string of entirely false claims. No: because their falsity is so open and palpable that they deceive no one, but have rather the status of fictional inventions. Is Hal's eventual rejection of him a conclusive authorial verdict? Yes: because he has never been shown as anything but lawlessly self-serving. No: because every spectator watches the rejection with pain and regret. And so on: as the foremost connoisseur of ambiguity put it, 'The whole joke of the great rogue is that *you* can't see through him, any more than the Prince could' (William Empson, 'Falstaff', in Empson 1986: 38). Falstaff's opacity is the guarantee of his substantial presence; in an audacious dramaturgic move, the authenticity of his being is derived from the unreliability of everything he says.

Shakespeare's ability to sustain this elusiveness depends on Falstaff's eccentric relation to the dramatic structure in which he figures, and this depends in turn on the fact that the structure itself is contradictory. As Benjamin points out in connection with *Trauerspiel*, drama and history are characterized by incompatible kinds of unity. Drama 'demand[s] closed form, in order to achieve that totality which is denied to all external temporal progression' (Benjamin 1977: 75–6). Drama, that is, is supposed to begin from nothing and end completely, in a way that historical narrative never can; while, on the other hand, a plot which claims to represent historical events is obliged by that function to 'follow an unequivocal line of development', to conform itself to a temporal sequence which is not generated within its own form, but determines it from outside. Not that the playwright is tied down to 'the facts' – many historical dramatists, including Shakespeare, treat these fairly freely. The point is rather that because of the play's explicit reference to a code beyond its own boundaries, the dramatic world is incapable of self-completeness. Whereas a tragedy or a comedy can in principle 'achieve totality' by exhausting all the possibilities implied in its initial situation, a play such as *Henry IV* is fragmented by its referential function, which admits into its structure the alien rhythm of chronicle.

Falstaff is not tied to this historical linearity, because he is fiction. Whereas the historical characters are weighty, carrying between them the burden of the plot, Falstaff is light, moving freely around and across the 'unequivocal line of development'. He is not a historical character but a comic one; and if he were in a comedy – as *The Merry Wives of Windsor* demonstrates – then he would be constrained in his turn by the 'closed form' of his proper genre, with its own requirements of development and denouement. But in *Henry IV* there is no comedy for him to be in: the autocracy of the historical plot makes it impossible for the comic elements to achieve autonomous form. So Falstaff gets away: exempt from both of the genres which might contain him, he flourishes like a luxuriant weed in the crack between them. He is structurally, as well as empirically, a rogue character – not so much autonomous as disorderly.

The archaeology of the role yields a similar story. If Gary Taylor is right, then Falstaff should not even be called Falstaff, but Sir John Oldcastle, the character having been intended to represent the Lollard knight of that name who was first favoured, but later imprisoned and executed, by the historical Henry V (see Taylor 1983). The name was changed because Oldcastle's powerful descendants objected to his being exhibited on the popular stage as a drunken buffoon, as no doubt did the many godly readers of Foxe's *Acts and Monuments*, who knew Oldcastle as a proto-Protestant martyr. This identification makes the fat knight a historical character after all, but one of a peculiar kind. The hagiographical record gives Oldcastle, conventionally enough, a dissolute youth to contrast with his later exemplary conduct; the anti-Lollard chroniclers, on the other hand, naturally represent him as a hypocrite and a traitor who was seeking to overthrow the law of the land. These originally distinct versions of Oldcastle's vices seem to have got mixed up with each other and with the powerful myth of Henry V's youthful wildness to produce an odd metamorphosis. Oldcastle's dissolute youth became Henry's, with Oldcastle himself (presumably because of his name) as an *older* companion of the prince's riots; and Oldcastle's loss of Henry's favour came to be attributed, not to his heresy, but to the stories about drinking and fornicating which his own admirers had put into circulation. Oldcastle's moral reformation was thus transferred to Henry, and his serious oppositionality demonized as the crudest and most picturesque kind of 'vice'.

Two further elements complicate this already complicated game of ideological whispers-round-the-table. One is Shakespeare's subtle finessing of the Wild Prince legend itself. Whereas the *Famous Victories* had shown the future king committing robbery and assaulting the Lord Chief Justice, *Henry IV* contrives to give the *impression* that Hal does these things without unequivocally saying so. The play immerses the prince in an atmosphere of illegality, but stops short of actually having him break the law of his future realm. This evasion requires a sort of dramatic surrogate, someone who can perform the actions which both must and must not belong to the Wild Prince (see Bevington 1987: 22–4). It is because this function devolves upon Oldcastle/Falstaff that the colourless and marginal companion of the *Famous Victories* moves to the centre of the lowlife scenes and becomes the radiant focus of their comic energy. Falstaff, who, as he explains to the Lord Chief Justice, is really a young gallant despite his elderly appearance (*2 Henry IV*, I.ii.147–52), is Henry V's wild youth in displaced form – displaced so that in the end it can be rejected.

The other complication is that when this demonized dissent moves on to the stage, it naturally takes the form of the Vice. As many critics have pointed out,[12] Falstaff is something of a compendium of Vice characters: visually he is Gluttony; politically he is Abuse (misusing his commission of impressment and trading on his intimacy with the prince); and as the father of lies and misleader of youth he is a kind of Satan. But what is really more to the point than these individual categories is Falstaff's access, through them, to the theatrical mode of being of the Vice. Stage Vices, after all, are not only personified kinds of wickedness; they are also clowns. They speak badly – swearing, stammering, punning, talking doggerel and nonsense. They are entertainers, doing songs and slapstick routines, wearing stunt costumes, claiming false identities, playing practical jokes on each other, scandalously inverting legal and religious ceremonies. These activities transgress not only the official ethical code, but also that of the drama: they move in and out of role, they impertinently interrupt even their own plots, they chat to the audience in a temporality which is obviously that of the performance rather than that of the story. They are not imitated human beings, but devised monsters who live, brashly and alienatingly, in the space of theatricality.

Falstaff carries a bottle in his pistol-case, orates in praise of cowardice and sack, passes himself off as the conqueror of Hotspur, evades the admonitions of Justice by feigning deafness, and so on: that the role is constructed at least partly out of Vice materials is a point which hardly needs labouring. What does have to be registered, rather more carefully, is the curious performance space in which Falstaff therefore moves – the space of the entertainer, even, in his flamboyant, wayward monologues, of the stand-up comic; curious, not because there is anything inherently paradoxical about it, but because it is not the same as the socially and historically determined space inhabited by most of the rest of the cast. What is coercively real for them is a matter of invention for him; he can turn diseases to commodity; he does not share their earnestness because he is a player. Here is a simple explanation for the spiralling ambiguities of Falstaff's character. The reason a coward can be so tranquil on the battlefield of Shrewsbury is that he is not only on the battlefield, but also on the stage, expounding his own terror with philosophical urbanity; the reason why critics can never decide whether the eleven buckram men are a lie or a knowingly extravagant entertainment is that they are both at once, because the name 'Falstaff' comprehends both the represented braggart and the representing wit. The enigma of his true nature, then, is the effect of projecting the duality of actor and role into the unitary category of realistic character: the resulting confusion looks like depth.

In one word, Falstaff's mode of being is parody. He is not a coward, but the accredited stage representative of cowardice itself, boldly seeking out the occasions of honour and meeting them with an abjectness which is no less consciously exemplary than Hotspur's courage. He is not Oldcastle, but a travesty of Oldcastle so gross and unfair that a simple change of name was enough to sever it from the original entirely. In memory of his distant origins in Protestant martyrology, he does an accurate and offensive imitation of the accents of the godly; but he is not only a parody-puritan; he also speaks as a parody-soldier, a parody-gallant, a parody-counsellor, a parody-philosopher. Even his misuse of the king's press is parodic: the scene (*2 Henry IV*, III.ii) is only marginally a realistic portrayal of corrupt impressment; most of its energy goes into taking the *gest* of official selection and turning it into a silly game with the candidates' names. Falstaff is not so much a bad recruiting officer as a *mockery* of a recruiting officer.

His sovereignty at the Boar's Head converts its staff and regulars into courtiers of misrule:[13] Hal deserts his father's court not, as the sentimental and novelistic version of the story would have it, in order to be with 'ordinary people', but in order to attend a travesty court. This is seen, for example, in the construction of Falstaff's grossness through Hal's tirelessly hyperbolical descriptions: just as royal majesty flows from the honouring flattery of courtiers, so Falstaff's majestic dishonour flows from Hal's assiduous stream of abuse. Chops, paunch, guts, hill of flesh, tun of man, roasted Manningtree ox – even Falstaff's most spectacularly organic attribute, his belly, derives its huge physical substance from the discourse of parody. From the start, their relationship is characterized by debasing metaphoric substitutions – cups of sack for hours, the false thief for the true prince, the king's tavern for the king's exchequer, a pitiful bald crown for the precious rich crown. Falstaff is made up of deliberate reversals. He is not accidentally the companion, but essentially the content, of Hal's delinquency; not just an ignoble person, but the programmatic negation of nobility as such.

And it is as the 'incarnation of parody' (Benjamin 1977: 124), not as a characterized individual, that Falstaff poses a threat to the dramatic and ideological order of the play. For example: the representational dimension of the recruiting scenes (an individual officer is shown taking bribes and getting his beggarly conscripts killed) amounts to no more than a loyal and responsible protest: the king would be better served if his recruiting officers were honest and conscientious. But Falstaff's cruel and fanciful performance parodies, not merely corruption, but the whole *gest*: after all, the honest officer, no less than the crook, is in the business of dragging people away from their more or less pleasant and imperfect lives to come and be killed for the sake of honour, or order, or something. The distinction between proper and improper ways of doing is dissolved in Falstaff's corrosive frivolity. In the end, then, rejecting Falstaff is a much more fundamental assertion of state power than, say, defeating Hotspur; because, although Falstaff represents no danger whatsoever to royal political stability, his capacity to undermine the royal order of meaning is unlimited. This is what the dying Henry IV understands:

> Harry the fifth is crowned, up, Vanity,
> Down, royal state . . .
> For the fifth Harry from curbed licence plucks
> The muzzle of restraint . . .
>
> (IV.ii.248–9, 259–60)

From the king's point of view, Falstaff is not an objectionable individual; he is Vanity, Licence, Idleness. In this respect, Henry is a better reader than Morgann: Falstaff's formidable presence is a matter, not after all of personality, but of allegory. His physical bulk is not so much a natural attribute as an emblem, which he carries before him into battle like a shameless banner.

For Benjamin, as for us, a powerful tradition of reception suppresses the allegorical dimension in Shakespeare:

> the *Sturm und Drang*, which discovered Shakespeare for Germany, had eyes only for the elemental aspect of his work, not the allegorical. And yet what is characteristic of Shakespeare is precisely that both aspects are equally essential. Every elemental utterance of the creature acquires significance from its allegorical existence, and everything allegorical acquires emphasis from the elemental aspect of the world of the senses.
>
> (Benjamin 1977: 228)

The duality of this formulation is crucial. The elemental and the allegorical do not merge, but are held in a polarity which is at once conflictual and complementary. The tension can be read most plainly in the language. The 'elemental utterance of the creature' is heard as speech, breath, cries and laughter; it is, as Benjamin says elsewhere, 'exposure, rashness, powerlessness before God' (Benjamin 1977: 201). But this voice is everywhere confronted, in Shakespeare as in the baroque, by the aggressive writtenness of the text within which it is displayed; that heavy, showy writing which is 'composure, ... dignity, superiority, omnipotence over the objects of the world'. Falstaff is this polarity in its most vivid form, with, on the one hand, his helpless enslavement to every sensual stimulus and his gradually deepening fear of death, and on the other, the elaborate, self-sufficient artifice of his prose. The critical discourse of the 'dramatic character' labours to reconcile the whole opposition, blending body and significance, creatural and artificial, speech and writing, in a single psychological entity which can then be called natural. It is the idea of allegory which opens up this synthetic nature and restores its component parts to the stage in the form of distinct, spaced gestures.

Yet if Falstaff is indeed the initiating object of character criticism, this is not an accident. As has been pointed out by Edward Burns (1990: 192–202), he is the paradigmatically non-Aristotelian character, because his dramatic being depends so little on action. In Aristotle, and consequently in neoclassical poetics, character is the effect of *proairesis* – a choice between courses of action which ethically defines the chooser because both alternatives are feasible. Falstaff makes no choices of that kind, but just behaves; and since he is, despite this lack of ethos, a highly differentiated figure, he provided the perfect occasion for the construction of character as an autonomous dramatic category. Benjamin, however, invites a quite different reading of Falstaff's inconsequential relation to the main action. As we have seen, it is a question of parody, inversion, mocking reflection. Falstaff is not a participant in the action, but a bundle of travestying discourses set athwart its progression, interrupting its tense, purposeful temporality with a leisurely and studied impertinence. He is everything base by turns – braggart, liar, hypocrite, drunkard, time-server – but if that list seems never to exhaust his potential however many items are added to it, the reason is not so much that his essence is ineffable as that the allegorical intention which generates the list cannot itself be listed. With no commitments to the economy of the plot, he fills up the time by describing, expounding and performing himself – but then that makes him the expositor as well as that which is expounded. So far from being a unified consciousness, he lives in the inherent duality of parody, which is always a composite of the imitated object and the imitating intelligence.

Nothing is so typical of this dramatic mode of existence – or so inconspicuous in the critical accounts of Falstaff's 'character' – as his addiction to disputation; the whole role is a tissue of opinions, persuasions, sentiments, wishes, praise and abuse. To argue is as constitutive of Falstaff as to drink. For the existentially defining practice of proairetic action, he substitutes the dispersing and convivial practice of reason. At this point Benjamin's mule track comes suddenly into view. In Falstaff, the untragic hero makes his estranging appearance in the family drama of the realm, arresting its continuities by bringing on to the stage the relaxed, 'undramatic' rhythms of pleasurable thought.

Conclusion

If there is a route from here into the theatre of Brecht, it connects not so much with the work Benjamin saw in the early 1930s as with the later untragic heroes such as Galileo and Azdak. Gluttonous sages, loquacious and dishonest, they engage in thought without incurring its accompanying melancholy because their thinking is materialist and does not open up the mournful gap between doctrine and the life of the senses. This figure – the comic *raisonneur*, the trickster, the philosopher of sensuality – is alien to the *Trauerspiel* world. It is at this point, you could say, that my attempt to assimilate *Trauerspiel* and epic theatre into a single theory of drama breaks down.

But Benjamin sees *Trauerspiel* as realizing itself most completely when, as in the theatres of Calderón and Shakespeare, it transgresses its own boundaries: 'The finest exemplifications of the *Trauerspiel* are not those which adhere strictly to the rules, but those in which there are playful modulations of the *Lustspiel*' (Benjamin 1977: 127). In Germany, however, a willed gravity meant that 'the expression of this significant relationship was left to the popular spectacle'. *Trauer* (mourning) and *Lust* (mirth) were not to appear on the same stage, even if, as Benjamin insists, they are intimately linked by the fact that the vanity of the world is the object of both. As the allusion to popular spectacle suggests, this separation is a socio-cultural matter. The German baroque drama was a designedly elite form, deploying (like Benjamin's study of it) a pedantic and ostentatious literariness against the felt chaos of its age, and closing its pseudo-classical doors against the debasing heterogeneity of popular entertainment.

These are the doors which, in *Henry IV*, are jammed open by the bulk of Falstaff. It is not only that he has theatrical affiliations with the Vice-buffoon tradition deplored by humanists such as Sidney and Jonson,[14] or even that his scenes, in carrying the rough picaresque comedy of the *Famous Victories* into the midst of the drama of state, bring about a hybrid of written chronicle and folk legend. It is also that, as title pages and contemporary allusions make clear, the stage character himself was a popular hit, whose otherwise implausible national celebrity in the *fictional* England of Part 2 reflects his actual fame among theatre audiences.[15]

Let us entertain the most vulgar solution to the 'structural problem' of the two parts of *Henry IV*: the hypothesis that a single play was expanded into two in order to milk the success of its comic star.[16] This would explain, for example, the curious fact that, until well into Act IV, Part 2 duplicates the basic structure of Part 1 practically scene by scene. Like many of the 'sequels' of the contemporary film industry, what presents itself as a linear continuation is really a structural repetition. This theory is not much liked in academic circles, possibly because it impugns Shakespeare's artistry; but the analogy with epic theatre invites us to question the conception of artistry which this nervousness implies.

The idea is that there is something discreditable about cooking up a sequel in response to a success – it is padding, filling out, producing a pot-boiler. This reproach (which makes the critic sound a little like the Lord Chief Justice on the subject of Falstaff) supposes a kind of literary economics. The good text is the *efficient* text, the one which achieves its corporate goals with the smallest possible expenditure of resources (the resources are words, scenes, *dramatis personae*, stage time). That is: we assume an *end* to which the spectacle is tending, and so can define its material elements as *means*. It is in order to subvert this textual hierarchy, and to license formal prodigality, that Brecht favours the 'scene-montage' principle summed up in his slogan 'each scene for itself' (Brecht 1964: 37).

For instance, he instructs an actor in the *Threepenny Opera* to play a beggar's choosing of a wooden leg in such a way that 'just for the sake of seeing this particular turn people will plan to revisit the show at the precise moment when it occurs' (Benjamin 1973b: 6). Historically, this advice is not as far-fetched as it sounds. In England, certainly from the Restoration through to the Victorian theatre, and probably in the Elizabethan theatre, too, it was quite normal to look in at the play for an act or so before going on to some other entertainment. It is perhaps only post-Romantic drama which has demanded its audience's continuous and undivided attention. Benjamin perceives the importance of Brecht's refusal to make that demand – 'For epic theatre, as a matter of principle, there is no such thing as a latecomer' – and relates it to new technical forms (radio, cinema) which have to live with an audience that drops unpredictably in and out. Since then, videotape has made Brecht's point about the wooden leg still less fantastic. A performer can now use the fact that film acting is shot precisely as a series of 'particular turns', to make something which can also be appreciated in this way, something to which people are going to want to rewind.

This ironic history of selective viewing is a neat image of an idea which informs much of Benjamin's, and Brecht's, interest in early modern theatre: the idea that modern conditions return to sixteenth- and seventeenth-century ones in ways that make the intervening 'massif' of bourgeois dramatic values an obstacle both to the understanding of the past and to the invention of the future. *Henry IV* is one of the best Shakespearian illustrations of this thesis. Falstaff choosing recruits, Northumberland hearing the bad news, Hotspur saying goodbye to his wife (twice), Hal stealing the crown – the plays are full of episodic values, cues for the actor to perform a quotable, revisitable 'turn'. The educational and theatrical processing of Shakespeare which irons out these cues, resolving the opportunistic irregularity of the spectacle into symbolic and thematic unity, has the effect of muting and suppressing the gestures so that their rich, material historicity disappears in the flow of abstract (ideological) meaning: they become means to an artistic end. Both Shakespeare's script and our theatres would be better served if we were to declare a moratorium on the idea that *Henry IV* is a great work of art, and resolve instead to see it – and perform it – not as a bad work of art, certainly, but as a great pot-boiler.

SUPPLEMENT

NIGEL WOOD: On page 129 you note how equivalent a contemporary *British* critical context could be to that of Brecht, who felt that it was time to embrace 'bad new' art at the expense of a complacent reliance on 'good old things'. Could you expand on this? Why is it now apposite to change our (British?) tastes and fabricate new aesthetic criteria?

PETER WOMACK: Let us formulate the idea a little more carefully. It is that in the arts there are times – moments of what is called decadence – when *it is better to be worse*. Exemplary classics exist – models of elegance, subtlety and wisdom – and it is possible to emulate them; but somehow this only leads to narcissistic elegance, pointless subtlety, reactionary wisdom. Then it is more productive to be perverse and go for awkwardness, crudity, folly. To put it extremely: better the real ugliness of Georg Grosz than the fake beauty of Nazi kitsch.

Why this now? Well, for one thing, as I said, what we have in our background, where Benjamin had neo-Kantian aesthetics in his, is that particular model of elegance, subtlety and wisdom which became famous as the Well Wrought Urn. (It was Cleanth Brooks who made it a slogan; he was quoting John Donne, but also referring to the better-known urn in Keats – the one that says (what Grosz is effectively denying) that beauty is truth.) Experts in theory may feel that this perfectly formed vessel was smashed, or at any rate deconstructed, many years ago; if so, they would have been surprised to find it in one piece in 1993, in the form of the British government's proposals for compulsory good literature in the National Curriculum for England and Wales. Only now, you might say, has the long-discussed crisis in English Studies actually arrived, rendering unmistakably audible the *political* overtones of a belief in the good old things.

But then I also think that the terms of this whole debate have been shaken up, more profoundly than we can see yet, by the virtual collapse of communist politics in Europe. Not, of course, that many of the organizations consigned to oblivion since 1989 had much to do, by that time at least, with what a socialist would call 'socialism'. But the whole débâcle has certainly been an unconditional triumph of capitalism; and if anyone thinks that academics in the capitalist heartlands can simply go on doing Marxist aesthetics as if nothing had happened – well, he/she is not thinking in a very materialist fashion. When Brecht made that remark about the bad new things, he was probably thinking about the Soviet state, which was, at the time, fairly new and undoubtedly bad. Now it is superannuated, and the Marxist writings which were always so much better than it was, in all their elegance, subtlety and wisdom, definitely look like a 'good old' tradition. Inside or outside the theatre, where are our bad new things?

NW: In Benjamin's essay on 'Surrealism' in *One-Way Street*, he wrote of the need to 'expel moral metaphor from politics and to discover in political action a sphere reserved one hundred per cent for images' (Benjamin 1979: 238). Benjamin's work is notoriously uneven and difficult to categorize, yet you seem here to stress that, in art, he favoured rather the opposite in discovering epic drama's allegorical metaphors so as to resist the seduction of autonomous, 'natural' images. Is there a potential split between Benjamin on politics and on art?

PW: Thinking about this question, I have decided, with some surprise, that the notion of metaphor is *irrelevant* to what Benjamin means by allegory. Common sense would suggest that it should be highly relevant: obviously allegory is a kind of metaphor, very often a 'moral' kind. But in fact that is not the point of Benjamin's interest in it at all. 'Allegory' in the *Trauerspiel* book is defined by its opposition with 'symbol'; both are, very broadly speaking, kinds of metaphor; the difference is that whereas the symbol discovers meaning within nature as a sort of inner transcendence, allegory breaks nature up and reads the bits as signs and clues of an external, preternatural meaning. Metaphor, in itself, does not necessarily either consolidate or disrupt the integrity of the natural – it all depends how it is done.

Allegory for Benjamin, then, is above all a destructive and ruinous force, especially in secular cultures where its disintegration of the profane world is not necessarily covered, so to speak, by the ulterior unity of the sacred. And if Benjamin usually seems to be 'on the side of' this destructive principle, against harmony, this is not only because he has a melancholic's taste for the fragmentary – though clearly he does. It is also because it is with him a point of revolutionary honour to regard all kinds of reconciliation with intense suspicion – the aesthetic reconciliation of spirit and matter no less than, and somewhat analogously to, the political reconciliation of classes in that 'bad poem on springtime' which is the programme of social democracy. He says all this in the essay you quote, where he is seeking to identify Surrealism as the literary movement that has the necessary degree of divisiveness. A year or two later, he found a more satisfying paradigm in epic theatre, not because it is metaphorical (it is not, particularly), but because, like baroque allegory, it reinterprets the world by wrecking its continuity.

NW: On p. 151 you point out how, where Falstaff is concerned, the actual 'duality of actor and role' tends to get subsumed both in a critical reading and an audience's responses in an appreciation of a 'unitary category of realistic character'. This inevitably produces an 'enigma', because Falstaff is a narrative function as well as a *dramatis persona*, and so what might be mistaken as psychological 'depth' is really the result of a 'confusion' of categories. Have I described your proposition accurately? In any case, is Falstaff a particularly marked example of this syndrome or is this *equally* true of all Shakespeare's work?

PW: Yes – that's more or less what I mean, though to me, at least, the paraphrase is no clearer than the original, and changes its emphasis in ways I do not recognize. For example, you say that Falstaff is a *dramatis persona* and also a 'narrative function'. That moves the point towards narratology and away from the stage. I meant that he is a *dramatis persona* and a comic entertainer. It is not a very refined point theoretically. Anyone can see that Edna Everage is not the same kind of stage phenomenon as Hedda Gabler; I am saying that Falstaff is more like Edna and less like Hedda than has often been supposed. Or again, my conclusion – 'the resulting confusion looks like depth' – becomes 'what might be mistaken as psychological depth is really the result of a confusion'. Your additions – 'mistaken', 'really' – give the proposition an epistemological dogmatism which is rather ridiculous in the context of a discussion of theatrical effects, and which I was seeking to avoid.

As for Falstaff's particularity: yes, he is a special case. As I have said, he has strong affiliations with the parodic Vice figures of the interludes, who inhabit a time and space which are as much those of the audience as those of a fictional world. Robert Weimann puts it very clearly when he says that the 'multi-conscious' mode of a play like *Henry IV* 'did not rest, ultimately, on a metaphysical principle, rather its vitality depended on the continuity of a style of acting that bridged the gap between play and audience, a stage position such as that occupied by the Garcio or Vice types, or the Elizabethan clown' (Weimann 1978: 190). That is, Falstaff's mode of being is not just the formal duality of all dramatic characters; it is a theatrically live and effectual doubleness because he is a clown, with the clown's irresponsible, half-in-half-out relation to the proper story. Of course, there are many Shakespearian clowns, but none of them is allowed Falstaff's licence to build a fictional environment around himself, or to dominate the stage in scene after scene. He is a unique collision of dramatic traditions, which Morgann rewrote, brilliantly, as a collision of psychological principles.

NW: I would like a little more on the suggestive comment you make on p. 140, that there is in both plays the sense of an 'arbitrarily imposed design' rather than some 'natural' extension of the narrative logic. Isn't this 'design' an author? If so, isn't the author responsible for *both* this base 'logic' *and* the 'willed, external agenda'?

PW: If you cut the Falstaff scenes from Part 1, you get a running order like this:

1 Opening scene, at the end of which a meeting of Council is announced.
2 Council meeting, at the end of which the Percy faction decides on insurrection.

3 Scene showing Hotspur organizing insurrection, at the end of which he and his wife set out to join the other rebels.
4 Scene showing Hotspur and his wife in the company of the other rebels . . .

And so on. Each scene lays out the ground which the next one then occupies; thus the ordering of events on the stage is, as it were, transparent; you seem to see straight through it to the order of events in the story. By interrupting this 'natural' sequence, so that each scene is followed, not by the one it made a space for, but by a different one which it was, so to speak, not expecting, the dramaturgy discloses an alien principle of composition, which is not implicit in the action but has been imposed upon it by a separate intention. No doubt this intention and the sequence it interrupts belong equally to the (individual or collective) 'author'; however, it is just that equality which makes the idea of the author irrelevant to the distinction I am trying to make. If the script were to suppress the alien principle and submit itself to a single story (as *Henry V* does, more or less), then it would be a different kind of show – not more or less 'authorial' but just differently structured. I am more interested in the dynamics of the play than I am in the metaphysics of authorship.

All the same, I do think it is interesting how chronicle drama proper – such as the non-Falstaff part of *Henry IV* – imposes external limits on the 'free' exercise of authorial invention. As I have said somewhere in the essay, it is not that facts are facts and you cannot change them: clearly dramatists do, and Shakespeare did. It is rather that in publicly adopting *information* as one of its functions, the theatre is presenting itself as secondary to the non-theatrical authority of its sources, which makes it impossible for the author to maintain his sovereignty in the realm of the text. In Part 2, for instance, actions like the tricking of the rebels at Gaultree Forest, or Hal's removal of his father's crown, are done with a sort of flat unexpectedness: they do not emerge 'organically' from the development of the drama, and they are not seriously 'explained'; rather, the scene's authority consists in the assurance that you are being shown something that actually did happen. I find this effect theatrically very exciting because of the hard externality of the style – you do not get any of the usual discreet guidance about what you are to make of these actions; the *gest* is, as it were, slammed down in front of you; the answer to the question 'Why are we watching this bit?' is not authorial ('because it illuminates so-and-so's character', 'because it balances the scene before') but scribal ('because that's how the book says it was').

Clearly a production which cultivated this explicit enslavement of drama by chronicle would be inviting its audience to watch in a very 'Brechtian' fashion.

NW: Do you discern a consistent ideology in both *Henry IV* plays? Or is this always a matter of performance?

PW: This is the question about subversion, isn't it? One says that *Henry IV* is a fundamentally subversive text; or that it generates subversion only in order to enact its containment and is therefore a fundamentally repressive text; or that it is a repressive text which inadvertently discloses the mechanisms of repression through its own formal slippages and can therefore be read as a fundamentally subversive text; etc. There is a strong tendency for this circular debate to get absurdly solemn. It is only a play, after all – it is not going to bring down the government, whatever we decide.

I prefer the model offered by Brecht's idealized version of the Berliner Ensemble at work on *Coriolanus*. After a long discussion of the first scene, the collaborators ask themselves what can be learned from a performance of it.

B. That the position of the oppressed classes can be strengthened by the threat of war and weakened by its outbreak . . .

P. That differences in income can divide the oppressed class.

R. That soldiers, and war victims even, can romanticize the war they survived and be easy game for new ones.

W. That the finest speeches cannot wipe away realities, but can hide them for a time.

R. That 'proud' gentlemen are not too proud to kowtow to their own sort.

P. That the oppressors' class isn't wholly united either.

B. And so on.

R. Do you think that all this and the rest of it can be read in the play?

B. Read in it and read into it.

(Brecht 1964: 264)

What does Brecht think is the 'consistent ideology' of *Coriolanus*? He has no interest in the question; there is no stage in the working process at which it needs answering. He and his associates are choosing to read the play for certain purposes and at a certain historical juncture (East Berlin in 1953), happily aware that other people, with different purposes at a different time and place, would come to quite different conclusions. Their discourse is light and pleasurable because no one is trying to decide what the play *is* – and this reveals by contrast the tense essentialism of the critical project which seeks to fix the relationship between 'the text' and 'power'. (What text? What power? Relationship for whom? etc.) Their attitude to the script is thus both more casual and more serious than that of our own left-critical establishment: more casual because they are perfectly prepared to misread it or rewrite it to suit their immediate purposes; and more serious because, in pursuit of those purposes, they subject this single scene to a minute analysis which makes most academic criticism, intent as it is on grander questions, look rushed and unspecific. As theatre people, they know that a play takes place moment by moment, and they are prepared to postpone totalization almost indefinitely. I am not sure that criticism would lose anything by following their example.

Endpiece

NIGEL WOOD

'To die is to be a counterfeit, for he is but the counterfeit of a man who hath not the life of a man; but to counterfeit dying, when a man thereby liveth, is to be no counterfeit, but the true and perfect image of life indeed' (*1 Henry IV*, V.iv.114–18) – but in what sense does Falstaff enjoy 'life'? Placed next to Hotspur's corpse, he receives Hal's familiar yet touching elegy, which places him in an unholy alliance with the newly slain chivalric hero, 'in blood' (V.iv.109), both by dint of the wash of shared blood that Hal expects from neighbours in death, but also with the association of the achieved consanguinity of martial fellowship. One line later, with Falstaff's resurrection, Hal's term is proved ironically apposite; 'in blood', as a hunting term, meaning 'in full vigour', now comes to be bathetically prescient. In A.R. Humphreys's (1960: 60, note to V.iv.109) crisp phrase, 'in this sense it is literally, and comically, true of the sham corpse'. The shock value of Falstaff's renewal also arrives from a different quarter. Just as it serves the plot as a basic necessity (he will be around for Hal to reject in Part 2), the irrepressible negation of Part 1's more heroic 'main' plot which Falstaff figures here takes actual physical shape. He may be visceral stuff, but, being thus, he is a 'true and perfect image' of life – not quite the thing itself.

It is one thing to enter this Hall of Mirrors and point out that Shakespeare dealt in fictions, quite another to catch its truth, either of representation or affective power. 'Counterfeiting', in any case, then embraced the acceptable action of imitating as well as the passing of false coin. One ought to call to mind just how Falstaff and Hotspur leave the stage, the one bearing the other on his back, much like the Morality devil hauling souls to Hell in, for example, Ulpian Fulwell's *Like Will to Like* (1562–8) or *Enough is as Good as a Feast* (*c*. 1560) (see Dessen 1974). Twenty-five lines earlier and Falstaff confounds Hal and his brother, by answering their consternation at his existence, 'Thou art not what thou seem'st', by protesting that he is no 'double man', and if not Jack Falstaff then a 'jack' or knave (V.iv.134–6). This is profound equivocation. There is no one else marching in Falstaff's coats that day (or since, unlike Henry IV) yet the verbal and visual associations we have just received establish his 'doubleness' (at least). It is as if the staging of Falstaff's 'reality' actually casts doubt on the identities of all those who come into close contact with him, and eventually of the realism of the whole dramatic event.

'In Dramatic composition the *Impression* is the *Fact*', according to Maurice Morgann in his famous *Essay on the Dramatic Character of Sir John Falstaff* (1777). As outlined in my Introduction, Morgann's significance in reassessing Falstaff's function in the *Henry IV* plays was to reclaim the characterization from outright ethical disdain. One might be able to select adequate textual testimony as to Falstaff's cowardice, yet still be unable to assess the register of purely verbal evidence. Falstaff managed to address an audience's immediate passions (one's '*mental Impressions*') rather than the '*Understanding*' (Morgann 1972: 146), or rather, he is a persona of such complexity that he provides opportunities for the judicial faculties (that 'condemn or applaud characters or actions on the credit of some logical process') to confront the obstinate singularity of unassimilable detail that causes our hearts to 'revolt' (Morgann 1972: 147). 'For the most part' we ought to 'look to the spirit rather than the letter of what is uttered', and involve ourselves in a discourse of 'humour, or folly, or jest' (Morgann 1972: 156).

The value of Morgann's approach lies in its refusal to regard Falstaff, or for that matter, most complex dramatic representations, simply as emblems or types. It is his '*Dramatic* Character' that should claim our attention, and this is composed of an effect on an audience as well as the calculations of a dramatist. While Morgann's work slots into critical historical place rather neatly as one of the first pieces of Character criticism, its emphases are not those of a naïve realism or an interest in some egoistic case study, the goals of contemporary examples of this strain of criticism, such as William Richardson's *Philosophical Analysis and Illustration of some of Shakespeare's Remarkable Characters* (1774) (see

Bate 1989: 144–6; and Vickers 1981). For Morgann, just as we may claim that his dramatic characters 'act and speak in strict conformity to nature', it is as much a reality of theatrical experience that they also exist 'in strict relation to us [as an audience]'. At the same time as Falstaff comes over as an original creation, his ethos is founded on nothing quite so distinct as an autonomous reflection of reality:

> The Chronicle, the Novel, or the Ballad; the king, or the beggar, the hero, the madman, the sot or the fool; it is all one; – nothing is worse, nothing is better: The same genius pervades and is equally admirable in all.
>
> (Morgann 1972: 171)

Intention here is not linear or even inexorable; it indicates a disinterested delight in aesthetic creation – not a programmatic and exclusive preoccupation with some isolatable thesis. Consequently, as Edward Burns has helpfully noted, it is vital for this notion that character remain distinct from action, and the ensuing potential for incongruity exploited (Burns 1990: 192–5). This is a far cry from A.C. Bradley's appreciation of tragedy as a reflection of some outer life: 'The centre of tragedy, therefore, may be said with equal truth to lie in action issuing from character, or in character issuing in action' (Bradley 1909: 7).

Morgann's complex account has been described in my Introduction. I here wish to use it as a point of entry into a particularly fraught debate that has raged recently about the supposed integrity of a work of art. For Morgann, Falstaff is both an individual and a representative, a testament to Shakespeare's original genius, that, to paraphrase Keats, in his letter to Richard Woodhouse (27 October 1818), is of no essential quality or 'character' and conceives as readily of the virtuous Imogen as the wicked Iago. What is radical about Morgann's *Essay*, according to A.D. Nuttall, is its development of a latent or 'under'-meaning, its bold assertion that an audience should infer what is deliberately not shown' (Nuttall 1983: 173–8). Nuttall quotes to good effect Morgann's note on the nature of Shakespeare's dramatic characters, where he so admires their 'certain roundness and integrity . . . a felt propriety and truth from causes unseen' (Morgann 1972: 167, 169), which truth we are encouraged to identify and bring to the dramatic experience. Nuttall's reading of this 'latency' is as follows:

> Morgann knew that if he could induce his reader to acknowledge a latent area, the business of exploring that area (by surmise and inference) would naturally involve some reliance on the known

character of the real world ... [He] is in fact proposing that where literature proposes probable human beings it is wholly natural and proper to apply one's sense of what is likely in real life ...

(Nuttall 1983: 174–5)

There is an important sense, here, wherein Nuttall's summary takes a direction not explicitly taken by Morgann – a signal case of creative 'inference'. Does Morgann expect us to find Falstaff emerging from 'the known character of the real world'? Is he 'probable', or even 'likely'? For all Nuttall's acute sense of the 'real' at this juncture, and his sensitive argument in favour of an enhanced mimesis, there is a current in the above argument that would return Falstaff to the 'known' and 'prob-able' – nearer to the typical than the exceptional. Morgann, in any case, is by no means consistent (as my commentary above indicates) in establishing a bridge that spans the fictive, contained in form, and the real, that provides our store of inspired guesses so that we may have some preliminary grasp of new meanings. In the same note from which Nuttall identifies Morgann's inferential method, there is just as much evidence to lead one to suppose that Falstaff was a great original, having his own 'first principles of *being*, and [having] an existence independent of the accidents, which form their magnitude or growth' (Morgann 1972: 168). Morgann is here very much more influenced by David Hume's departures from John Locke's empiricism in his 'borrowing' of his term, 'impressions' (found in the *Treatise of Human Nature* (1739–40)), than any convergence of view. For Hume, identity and a *substantial* nature were unknowable, open only to belief and the pas-sions. Morgann expends more effort in trying to trace this 'secret rela-tion' of nature than in embedding Falstaff in the 'probable' or 'likely'.

If this is admitted, then the range of permissible inference is con-siderably expanded, and this collection of essays could be said to exploit this. As Jonathan Goldberg reminds us, there is always an urgency in reminding ourselves that Shakespeare is not our contemporary. Our sexual norms, and thus our store of probabilities and types, appear to provide access to the past (our terms of reference seem to be linguis-tically similar), yet we are imperceptibly barred thereby from its alien assumptions. The path to this rediscovery has to be counter-intuitive. For Peter Womack, Falstaff's 'mode of being is parody' (this volume, p. 151), in that he is an awkward, yet salutary, reminder that the abstractions of exclusively textual interpretation rarely render the myriad of reversals he signifies – and *is*. Ronald Macdonald, in turning to Bakhtin's own understanding of 'heteroglossia', allows us to resist the imposition of premature critical closure, which enlists the plays all too readily to serve in royalist ranks, whereas Kiernan Ryan advances the initially unlikely proposition that the plays exhibit a prophetic and utopian power that is both historical *and* the stuff of hope and desire. As Ryan concludes, we ought to comprehend 'all the devices deliberately constructed [in the plays] to colour our vision and complicate our judgement' (p. 121). This is not obscurantist meandering, for, if it is granted that the most error-free mimetic model in this regard is not a direct brand that embraces an essentially unchanged human nature, then there has to be some violence of means to construct an alternative.

The more we consider the divisions of opinion on the point of just what constitutes a fictive 'character' the more we may be drawn into what might lie beneath the wider debates on the *Henry IV* plays. Nuttall's main targets are those who attempt to approach literature by resolving 'substance into form, fact into convention . . . in a fundamentally uncritical manner' (Nuttall 1983: 191). The aim of this collection is surely no different, and there may be an uncanny degree of convergence where certain preliminary forms of critical practice are concerned: the reference to areas of historical evidence, the attempts to realize past forms of knowing and being. Nuttall is persuasive and generous, to my mind, when he admits that the power of (and reason for) the seedy panorama of Eastcheap types that people both plays cannot be said to rest 'on psychological probability. It is thematic. It is Falstaff that Shakespeare needs and all the rest is a sort of moving cloud of circumambient Falstaffiana' (Nuttall 1983: 144). Alive to the layers of parody to which Falstaff inveterately gestures, Nuttall eventually concludes that the mutivalent aspect of the characterization 'is partly an effect of style' (Nuttall 1983: 151). The 'partly', however, should not be glossed over. For Alan Sinfield, 'essentialist humanism' is a form of critical short-circuit, where the identification of a distinct set of traits and thus of a subjectivity does not imply that the description 'Falstaffian' is a perennial feature and undergoes no significant alteration in the passage of time: 'This effaces the mechanisms of cultural production and their implication in power structures' (Sinfield 1992: 62).

What is really at stake emerges as a disagreement about the degree of due humility to pay to past monuments of intellect and feeling. To keep them unageing either entails a vast removal of pointless critical lumber to allow the perfectly sufficient artistic intention to shine through, on the one hand, or a constant vigilance to resist the critical entropy of antiquarianism *or* anachronism, on the other. To this end, two unhelpful and yet tenacious caricatures are tempting and often near at hand: historicists are not supposed to possess the requisite sensitivity to ambiguity and play in art, whereas deconstructive commentators are supposed to see nothing else as they collapse all into text. There are powerful vested interests at work here, and, one might note, neither Nuttall nor Sinfield actually fills either of these critical roles. Just as Nuttall distrusts the *esprit de système* of the structuralist paradigm that stresses relations between items at the expense of a recognition that such items can exist independently, his noting of hybridity and fictive *jeux d'esprit* is hardly formulaic. On the other hand, Sinfield, while resisting the lures of fixing on, to borrow a term from Jacques Derrida, some notion of a 'transcendental signified' (of ego or original meaning; see Derrida 1981: 49–50), still opens the text up to History (see Sinfield's treatment of Renaissance Protestantism and Puritan Humanism in Sinfield 1992: 143–213). Just because one loses faith in *meaning* does not mean that *meanings* cease to exist:

> continuous interiority in a dramatis persona can only be an effect of culture and its multiple discourses, and those can never be held to a determinate meaning ... There is no essential woman or man, but there are ideas of women and men and their consciousnesses, and these appear in representations.
>
> (Sinfield 1992: 63)

These are History too.

It would be disingenuous for me to appear neutral in this debate (the interests of the *Theory in Practice* series and my Introduction in this volume give the lie to that), but one's critical interests are not best served by creating paper tigers out of those who hold alternative views. Hal and Falstaff, however much we may feel that they have signified more, not less, consistently in productions of *Henry IV*, are not impervious to the present moment of their staging – 1795, 1895 or now. Renaissance concepts of character, in any case, advance far less unitary ideas of being. There are few more comprehensive accounts of this than Edward Burns's (1990: 6–38) careful identification of the classical heritage that formed a mix of rhetoric and self-identification in the period, the division between a 'substantive' concept (nearer to our more recent concern with a potentially autonomous self, defined by its ethical being) and a 'transactional' model (formed in a process of social interaction, an assumption of available personae that fit a variety of occasions):

> 'Character' is ... a central concern of rhetorical study. But the term is tied very closely to its original meaning, as an example,

metaphorically extended and elaborated, of one of the processes by which human beings recognise and are recognised as themselves.

(Burns 1990: 6; see also Weimann 1978)

This traversing of what in practice turn out to be separate meanings we are inclined clumsily to call simply 'character', yet the Aristotelian categories of *praxis* (what individuals do), *pathos* (what occurs to individuals) and *ethos* (what they are) were vital distinctions – and more exact descriptions of rhetorical function. It should not be alarming to liken Falstaff's dramatic power to the reception of Chinese boxes, when the search for content (a core personality) comes increasingly to appear beside the point, as the unwrapping is so rewarding.

What this consideration opens up to view is how Falstaff *affects* the narrative of the plays, and how he is implicit in several scenes where he is not physically present. One does not completely relinquish the delight at ironic reversal, verbal play and situational travesty once kings and rebels take the stage. For Stephen Greenblatt, this involves an appreciation of the theatrical display of royal power – and its obverse, the potentially destructive realism voiced by Falstaff. This tension actually adds to an audience's vigilance:

> prodded by constant reminders of a gap between real and ideal, the spectators are induced to make up the difference, to invest in the illusion of magnificence, to be dazzled by their own imaginary identification with the conqueror. The ideal king must be in large part the invention of the audience.
>
> (Greenblatt 1988: 63)

However, in a less reassuring reflection, Greenblatt also recognizes that the 'yoking of the unstable and the inevitable' also creates a significant space for 'voices that seem to dwell outside the realms ruled by the potentates of the land' (Greenblatt 1988: 43; but see the less convinced perspective advanced by Graham Bradshaw 1993: 80–122). This mix of styles carries its own political potential. As Erich Auerbach noticed in 1953, the element of 'physical creaturalness' and idiomatic diction takes from the sublime its unquestioned authority to *be*, naturally and effortlessly (Auerbach 1953: 312–33; see also, on the opportunities for parody in the Elizabethan theatre, Weimann 1978: 208–55). It survives, but only in a valley of its own making.

It is quite possible, therefore, to regard the demand for varying degrees of simple mimesis or the irreducibility of Falstaff ('What a character!') as a critical divide-and-rule, leaving the grand historical narrative towards Henry V relatively untouched. In holding to this more politicized approach to the Histories, one is inevitably laying less store by pure aestheticism. Consequently, when Barbara Everett applauds 'The Fatness of Falstaff', she poses an alternative to political codifying, using Falstaff and Launce's dog from *The Two Gentlemen of Verona* as prime examples. 'The thing worth knowing' is often in danger of a standardizing by the academic community into 'the thing capable of proof': the dog '*is,* beyond analysis: to be is as much the dog's function as it is Hamlet's. He is character as an end more than a means, the thing in itself'. This is capable of some flexibility, as Everett also notes that 'a character in his work is less a person than an insight, but an insight embodied into brilliant forms of the real' (Everett 1990: 18) – if the everyday 'real', then Falstaff is surely not 'brilliant', either in his stature or depiction; if the exceptional 'real', then why may this not be a fictional proposition, that departs from the expected to make a particular point, or offer an insight? Is it still (without qualification or necessary definition) 'real'? Furthermore, the evidence to hand is that Shakespeare created Falstaff and Launce's dog in a theatrical tradition quite distinct from nineteenth-century realism, where the integrity of an individual novelistic subjectivity is the result of an often carefully calculated strategy. As Burns and Weimann have discovered, strong 'character' is frequently a confluence point of associations that can be deployed for local effect or thematic development and that comprises *praxis* and *pathos* quite as much as *ethos.*

When in Act III, scene iv of *King Lear*, Lear comprehends perhaps for the first time 'the thing itself', 'Unaccommodated man', this 'poor, bare, forked animal' (III.iv.95–6) is not quite 'poor Tom', but, *in propria persona*, Edgar, the wronged son of Gloucester, who will inherit power at the play's conclusion. 'The thing itself' is here a notoriously unreliable entity, but that does not mean that Lear's insight is questioned by Edgar's disguise. The beauty of the torchlight plaints at Leonato's monument in *Much Ado About Nothing* (Act V, scene iii) and the elegies in Act IV, scene ii of *Cymbeline* are not rendered gratuitous because the audience knows that Hero, Posthumus and Imogen are in fact still alive. Portia's sentiments on mercy (*The Merchant of Venice*, IV.i) are no less resounding because she, too, has adopted a 'counterfeit' persona through which to utter them. What is more probable is that there are frequent occasions when the verbal texture of a Shakespeare play need not take its rise from the 'character' of its spokesperson or, with Launce's dog in mind, the immediate exigencies of the plot – and, to my mind, this makes Falstaff more, not less, interesting.

Notes

Introduction

1 As Melchiori (1989: 116) notes, there is here an allusion to Ovid's *Metamorphoses* 15: 287–90 – here in Golding's translation (1567):

> Euen so haue places oftentymes exchaunged theyr estate.
> For I haue seene it sea which was substanciall ground alate,
> Ageine where sea was, I haue seene the same become dry lond,
> And shelles and scales of Seafish farre haue lyen from any strond.
> (Golding 1961: 300).

The expression of mutability also stems from Spenser's *Mutabilitie Cantos* (pub. 1609) (Books vi and vii). There, in terms similar to those deployed in Hooker's *Ecclesiastical Polity*, Spenser has Nature drive out the corruption of Mutability (see Book VII, canto viii, sts 1–2). In Shakespeare's account, there is no natural standard against which to identify the limits of Chance.

2 As Ricardo Quinones makes clear, the ideology of self-improvement compensated for a weakening of faith in linear concepts of history, at the same time as it was threatened by a revival of *Fortuna*'s power (see Quinones 1972: 181–6). See also Kastan (1982: 3–36 – and on the Histories, 37–55), and Rackin (1990: 16–18, 137–8). History, thus, could become something 'made' (see Bergeron 1991; and Rackin 1990, 1–39).

3 The tract most favoured by Tillyard (1944; 72–6) was the anonymous *Sermon of Obedience or An Exhortation concerning good Ordre and Obedience to Rulers and Magistrates* (*c*. 1574), which took rebellion as the chief example of human presumption. See also John Ponet's *A Short Treatise of Politic*

Power (1556), sigs. Gviii–Gviii ᵛ, and the homily issued by Elizabeth and her Council in 1570 just after the suppression of the Northern Rebellion of 1569: *An Homilie Agaynst Disobedience and Wylful Rebellion*, sigs. Bi–Bi ᵛ. See also Reed (1984: 43–65) (although the identification of a fully conceptualized artistic framework in the Histories seems too schematic), and Rozett (1984: 41–73).

4 Once again, Melchiori (1989: 118) identifies a familiar basis for the sentiment, here pointing to Warwick's embrace of the classical concept of *Historia magistra vitae*, History instructing life.

5 The Quarto description of Rumour, 'painted full of tongues', points directly to a Morality dramatic tradition, and links the figure with Fame or Report. See Melchiori (1989, 15–18), and also Abrams (1986).

6 George Daniel of Beswick's *Trinarchodia* (1647) testifies to the long-standing understanding of the possible calumny:

> Here to evince the scandal, has been thrown
> Upon a name of honour (charactered
> From a wrong person, coward, and buffoon);
> Call in your easy faiths, from what ye have read
>   To laugh at Falstaff, as an humour framed
>   To grace the stage, to please the age, misnamed.
>   (Daniel 1878, 4: 113)

7 The best review of these comments can be found in Dollimore and Sinfield's 'History and Ideology: The Instance of *Henry V*', in Drakakis (1985: 206–27), to be supplemented by Dollimore's own identification of the decentring of Man in Dollimore (1989: 53–69), and in 'The Disintegration of Providentialist Belief' (1989: 83–108).

8 It ought to be pointed out how partial Shakespeare's view was, given the unflattering portrait of the corrupt Richard in the anonymous *Woodstock* (*c.* 1592) and the honour accorded the rebels – in a text that Shakespeare used in the writing of *Richard II* (see Gurr 1984: 11–16). This was also the view of *The Mirror for Magistrates* (1559), which otherwise proclaims against rebellion: Richard 'wurketh his wil, and shunneth wisedomes sawes,/In flateries clawes, and shames foule pawes shal light' (Campbell 1938: 120).

9 Man's helplessness is noted in Article X, 'Of Free Will', in the Thirty-nine Articles:

> The condition of man after the fall of Adam is such, that he cannot turn and prepare himself, by his own natural strength and good works, to faith, and calling on God; Wherefore we have no power to do good works pleasant and acceptable to God, without the grace of God by Christ preventing us . . .
>   (Rivers 1979: 128)

10 The controversy over the interpretation of this Article provoked the Archbishop of Canterbury, John Whitgift, to issue the Lambeth Articles in 1595, which reaffirmed Calvinist orthodoxy. Article 9 made it clear that 'It is not placed in the will or power of every man to be saved' (Pincess and Lockyer 1990: 48).

11 Thomas Starkey's elevation of Natural Law, for example, perceived 'a certain wit and policy by nature given to man' that could order civil rule. These 'virtues', indeed, stood not 'in the opinion of man, but by the benefit and power of nature in his heart are rooted and planted, inclining him ever to the civil life, according to the excellent dignity of his nature' (Starkey 1948: 30–1). It was evidently a commonsensical course to obey this *inner* prompting.

12 Holinshed has it that Oldcastle was eventually sent to the Tower, and escaped to Wales, leaving behind him riots provoked by his Lollard supporters. Oldcastle was subsequently outlawed, until captured and executed in 1417. Henry V's clemency and devotion to the idea of a Christian king is clear in Holinshed's account. Oldcastle was guilty of 'heresie', and he is allowed to enter the new king's presence to be examined on this count: 'The king first having compassion of the noble man, required the prelats, that if he were a straied sheepe, rather by gentlenes than by rigor to reduce him to the fold' (Bullough 1957–75, 4: 376). Shakespeare has Hal resort far more to 'rigor' than 'gentlenes'.

13 The quibble on 'instinct' at II.iv.345–6 is not, to my mind, simply taproom badinage. Hal picks this up in a subtly different context when Falstaff imagines the thrill in the blood at the prospect of meeting Hotspur and Glendower – a return but with interest:

> FALSTAFF: . . . Art thou not horribly afraid? Doth not thy blood thrill at it?
> PRINCE HENRY: Not a whit, i'faith. I lack some of thy instinct.
>
> (II.iv.357–9)

14 See note 12. Stow, however, is detailed in his account of Oldcastle's misdemeanours afterwards. See Bullough (1957–75, 4: 291–2) for the description of what amounted to a Lollard rebellion. Oldcastle was eventually 'hanged by the necke in a chayne of iron, and after consumed with fire' (Bullough 1957–75, 4: 292).

15 A detailed version of this point can be found in Jeffrey Stern's 'The Sins of the Fathers: "Prince Hal's Conflict" Reconsidered', in Moraitis and Pollock (1987: 487–502).

16 This is probably the scope of the allusion at *2 Henry IV*, II.ii.114, where the Page tells Hal that Falstaff is keeping Ephesian company at Eastcheap.

17 Tillyard's thesis neglected the opportunities for satire and irony. Disorder was portrayed so that the 'larger principle of order in the background' could eventually reassert itself: 'In his most violent representations of chaos

Shakespeare never tries to persuade that it is the norm: however long and violent is its sway, it is unnatural; and in the end order and the natural law will reassert themselves' (Tillyard 1944: 319, 23).

18 Grady's general picture is one of a long trek to postmodernism. His views on early Marxist readings of Falstaff can be found in Grady (1991: 8–14). See also his description of the context for Tillyard's work in Grady (1991: 158–89).

1 Hal's Desire, Shakespeare's Idaho

This essay includes materials (mainly drawn from a chapter entitled 'Desiring Hal') reworked from my *Sodometries* (Goldberg 1992b). The earliest drafts of this essay profited from the advice and enthusiasm of Michael Moon and Eve Kosofsky Sedgwick, while its current state would not have been possible without Jonathan Brody Kramnick.

1 For the purposes at hand, the most notable exception would be Findlay (1989). Findlay reads Hal as the locus of a homophobia inflicted upon the more or less sodomitical Falstaff, an argument which mine seeks to further by marking ways in which the play fails to deliver the exemplary Hal that Findlay's reading assumes. By so doing, I hope to move sodomy from the archaic and marginal position that it occupies in Findlay's essay, and to allow it the space of a recognition that would trouble received readings of the play of various critical stripes.

2 'For the respectes aforesayd in all former ages and in the most civill coun-treys and commons wealthes, good Poets and Poesie were highly esteemed and much favoured of the greatest Princes ... king *Henry* the 8, her *Majesties* father, for a few Psalmes of *David* turned into English meetre by Sternhold, made him groome of his privy chamber & gave him many other good gifts' (Smith 1904, 2: 16–17).

3 In 'Fetishizing Gender: Constructing the Hermaphrodite in Renaissance Europe' (Epstein and Straub 1991: 80–111), Ann Rosalind Jones and Peter Stallybrass have suggested that the biologistic bias in gender definition (the assumption that genitals are the physical bedrock upon which gender is founded) is questionable not only theoretically, as has often been argued, but also historically; the assumption is, they claim, a modern one and not to be found in Renaissance texts about the body which posit socio-legal definitions of gender as the bedrock of difference.

4 These patriarchal fantasmatics are traced in Montrose (1983: 70–1). Although Montrose connects the lines that Theseus speaks in I.i.47–51 to the fight over the Indian boy, he is silent about the sexual connection that the child represents; for that point, one can turn to Crewe (1986: 148–51) for a somewhat pathologizing view of Oberon's desire for the boy as, in

Crewe's terms, his 'pathic'. Nevertheless, Crewe sees that the boy is written much as the young man is in the sonnets, and that as changeling he is the very locus for a series of crossings in the play.

5 Hal's imagery answers his initial accusation that Falstaff is 'fat-witted with drinking of old sack' (I.ii.2–3); the connection between 'vapors' and flatulence is made over and again in Ben Jonson's *Bartholomew Fair* (1614, pub. 1631; in Jonson 1981–2). See especially IV.iv.45–98.

6 See Empson (1950: 102–9), in the essay on 'They that have power to hurt'.

7 These are not unlike the terms of patriarchy described by Luce Irigaray in *This Sex Which Is Not One* (Irigaray 1985: 192–3). Where this critique parts company with Irigaray is in her supposition that such male–male relations (for example, the pederasty that lurks in father–son relations) mask homosexuality *tout court* as the secret of homosociality (this is the argument that her nonce word 'hom[m]osexuality' conveys), since it leaves no room for the recognition that the policing of homosexuality is complicit with the policing of women, and that there is a world of difference between homosexuality and homophobia. This is a point argued against Irigaray by Craig Owens in 'Outlaws: Gay Men in Feminism', in Jardine and Smith (1987: 223–4), which draws upon the exemplary discussions of Eve Kosofsky Sedgwick such as the one in the introduction to Sedgwick (1985: 19–20).

8 I am grateful to Jonathan Brody Kramnick for suggesting to me this crucial overlap.

9 This is much less true for women given their position under patriarchy and their definitional status acquired through marriage. But it is not entirely untrue, as Valerie Traub begins to suggest in 'Desire and the Difference It Makes', in Wayne (1991: 81–114), an essay included in Traub (1992: 91–116).

10 See W.H. Auden, 'The Prince's Dog', in Auden (1948), which does make some valuable connections between the sonnets and the relationship in the play, but which also insists on the fat knight's narcissism, infantilism, feminization and alcoholism.

11 Patricia Parker (1987: 20) declares Falstaff an 'obvious Shakespearean "fat lady"' on the basis of his girth and his tongue; it is difficult to see in whose interest such an identification is made.

12 Michael Moon and Eve Kosofsky Sedgwick (1990–1) offer a sustained meditation on these questions. For the relationships between body size and social organization in the transition to capitalist social organization – towards the modernity incipient in Shakespeare's plays, see Mennell (1987), especially his discussion on p. 397 of the ways in which an older aristocratic corpulence becomes the body of the poor as the new regimes of civilization preach restraint. Falstaff's body is, in these terms, legible under both the old and new regimes.

13 This is Valerie Traub's (1989) argument. 'The homoerotics of the Henriad

deserve fuller treatment', Traub notes, only immediately to figure that sexuality as Hal's masculinity played in relation to Falstaff's femininity (p. 465).

14 I owe this connection to Jonathan Brody Kramnick.

15 For example:

> A woman's face, with Nature's own hand painted,
> Hast thou, the master-mistress of my passion;
> A woman's gentle heart, but not acquainted
> With shifting change, as is false women's fashion; . . .
>
> (ll.1–4)

See also Bruce Smith (1991: 248–52) for a reading which stresses the way that the homosocial becomes homosexual at this point.

16 Fantasmatic since the mechanisms of repression are, as Foucault argued, productive, but fantasmatic, too, because the private is continually policed and regulated to this day, and the sanctioned forms of sexuality that are secured are the ones that ensure the perpetuation of procreative sex within a compulsory heterosexuality. The 1986 US Supreme Court decision in *Bowers* v. *Hardwick*, denying any constitutional right to private consensual acts of what the Court termed 'homosexual sodomy', makes this all too clear.

17 The man 'who'd given him the poison, . . . pinched his foot hard, and asked him if he could feel it, and Socrates said not. After that he felt his shins once more; and moving upwards in this way, he showed us that he was becoming cold and numb' (Plato 1975: 72). I am aware of the caveat offered by Gary Taylor in his note to the Oxford *Henry V*, II.iii.22–4, but the resemblance seems too striking to ignore.

18 Porter (1988) reads Mercutio as a figure for Marlowe, and his relationship with Romeo in counterpoint to Romeo's relationship with Juliet.

2 Uses of Diversity

1 The brief story is told in Genesis 11: 1–9. Quotations are from the Authorized Version.

2 The distinction between what is given and what is posited, a central one in Bakhtin's work, may be traced to his early immersion in the neo-Kantian thought of the Marburg School in Germany, which flourished in the first years of the twentieth century, and particularly to the ideas of Hermann Cohen, who summed up his position by asserting that 'the world is not given, but conceived' ('Die Welt ist nicht gegeben, sondern aufgegeben'). Cited by Katerina Clark and Michael Holquist (1984: 59).

3 I say 'colleague' as the safest sort of generalization. There are those, including his English translators, who maintain that the work Voloshinov

signed properly belongs to him, while others believe it is actually work which Bakhtin published under Voloshinov's name for prudential reasons. The case for Voloshinov's authorship may be consulted in Morson and Emerson (1990: 101–20); the case for Bakhtin's in Clark and Holquist (1984: 146–70). For the present study, it is enough to recognize that Bakhtin and Voloshinov had much in common, including terminology.

4 I have preserved the more usual transliteration of Voloshinov's name, substituting 'sh' for the translators' diacritically modified 's'.

5 I except Voloshinov from the denial of final words, because he seems to have been a committed materialist dialectician and thus would have antic- ipated a dialectical resolution to the historical process at some point in the future. Bakhtin, on the other hand, seems to have been sceptical about any kind of 'finalization', any kind of utopian thinking in whatever guise. For an account of Bakhtin's Marxism, or the lack of it, see Morson's and Emer- son's account of the disputed texts in Morson and Emerson (1990: 101–19).

6 It should be noted that Bakhtin specifically classed drama among the 'monologically deaf' genres, those, like lyric poetry, that in his estimation exclude heteroglossia and attempt to place a single voice beyond dispute or rejoinder. 'Pure drama strives toward a unitary language, one that is individualized merely through dramatic personae who speak it' (Bakhtin 1981: 405). But Bakhtin allows in a footnote to this passage that he is speaking of 'the ideal extreme of the [dramatic] genre'. 'Contemporary realistic social drama', he continues, 'may, of course, be heteroglot and multi-languaged.' Surely he would have recognized Shakespeare's plays, notorious hybrids in which highbrow and lowbrow strains, classical and native traditions are joined, as participating in authentic heteroglossia.

7 The term for such reflexiveness, 'metatheatrics', was introduced by Lionel Abel (1963). Since this inauguration, many studies have pursued the topic of drama about drama, important among them Calderwood (1971). The title of Calderwood's chapter on *Richard II*, 'The Fall of Language', suggests the common ground between his approach and that of the current study.

8 Louis Adrian Montrose has suggested that the frequency with which we encounter some version of the Elizabethan World Picture in fifteenth- century documents is evidence not of its universal and uncritical acceptance, but of its tenuousness. See Montrose (1980).

9 'Si un homme qui se croit un roi est fou, un roi qui se croit un roi ne l'est pas moin' (Lacan 1966: 170).

10 See 'Invisible Bullets', collected along with several other of Greenblatt's altogether interesting essays in Greenblatt (1988). The point concerning Falstaff's unfortunate anticipation of Henry's sententious lament about the burdens of the dominant classes may be found on pp. 54–5 of that volume.

11 See Bakhtin's essay 'Epic and Novel', in Bakhtin (1981: 31). In this same passage Bakhtin remarks: 'Prophecy is characteristic for the epic, prediction for the novel.'

4 *Henry IV* and Epic Theatre

1 There are two German words for tragedy – *Tragödie* and *Trauerspiel*. The first is the classical term, which therefore suggests Attic tragedy; it is, for example, the word used in Nietzsche's title *The Birth of Tragedy* (1872), a book with which Benjamin is in dialogue. *Trauerspiel* is a purely Germanic word: *Trauer* means grief or mourning, and *Spiel* means a play, so the term could be said to eschew fomal implications and simply denote, as George Steiner elegantly puts it, a play of sorrow (Benjamin 1977: 24). In ordinary speech the two words are used almost interchangeably, but Benjamin's monograph sets out to establish German *Trauerspiel* as an autonomous genre: not Aristotelian *Tragödie* which fails to master its form, but non-Aristotelian tragic drama.

His particular primary texts are the *Trauerspiele* of the period during and after the Thirty Years' War (1618–48) which left much of Germany materially and culturally devastated. The best-known names (even these are not particularly well known outside the sphere of German literary study) are those of Andreas Gryphius (1616–64) and Daniel Caspar von Lohenstein (1635–83). The plays mostly present historical, biblical or legendary monarchs, whose stories they resolve into the terms of Court intrigue; the characteristic figures of the drama are the tyrant, the martyr, the scheming courtier. They are baroque in their combination of physical horror, erudite linguistic artifice, and the unrestricted use of allegory in the formation both of the *dramatis personae* and of the imagery. Informed by an intense and usually Protestant piety, they dwell moralistically on the falsity and transience of the world and the destructive effects of passion, themes which they ennoble through the rank of their protagonists and through an addiction to apotheosis, divine intervention, and magical evocations of the spirit world.

For an English reader, much of this suggests an analogy with Jacobean tragedy, which may indeed have influenced the German genre through the tours of English actors in the early part of the seventeenth century. Benjamin seems not to have come across writers such as Marston and Webster, whom he would have found interesting; he does argue that the ultimate *Trauerspiel*, the play in which the genre realizes itself way beyond the scope of any of the German practitioners, is *Hamlet*. The decisive difference between England and Germany is that England had a living public theatre, whereas the German writers, surviving as Court protégés in the fragmented world left by the war, were forced back on an academic conception of the dramatic. It is not certain that the plays were ever staged; whether they were or not, the dramatists thought of themselves not as playmakers, but as poets, making use of a dignified form to raise German letters above a prevailing barbarism.

2 That is, Brooks (1949). See also Eagleton (1981: 3–19).

3 The other versions are on pp. 18–19 and 100.

4 'Tragedy is the representation of an action, and it is chiefly on account of the action that it is also a representation of persons' (Aristotle, *On the Art of Poetry*, Chapter 6, quoted from Dorsch 1965: 40). It follows that the *dramatis persona* should be constructed first and last as the doer of his deed. Consequently the sage, whose distinctiveness consists not of his action but of his thought, is excessive or even disruptive to the economy of the 'dramatic'. It is true that here, as usual, Aristotle is speaking specifically about tragedy. But a long tradition has extended his principles to drama in general; it is precisely to resist this generalization that Benjamin insists that *Tragödie* and *Trauerspiel* are not the same thing.

5 This passage appears in Benjamin (1973b: 17–18); but I have preferred the translation by Harry Zohn in Benjamin (1973a: 151–2).

6 Victor Hugo (1864), in Bate (1992: 227).

7 From Coleridge's *Table Talk*, in Bate (1992: 161).

8 Adrian Noble's production of both parts at the Royal Shakespeare Theatre, Stratford, in 1991, and the Barbican Theatre, London, in 1992. The critical orthodoxy can be seen, strikingly, at the end of Smidt's own book (Smidt 1982: 162–6), which recuperates Shakespeare from his errors in terms not very different from those of Johnson's 1765 Preface.

9 'The one question left open in Tudor divine right teaching was this: who is the king appointed by God? The Tudor answer was pragmatic: whoever happens to be recognized as king. Anything more philosophical would have been awkward for a dynasty whose original claim was very weak' (G.R. Elton, 'The Divine of Right of Kings', in Elton 1974, 2: 204).

10 Benjamin himself quotes a relevant account of the south German *Haupt- und Staatsaktion*: see Benjamin (1977: 123–4).

11 The point is made by William Empson in his essay 'Falstaff', in Empson 1986, 29–78 (38).

12 For a well-informed version of a widely advanced thesis, see Dessen (1986).

13 This way of looking at Falstaff begins with Barber (1957: 192–221).

14 See Sir Philip Sidney on 'naughty play-makers and stage keepers' who 'stir laughter in sinful things, which are rather execrable than ridiculous' (Sidney 1965: 117, 137); and Jonson's attack on 'theatrical wit, right stage-jesting, and relishing a play-house' in *Discoveries*, accessibly in Jonson (1975: 454).

15 See *2 Henry IV*, I.i.19; II.ii.101–3; IV.i.367–8. Ingleby *et al.* (1909), contains more early seventeenth-century allusions to Falstaff than to any other character, or than almost any entire play. The compilers' headnote to their index of Shakespeare's works (1909, 2: 536) sums up the situation: 'For the purposes of this index, Falstaff is treated as a work.'

16 This hypothesis informs Melchiori's edition of Part 2 (Melchiori 1989). The idea that Part 2 is therefore a 'pot-boiler' appears in David (1953).

References

Unless otherwise stated, place of publication is London.

Abel, Lionel (1963) *Metatheatre: A New View of Dramatic Form*. New York.

Abrams, Richard (1986) Rumor's reign in *2 Henry IV*: The scope of a personification, *English Literary Renaissance*, 16: 467–95.

Adorno, Theodor (1974) *Minima Moralia*, trans. E.F.N. Jephcott.

Althusser, Louis (1977) *Lenin and Philosophy and Other Essays*, trans. Ben Brewster. (1st edn, 1971.)

Auden, W.H. (1948) *The Dyer's Hand*. New York.

Auerbach, Erich (1953) *Mimesis: The Representation of Reality in Western Literature*, trans. Willard R. Trask. Princeton, NJ.

Bakhtin, Mikhail (1981) *The Dialogical Imagination: Four Essays by M.M. Bakhtin*, ed. Michael Holquist and trans. Caryl Emerson and Michael Holquist. Austin, TX.

Bakhtin, Mikhail (1984a) *Rabelais and his World*, trans. Helene Iswolsky. Bloomington, IN.

Bakhtin, Mikhail (1984b) *Problems of Dostoevsky's Poetics*, ed. and trans. Caryl Emerson. Minneapolis, MN.

Barber, C.L. (1959) *Shakespeare's Festive Comedy: A Study of Dramatic Form and Its Relation to Social Custom*. Princeton, NJ.

Barish, Jonas (1981) *The Antitheatrical Prejudice*. Berkeley, CA.

Bate, Jonathan (1989) *Shakespearean Constitutions: Politics, Theatre, Criticism, 1730–1830*. Oxford.

Bate, Jonathan (ed.) (1992) *The Romantics on Shakespeare*. Harmondsworth.

Benjamin, Walter (1973a) *Illuminations*, ed. Hannah Arendt, trans. Harry Zohn. (1st English edn, 1968; orig. pub. as *Schriften*, 1955.)

Benjamin, Walter (1973b) *Understanding Brecht*, trans. Anna Bostock.

Benjamin, Walter (1977) *The Origin of German Tragic Drama*, trans. John Osborne.

Benjamin, Walter (1978) *Reflections: Essays, Aphorisms, Autobiographical Writings*, ed. Peter Demetz, trans. Edmund Jephcott.

Benjamin, Walter (1979) *One-Way Street, and Other Writings*, trans. Edmund Jephcott and Kingsley Shorter (orig. pub. as *Einbahnstrasse*, 1955).

Berger, Harry, Jr (1989) *Imaginary Audition: Shakespeare on Page and Stage*. Berkeley, CA.

Bergeron, David (1991) Shakespeare makes history: 2 Henry IV, *Studies in English Literature*, 31: 231–45.

Bevington, David (1968) *Tudor Drama and Politics: A Critical Approach to Topical Meaning*. Cambridge, MA.

Bevington, David (1987) Introduction, in David Bevington (ed.), *Henry IV, Part 1*. Oxford.

Bloch, Ernst (1959) *Das Prinzip Hoffnung*. Frankfurt.

Boone, Joseph A. and Cadden, Michael (eds) (1990) *Engendering Men: The Question of Male Feminist Criticism*. New York.

Bradley, A.C. (1909) *Oxford Lectures on Poetry*.

Bradshaw, Graham (1993) *Misrepresentations: Shakespeare and the Materialists*. Ithaca, NY.

Braunmuller, A.R. and Hattaway, Michael (eds) (1990) *The Cambridge Companion to Renaissance Drama*. Cambridge.

Bray, Alan (1982) *Homosexuality in Renaissance England*.

Bray, Alan (1990) Homosexuality and the signs of male friendship in Elizabethan England, *History Workshop*, 29: 1–19.

Brecht, Bertolt (1964) *Brecht on the Theatre*, ed. John Willett.

Brecht, Bertolt (1976) *Poems*, ed. John Willett and Ralph Manheim.

Bredbeck, Gregory W. (1991) *Sodomy and Interpretation: Marlowe to Milton*. Ithaca, NY.

Brooks, Cleanth (1949) The *Well-Wrought Urn*.

Bullough, Geoffrey (1957–75) *Narrative and Dramatic Sources of Shakespeare*, 8 vols.

Burckhardt, Sigurd (1968) *Shakespearean Meanings*. Princeton, NJ.

Burns, Edward (1990) *Character: Acting and Being on the Pre-Modern Stage*.

Butler, Judith (1992) The lesbian phallus and the morphological imaginary, *differences*, 4: 133–75.

Calderwood, James L. (1971) *Shakespearean Metadrama: The Argument of the Play in Titus Andronicus, Love's Labour's Lost, Romeo and Juliet, A Midsummer Night's Dream, and Richard II*. Minneapolis, MN.

Campbell, Lily B. (ed.) (1938) *The Mirror for Magistrates*. Cambridge.

Campbell, Lily B. (1947) *Shakespeare's Histories: Mirrors of Elizabethan Policy*. San Marino, CA.

Cave, Terence (1979) *The Cornucopian Text: Problems of Writing in the French Renaissance*. Oxford.

Clark, Katerina and Holquist, Michael (1984) *Mikhail Bakhtin*. Cambridge, MA.

Crane, Mary Thomas (1985) The Shakespearean tetralogy, *Shakespeare Quarterly*, 36: 282–99.

Crewe, Jonathan (1986) *Hidden Designs: The Critical Profession and Renaissance Literature*. New York.

Crewe, Jonathan (1990) Reforming Prince Hal: The sovereign inheritor in 2 *Henry IV*, *Renaissance Drama*, n.s. 21: 225–42.

Daniel, George (1878) *The Poems of George Daniel (1616–1657)*, ed. Alexander B. Grosart, 4 vols. Boston, MA.

David, Richard (1953) Shakespeare's history plays – epic or drama?, *Shakespeare Survey*, 6: 129–39.

Dean, Paul (1990) Forms of time: some Elizabethan two-part history plays, *Renaissance Studies*, 4: 410–30.

Derrida, Jacques (1981) *Positions*, trans. Alan Bass. Chicago (1st edn 1972).

Dessen, Alan (1974) The intemperate knight and the politic prince: Late morality structure in *1 Henry IV*, *Shakespeare Studies*, 7: 147–71.

Dessen, Alan (1986) *Shakespeare and the Late Moral Plays*. Lincoln, NB.

Dollimore, Jonathan (1989) *Radical Tragedy: Religion, Ideology and Power in the Drama of Shakespeare and his Contemporaries*. Hemel Hempstead (1st edn 1984).

Dollimore, Jonathan (1991) *Sexual Dissidence: Augustine to Wilde, Freud to Foucault*. Oxford.

Dollimore, Jonathan and Sinfield, Alan (1990) Culture and textuality: Debating cultural materialism, *Texual Practice*, 4(1): 91–101.

Dorsch, T.S. (ed.) (1965) *Classical Literary Criticism*. Harmondsworth.

Drakakis, John (ed.) (1985) *Alternative Shakespeares*.

Eagleton, Terry (1981) *Walter Benjamin, or, Towards a Revolutionary Criticism*.

Eagleton, Terry (1986) *Shakespeare*. Oxford.

Eagleton, Terry (1990) *The Ideology of the Aesthetic*. Oxford.

Eagleton, Terry (1991) *Ideology: An Introduction*.

Elton, G.R. (1974) *Studies in Tudor and Stuart Politics and Government*, 2 vols. Cambridge.

Empson, William (1950) *Some Versions of Pastoral*. (1st edn 1935.)

Empson, William (1986) *Essays on Shakespeare*, ed. David B. Pirie. Cambridge.

Epstein, Julia and Straub, Kristina (eds) (1991) *Body Guards: The Cultural Politics of Gender Ambiguity*. New York.

Evans, Malcolm (1986) *Signifying Nothing: Truth's True Contents in Shakespeare's Text*. Brighton.

Everett, Barbara (1990) The fatness of Falstaff, *London Review of Books*, 12: 18–22.

Findlay, Heather (1989) Renaissance pederasty and pedagogy: The 'case' of Shakespeare's Falstaff, *Yale Journal of Criticism*, 3: 229–38.

Foucault, Michel (1972) *The Archaeology of Knowledge and the Discourse on*

Language, trans. A.M. Sheridan Smith. (1st edn 1969, pub. as *L'Archéologie de Savoir*.)

Foucault, Michel (1978) *The History of Sexuality* Vol. 1, *An Introduction*, trans. Robert Hurley. (1st edn 1976.)

Foucault, Michel (1988) *Politics, Philosophy, Culture: Interviews and Other Writings, 1977–1984*, ed. Lawrence D. Kritzman. New York.

Garber, Marjorie (1992) *Vested Interests: Cross Dressing and Cultural Anxiety*. New York.

Goldberg, Jonathan (1986) *Voice – Terminal – Echo: Post-Modernism and English Renaissance Texts*.

Goldberg, Jonathan (1990) *Writing Matter: From the Hands of the English Renaissance*. Stanford, CA.

Goldberg, Jonathan (1992a) The commodity of names: 'Falstaff' and 'Oldcastle' in *1 Henry IV, Bucknell Review*, 35: 76–88.

Goldberg, Jonathan (1992b) *Sodometries: Renaissance Texts, Modern Sexualities*. Stanford, CA.

Golding, Arthur (1961) *Shakespeare's Ovid: Being Arthur Golding's Translation of the Metamorphoses* [1565–76], ed. W.H.D. Rouse.

Goldmann, Lucien (1964) *The Hidden God*, trans. Philip Thody.

Grady, Hugh (1991) *The Modernist Shakespeare: Critical Texts in a Material World*. Oxford.

Greenblatt, Stephen (1988) *Shakespearean Negotiations*. Oxford.

Gurr, Andrew (1984) Introduction, in Andrew Gurr (ed.), *Richard II*. Cambridge.

Harvey, Elizabeth D. and Maus, Katharine Eisaman (eds) (1990) *Soliciting Interpretation: Literary Theory and Seventeenth-Century Poetry*. Chicago.

Hayman, Ronald (1983) *Bertolt Brecht: A Biography*.

Hodgdon, Barbara (1991) *The End Crowns All: Closure and Contradiction in Shakespeare's History*. Princeton, NJ.

Hodgdon, Barbara (1993) *Henry IV, Part Two* (Shakespeare in Performance series). Manchester.

Holderness, Graham (1992) *Shakespeare Recycled: The Making of Historical Drama*. Hemel Hempstead.

Holinshed, Raphael (1907) *Shakespeare's Holinshed*. New York.

Hooker, Richard (1989) *Of the Laws of Ecclesiastical Polity*, ed. Arthur Stephen McGrade. Cambridge.

Horst, Carl (1912) *Barockprobleme*. Munich.

Howard, Jean (1994) *The Stage and Social Struggle in Early Modern England*.

Humphreys, A.R. (ed.) (1960) *The First Part of King Henry IV*.

Ingleby, C.M., Toulmin-Smith, L. and Furnivall, F.J. (eds) (1909) *The Shakspere Allusion Book: A Collection of Allusions to Shakspere from 1591–1700* (re-edited by John Munro), 2 vols. (Orig. edn 1874.)

Irigaray, Luce (1985) *This Sex Which Is Not One*, trans. Catherine Porter. Ithaca, NY.

Iser, Wolfgang (1993) *Staging Politics: The Lasting Impact of Shakespeare's Histories*, trans. David Henry Wilson. New York.

Jakobson, Roman (1962–85) *Selected Writings*, 6 vols. The Hague.

Jameson, Fredric (1971) *Marxism and Form*. Princeton, NJ.

Jameson, Fredric (1972) *The Prison-House of Language: A Critical Account of Structuralism and Russian Formalism*. Princeton, NJ.

Jameson, Fredric (1981) *The Political Unconscious: Narrative as a Socially Symbolic Act*. Ithaca, NY.

Jameson, Fredric (1988) *The Ideologies of Theory: Essays, 1971–1986*, 2 vols.

Jardine, Alice and Smith, Paul (eds) (1987) *Men in Feminism*.

Jardine, Lisa (1989) *Still Harping on Daughters: Women and Drama in the Age of Shakespeare*. New York (1st edn pub. in Brighton, 1983).

Jenkins, Harold (1956) *The Structural Problem in Shakespeare's 'Henry IV'*.

Johnson, Samuel (1986) *Selections from Johnson on Shakespeare*, ed. Bertrand H. Bronson with Jean M. O'Meara. New Haven, CT.

Jonson, Ben (1975) *The Complete Poems*, ed. George Parfitt. Harmondsworth.

Jonson, Ben (1981–2) *The Complete Plays of Ben Jonson*, ed. G.A. Wilkes, 4 vols. Oxford.

Kahn, Coppélia (1981) *Man's Estate: Masculine Identity in Shakespeare*. Berkeley, CA.

Kamps, Ivo (ed.) (1991) *Shakespeare Left and Right*. New York.

Kastan, David Scott (1982) *Shakespeare and the Shapes of Time*.

Kerrigan, John (1990) Henry IV and the death of old Double, *Essays in Criticism*, 40: 24–53.

Knight, G. Wilson (1944) *The Olive and the Sword*. Oxford.

Knowles, Ronald (1992) *Henry IV, Parts I and II* (*The Critics' Debate* series).

Lacan, Jacques (1966) *Écrits*. Paris.

Macdonald, Ronald R. (1984) Uneasy lies: Language and history in Shakespeare's Lancastrian tetralogy, *Shakespeare Quarterly*, 35: 22–39.

Macherey, Pierre (1978) *A Theory of Literary Production*, trans. Geoffrey Wall (1st edn, 1966, pub. as *Pour une théorie de la production littéraire*).

McMillin, Scott (1991) *Henry IV, Part One* (*Shakespeare in Performance* series). Manchester.

Marotti, Arthur (1982) 'Love is not love': Elizabethan sonnet sequences and the social order, *Journal of English Literary History*, 49: 396–428.

Marx, Karl and Engels, Friedrich (1959) *Marx and Engels: Basic Writings on Politics and Philosophy*, ed. Lewis S. Feuer.

Masefield, John (1911) *William Shakespeare*.

Melchiori, Giorgio (1989) Introduction, in Giorgio Melchiori (ed.), *The Second Part of King Henry IV*. Cambridge.

Mennell, Stephen (1987), On the civilizing of appetite, *Theory, Culture and Society*, 4: 373–403.

Montrose, Louis Adrian (1980) The purpose of playing: Reflections on Shakespearean anthropolgy, *Helios*, n.s. 7: 51–74.

Montrose, Louis Adrian (1983) 'Shaping fantasies': Figurations of gender and power in Elizabethan culture, *Representations*, 2: 61–94.

Moon, Michael and Sedgewick, Eve Kosovsky (1990–91) Divinity: A dossier/a performance piece/a little-understood emotion, *Discourse*, 13: 12–39.

Moraitis, George and Pollock, George H. (eds) (1987) *Psychoanalytic Studies of Biography*. Madison, WI.

Morgann, Maurice (1972) *Shakespearean Criticism*, ed. Daniel A. Fineman. Oxford.

Morson, Gary Saul and Emerson, Caryl (1990) *Mikhail Bakhtin: Creation of a Prosaics*. Stanford, CA.

Nuttall, A.D. (1983) *A New Mimesis: Shakespeare and the Representation of Reality*.

Odell, George C.D. (ed.) (1963) *Shakespeare from Betterton to Irving*, 2 vols. New York (1st edn, 1920).

Ornstein, Robert (1972) *A Kingdom for a Stage: The Achievement of Shakespeare's History Plays*. Cambridge, MA.

Parker, Patricia (1987) *Literary Fat Ladies: Rhetoric, Gender, Property*.

Pequigney, Joseph (1985) *Such Is My Love*. Chicago.

Pincess, Gerald M. and Lockyer, Roger (eds) (1990) *Shakespeare's World: Background Readings in the English Renaissance*. New York.

Pittenger, Elizabeth (1991) Dispatch quickly: The mechanical reproduction of pages, *Shakespear Quarterly*, 42: 389–408.

Plato (1975) *Phaeto*, trans. David Gallop. Oxford.

Porter, Joseph A. (1988) *Shakespeare's Mercutio: His History and Drama*. Chapel Hill, NC.

Quinones, Ricardo J. (1972) *The Renaissance Discovery of Time*. Cambridge, MA.

Rabkin, Norman (1981) *Shakespeare and the Problem of Meaning*. Chicago.

Rackin, Phyllis (1990) *Stages of History: Shakespeare's English Chronicles*. Ithaca, NY.

Reed, Robert Rentoul Jr (1984) *Crime and God's Judgment in Shakespeare*. Lexington, KY.

Ribner, Irving (1957) *The English History Play in the Age of Shakespeare*. Princeton, NJ.

Rivers, Isabel (ed.) (1979) *Classical and Christian Ideas in English Renaissance Poetry*.

Rozett, Martha Tuck (1984) *The Doctrine of Election and the Emergence of Elizabethan Tragedy*. Princeton, NJ.

Ryan, Kiernan (1989) *Shakespeare*. Hemel Hempstead.

Sanders, Wilbur (1968) *The Dramatist and the Received Idea: Studies in the Plays of Marlowe and Shakespeare*. Cambridge.

Saussure, Ferdinand de (1959) *Course in General Linguistics*, ed. Charles Bally and Albert Sechshaye, trans. Wade Baskin. New York.

Sedgewick, Eve Kosovsky (1985) Between Men: English Literature and Male Homosocial Desire. New York.

Sedgewick, Eve Kosovsky (1990) *Epistemology of the Closet*. Berkeley, CA.

Sidney, Philip (1965) *An Apology for Poetry*, ed. Geoffrey Shepherd. Manchester.

Simmons, J.L. (1993) Masculine negotiations in Shakespeare's history plays: Hal, Hotspur, and 'the foolish Mortimer', *Shakespeare Quarterly*, 44: 440–63.

Sinfield, Alan (1992) *Faultlines: Cultural Materialism and the Politics of Dissident Reading*. Oxford.

Smallwood, R.L. (1974) Introduction, in R.L. Smallwood (ed.), *King John*. Harmondsworth.

Smidt, Kristian (1982) *Unconformities in Shakespeare's History Plays*.

Smith, Bruce (1991) *Homosexual Desire in Shakespeare's England: A Cultural Poetics*. Chicago.

Smith, Gary (ed.) (1991) *On Walter Benjamin: Critical Essays and Recollections*. Cambridge, MA.

Smith, G. Gregory (ed.) (1904) *Elizabethan Critical Essays*, 2 vols. Oxford.

Spenser, Edmund (1977) *Spenser: The Faerie Queene*, ed. A.C. Hamilton.

Starkey, Thomas (1948) *Dialogue between Reginald Pole and Thomas Lupset*, ed. K.M. Burton (1st edn, c. 1534).

Stoll, E.E. (1927) *Shakespeare Studies*. New York.

Stow, John (1592) *The Annals of England*.

Taylor, Gary (1983) The fortunes of Oldcastle, *Shakespeare Survey*, 38: 85–100.

Taylor, Gary (1982) Introduction, in Gary Taylor (ed.), *Henry V*. Oxford.

Tennenhouse, Leonard (1986) *Power on Display: The Politics of Shakespeare's Genres*.

Thomson, Peter (1992) *Shakespeare's Theatre*, 2nd edn (1st edn 1983).

Tillyard, E.M.W. (1943) *The Elizabethan World Picture*.

Tillyard, E.M.W. (1944) *Shakespeare's History Plays*.

Traub, Valerie (1989) Prince Hal's Falstaff: Positioning psychoanalysis and the female reproductive body, *Shakespeare Quarterly*, 40: 456–74.

Traub, Valerie (1992) *Desire and Anxiety: Circulations of Sexuality in Shakespearean Drama*.

Turner, James Grantham (ed.) (1993) *Sexuality and Gender in Early Modern Europe: Institutions, Texts, Images*. Cambridge.

Ulrici, Hermann (1876) *Shakespeare's Dramatic Art* (1st edn 1838).

Vickers, Brian (ed.) (1974–81) *Shakespeare: The Critical Heritage, 1623–1801* 6 vols.

Vickers, Brian (1981) The emergence of character criticism, 1774–1800, *Shakespeare Survey*, 34: 11–21.

Voloshinov, V.N. (1986) *Marxism and the Philosophy of Language*, trans. Ladislav Matejka and I.R. Titunik. Cambridge, MA (1st edn 1929).

Wayne, Valerie (ed.) (1991) *The Matter of Difference: Materialist Feminist Criticism of Shakespeare*. Ithaca, NY.

Weeks, Jeffrey (1981) *Sex, Politics and Society: The Regulation of Sexuality since 1800*.

Weeks, Jeffrey (1990) *Coming Out: Homosexual Politics in Britain from the Nineteenth Century to the Present* (1st edn 1977).

Weimann, Robert (1978) *Shakespeare and the Popular Tradition in the Theatre*, ed R. Schwartz. Baltimore, MD.

Wells, Stanley (ed.) (1986) *The Cambridge Companion to Shakespeare Studies*. Cambridge.

Wilders, John (1978) *The Lost Garden: A View of Shakespeare's English and Roman History Plays*.

Willett, John (1978) *The New Sobriety, 1917–33*.

Wilson, John Dover (1943) *The Fortunes of Falstaff*.

Yachnin, Paul (1991) History, theatricality, and the 'structural' problem in the *Henry IV* plays, *Philological Quarterly*, 70: 163–79.

Yeats, W.B. (1961) At Stratford-on-Avon, in Yeats, *Essays and Introductions*, pp. 96–110.

Zimmerman, Susan (ed.) (1992) *Erotic Politics: Desire on the Renaissance Stage*.

Zimmerman, Susan and Weissman, Ronald F.E. (eds) (1989) *Urban Life in the Renaissance*. Newark, DE.

Further Reading

1 Hal's Desire, Shakespeare's Idaho

Alan Bray, *Homosexuality in Renaissance England* (1982).
The most careful and fullest investigation of the problem of talking about a form of sexuality in a cultural situation in which the identity formation of 'the homosexual' does not exist.

Michel Foucault, *The History of Sexuality* Vol. 1, *An Introduction* (1978).
An argument against the 'repressive hypothesis' that details a modern deployment of sexuality and offers a broad historical genealogy of its emergence and points of contrast to earlier formations.

Jonathan Goldberg, *Sodometries: Renaissance Texts, Modern Sexualities* (Stanford, CA, 1992).
An investigation of a number of Renaissance literary texts (by Shakespeare, Spenser, Marlowe and others) in terms of emerging spheres of high literary culture, of antitheatrical polemic, and within the domains of colonial expansion and their co-implication with domains of sexuality and gender formation.

Jonathan Goldberg (ed.), *Queering the Renaissance* (Durham, NC, 1993).
Offers more than a dozen essays, with focus on Renaissance England, but also including continental European and American texts, with contributions by literary critics as well as by legal and social historians, each of which, through a variety of methodologies, seeks to enquire into the imbrication of questions of sexuality with a range of genres and historico-literary problematics, including the question of lesbianism in the Renaissance.

Eve Kosofsky Sedgwick, *Between Men: English Literature and Male Homosocial Desire* (New York, 1985).

A magisterial mobilization of feminist theory to antihomophobic work; while its focus is on the eighteenth and nineteenth centuries, it offers a brilliant reading of Shakespeare's sonnets within the complex terrains of male homosocial desire; there are also important caveats about Bray's work that point the way forward for future historians.

Valerie Traub, *Desire and Anxiety: Circulations of Sexuality in Shakespearean Drama* (1992).

The most recent contribution to the powerful nexus of feminist/gay studies work in the Renaissance; Traub reads a number of Shakespeare plays (including *Henry IV*) and offers the most fully articulated discussion to date of the relations between feminist, psychoanalytic, and gay and lesbian studies in the field.

2 Uses of Diversity

Katerina Clark and Michael Holquist, *Mikhail Bakhtin* (Cambridge, MA, 1984).

A detailed account of Bakhtin's life, work, and the relations between them.

Ken Hirschkop and David Shepherd (eds), *Bakhtin and Cultural Theory* (Manchester, 1989).

Among a number of valuable essays, Tony Crowley's 'Bakhtin and the History of the Language' is particularly pertinent here, especially in its emphasis on the spring of dialogism that never runs dry.

Aileen Kelly, 'Revealing Bakhtin', *New York Review of Books* (24 September 1992).

This review of Morson's and Emerson's book (see below) is a most penetrating short account of dialogism, particularly of the phenomenon of 'false monologization'.

Alexander Leggatt, *Shakespeare's Political Drama: The History Plays and the Roman Plays* (1988).

Astutely suggests that in the *Henry IV* plays the principals' attempts to present themselves in neat formulae send us looking for other ways to read them, a search that results in no certainties.

Gary Saul Morson and Caryl Emerson, *Mikhail Bakhtin: Creation of a Prosaics* (Stanford, CA, 1990).

The best general account of all aspects of Bakhtin's thought and a bit more balanced and sceptical than Clark and Holquist (see above), particularly on questions of authorship.

Phyllis Rackin, *Stages of History: Shakespeare's English Chronicles* (Ithaca, NY, 1990).

Particularly fine concerning the way the world of *Henry IV* replaces a nostalgic opposition of a mundane present to an idealized past with multiple divisions, distinct spheres of action marked by different languages and diverse representational modes.

3 The Future of History in *Henry IV*

Catherine Belsey, 'Making Histories Then and Now: Shakespeare from *Richard II* to *Henry V*', in Francis Barker, Peter Hulme and Margaret Iverson (eds), *Uses of History: Marxism, Postmodernism and the Renaissance* (Manchester, 1991).
   A provocative reading of the second tetralogy as postmodern historiography *avant la lettre*, designed to undo the 'grand narratives' of its day by telling 'a story of change which begins in nostalgia for a lost golden world and ends in indeterminacy'.

Ernst Bloch, *The Utopian Function of Art and Literature: Selected Essays* (Cambridge, MA and London, 1988).
   The best introduction to the aesthetic dimension of Bloch's 'philosophy of the future'. See in particular 'Art and society', 'Art and utopia' and 'On the present in literature'.

James L. Calderwood, *Metadrama in Shakespeare's Henriad: Richard II to Henry V* (Berkeley, CA, 1979).
   An illuminating analysis of the parts played by verbal and theatrical self-consciousness in the Lancastrian cycle.

William C. Dowling, *Jameson, Althusser, Marx: An Introduction to 'The Political Unconscious'* (1984).
   An indispensable guide through the often tortuous complexities of Jameson's argument, whose intellectual genealogy and tacit assumptions about language, culture and hermeneutics are lucidly unpacked and explained.

Steven Mullaney, *The Place of the Stage: License, Play and Power in Renaissance England* (Chicago and London, 1988).
   Chapter 3 offers a further variation on the new-historicist view of *Henry IV* as the double agent of the dominant culture. Mullaney discerns in Hal's Eastcheap interlude an intriguing paradigm of the way both stage and state in Shakespeare's time incorporate difference and dissent.

Phyllis Rackin, *Stages of History: Shakespeare's English Chronicles* (Ithaca, NY, 1990).
   Situates the plays in the context of changing Renaissance conceptions of history, and shows how orthodox, univocal historiography is transformed by Shakespeare into theatrical scripts exposing Elizabethan culture as 'a cacophony of contending voices'. A superb, ground-breaking study.

4 *Henry IV* and Epic Theatre

Benjamin's *One-Way Street*, which appeared in Germany in 1928 and is translated in *One-Way Street and Other Writings* (1979), was the book he wrote after *The Origin of German Tragic Drama*, and complements it by the method of contrast. Witty, discontinuous, and aggressively modernist, it nevertheless explores many of the same issues; see, for example, the extraordinary section called 'Toys'.

For Brecht, the main source remains John Willett's selection of theoretical writings *Brecht on Theatre* (1964). For our purposes here, it could be supplemented by Margot Heinemann's excellent essay, 'How Brecht Read Shakespeare', in Jonathan Dollimore and Alan Sinfield (eds), *Political Shakespeare* (Manchester, 1985: 202–30); and some account of the 1924 *Edward II*, e.g., John Fuegi, *Bertolt Brecht* (Cambridge, 1987), chapters 1 and 2; and Bernhard Reich in Hubert Witt (ed.), *Brecht As They Knew Him* (1974: 39–44).

On the whole, I find that Benjamin explains himself better than those who seek to explain him. (The English translations of his writings often feature introductions by such luminaries as Hannah Arendt, Susan Sontag and George Steiner, which should be treated with extreme caution.) However, I would recommend Richard Wolin, *Walter Benjamin: An Aesthetic of Redemption* (New York, 1982), and Julian Roberts, *Walter Benjamin* (1982).

Index